# Two Literary Riddles in the Exeter Book

HVRV ÐÆS BE HOFAÞ

# Two Literary Riddles in the Exeter Book

## Riddle 1 and The Easter Riddle

### A Critical Edition with Full Translations

### By James E. Anderson

UNIVERSITY OF OKLAHOMA PRESS : NORMAN AND LONDON

Library of Congress Cataloging-in-Publication Data

Anderson, James E. (James Edward), 1941–
    Two literary riddles in the Exeter book.

    Bibliography: p. 255
    Includes index.
    1. Riddles, Anglo-Saxon—History and criticism.
2. Christian poetry, Anglo-Saxon—History and criticism.
3. Anglo-Saxon poetry—History and criticism.
4. Riddles, Anglo-Saxon. 5. Christian poetry, Anglo-Saxon.
6. Anglo-Saxon poetry. 7. English poetry—Translations from
Anglo-Saxon. 8. Exeter book.
I. Title.
PR1764.A53    1986         829'.1         85–40471
ISBN 0–8061–1947–0

Publication of this book has been made possible in part by grants
from the Andrew Mellon Foundation and Vanderbilt University.

To Erika, Kristin, Tanya, and Erik,
who helped me to be . M . *dreama full* in this work

# CONTENTS

# ILLUSTRATIONS

# PREFACE

The *Codex exoniensis*, or Exeter Book, named after its domicile of now more than nine hundred years, is a vast and ostensibly various collection of poems assembled sometime in the last half of the tenth century. The anonymous scribe who copied the book, probably in a modest scriptorium, faced no small task. Not counting its missing pages, perhaps a dozen or more, the Exeter Book contains 123 large folios of poetry written continuously as if it were prose, in all 5,374 manuscript lines, or 8,089 poetic lines, of vernacular verse—about one-fourth of our surviving Old English poetry.

Like most other early English manuscripts the Exeter Book has no headings or titles for individual texts, which have nevertheless acquired editorial titles in modern scholarship. Virtually all of the poems are closed by extra spacing and a simple colophon (:7) sometimes elaborated with additional points and horizontal strokes of the pen. The single poems, or in a few instances major sections of longer poems, begin with spare, mostly uncolored initials of various styles and sizes, sometimes followed by all or part of a line of enlarged and emboldened script. Only seven poems or sections in the manuscript end with lexical signals: *Amen* six times and the word *finit* in minuscule once, after *Physiologus*, on folio 98a.

At various times damaged by fire, abuse, neglect, and loss of some leaves, the Exeter Book was eventually bound together with seven folios from another manuscript, which probably now resides in Cambridge. Among these interpolated first pages, various legal records and lists of properties donated to Exeter, is the itemized bequest of Leofric, first bishop of Exeter (+1072), to his cathedral and its library. The list of Leofric's property mentions his sixty-six books, including *1 mycel englisc boc be geh-wilcum þingum on leoðwisan geworht* 'one great book in English about diverse things, done in the poetical manner.' These words are generally thought, if not altogether proved, to describe the

Exeter Book itself, with its large number of separate poems on many subjects.

Even if the Exeter Book is a poetic miscellany, however, it is not necessarily of wholly arbitrary or random order. Like many other medieval collections it was probably assembled on some more or less definite but unstated plan. This book deals with only a small part of that lost scheme, some eight hundred lines of poetry in all. The texts in question are discussed and edited (and translated for the nonspecialized reader) as two groups of poems, one group bordering on and the other interrupting the famous Old English riddles of the codex. From such telltale locations and from plays of word and theme across their individual texts, both groups are interpreted as riddlic arrangements themselves and accordingly designated *Riddle 1* and *The Easter Riddle*. Their constituent poems—apparently of such widely mixed genres as elegies, didactic-devotional poems, riddles or parts of riddles, and poems of homiletic and liturgical focus—are considered as members of their riddlic groups and therefore essentially as riddles in themselves. By thus expanding and unifying the Old English riddles, *Riddle 1* and *The Easter Riddle* would also seem to impart a certain measure of hidden coherence to the manuscript as a whole.

This book began with several frustrated attempts to read nineteen lines of folios 100b–101a—that most obscure Old English refrain poem known as *Wulf and Eadwacer*—as an isolated text. Gradually I became convinced that this little poem was deliberately incomplete and that P. J. Frankis's proposal for reading it together with *Deor*, the adjacent refrain poem in the manuscript, was correct in the main if not in every detail. Through trial and error I discovered first how *Deor* played internally on its own refrain and then how *Wulf and Eadwacer* with its refrain concealed the feminine response. I was now sure, despite some vociferous published objections to Frankis's work, that *Deor* and *Wulf and Eadwacer* constituted a double riddle that ended with the eighth-century author's sly boast of joining together what had never been joined before. Next, by pure chance my skimming eye caught something it had never caught before: first the strong lexical and thematic similarities to *Wulf and Eadwacer* in the opening lines of *The Soul's Address* about the violent separation of body and soul at death, and then the unifying themes, sustained by repeated words and formulaic expressions, of wolfish predation and of bestial rending and eating. These ideas quickly appeared to be the major conceptual unity of all three poems of *Riddle 1*.

What I had therefore also stumbled upon, without quite knowing it at the time, was the adaptation of ancient oral formulaic tradition to a special literary context—the sequential riddle, which uses repeated words and formulas as clues for the hidden thematic unity of a number of paleographically separate texts. Since by its very subject matter *The Soul's Address* seems to be poetry of the tenth-century Benedictine Reform but *Deor* and *Wulf and Eadwacer* appear to be made of heroic legends reworked in a much earlier age, the somewhat insoluble question of method of authorship arises. Did a tenth-century riddler compose all or most of the newer poetry himself, with witty turns on the words and verse formulas of the older poetry constantly in mind? Or was the Exeter Book riddler mainly a compiler who successfully joined together finished newer and older poems by exploiting their common formulas and themes? At present, though I incline toward the latter possibility, I cannot fully exclude either one. On the one hand, some small passages at least look like the riddler's own rather crude interpolations meant to echo and sustain major themes throughout his large composite texts. On the other hand, such far-flung likenesses as the secular *wrætlic weallstana geweorc* 'wondrous works of wall stones' in *Cotton Maxims* 3a, the *weallstan* 'wall stone' who is the scriptural 'cornerstone' himself in the Exeter Book *Christ I*, and the *wrætlic . . . wealstan* of the allegorical *Ruin* at the end of *The Easter Riddle* suggest a large store of traditional images and expressions available to early and late Anglo-Saxon poets alike. From this lexical meeting ground of heroic and Christian poetry a tenth-century riddler could probably have built grand schemes several poems long almost without writing an original word, merely by fitting together the right old and new texts.

Whatever poetic resources the Exeter Book riddler used, whether or not he was the largely derivative genius that his texts make him seem to be, it was becoming clearer and clearer to me that at least in *Riddle 1* and *The Easter Riddle* the repeated words and verse formulas gather ostensibly separate poems into larger works with invisible thematic boundaries. Even before I could articulate this hypothesis, I had roughly outlined the boundaries and the logical progression of *The Easter Riddle*, from the allegorical Bride's complaint of abandonment on Good Friday to the Bridegroom's return in the Eucharist on Easter and a final glimpse of the wondrous ruin of all flesh. But I could not have finished this rough argument without substantial help from other scholars. In particular, my view of the vital dramatic roles of penitent and confessor in *The Easter Riddle* is greatly indebted to Allen J. Frantzen's recent study of Anglo-Saxon penitential literature. There are still other areas of investigation which for want of time or skill I have not finished. I have barely sketched, for example, the concealed operation of liturgical themes in the middle poems of *The Easter Riddle*. On that very exciting subject there is still much work for other scholars, especially historical liturgists.

Yet another point of method, closely linked to the nature of riddling, has gradually emerged in my work. As the texts in question showed more and more of their riddlic intent, the attraction of a patrological approach yielded somewhat to the greater force of scriptural allusions in the poems. After all, the best riddles work by giving a sudden and startling new perspective to an old, familiar subject; and what material, including even the church fathers, could have been more widely and intimately known to Anglo-Saxon monastic audiences than the Scriptures themselves? Perhaps the best rewards of reading these poems with Scripture in mind are seen in *The Wife's Lament*, where the typological story of Susanna illuminates even certain Germanic features of the text, and *The Ruin*, in which the biblical Temple in all its meanings is nothing less than the concealed central figure.

Finally, that part of my work which I have called trial and error can be briefly and, I hope, usefully described. Since riddling, more than any other literary form, is openly combative in nature, solving a difficult riddle would seem to require an especially competitive frame of mind. The intricate literary riddle challenges the reader, among other things, to relax some of the critical caution that would normally govern his work. He becomes for the nonce an adventurer who dares to overvalue apparently flimsy evidence, such minor word clues, for example, as the almost negligible occurrence of *deor* 'beast' and *werga* 'wolf, outlaw' in the first poem of *Riddle 1*. Nevertheless, the riddle solver cannot afford to be reckless. He must watch until he is reasonably sure that echoed words such as *deor*, *wulf*, *wylfenne*, and *werga* are not merely neutral formulaic devices in unrelated contexts. He must see such words or formulas also accumulating into matching themes: the many plays on *wulf* as man and beast of exile, the turns on blood and rending and eating, on predatory thinking and bestial sexuality throughout the poems of *Riddle 1*. Then he must work to reduce those accumulated themes to a system of meaning and, finally, to an answer which in turn explains all the words and themes he has found. *Riddle 1* has an at least implicit answer: eternal Death, which is prefigured in violent feuds on earth and foreshadowed in the mutual hatred of a feuding body and soul. *The Easter Riddle* has, I believe, an even more satisfying single answer in the end.

This is the ideal method and result which this book pursues, but readers will want to decide for themselves whether it settles for less. For those who will still object to calling many of the individual poems riddles, I would point to my frequent use of the awkward term *riddlic*, etymologically 'riddlelike.' To my own minor discomfort 'riddlelike' is how the poet forces us to think of originally nonriddling poetry which he has bent to new use in a riddling scheme. But some discomfort is a risk that the riddle-solver has to take. I hope that the methodological risks in this book will compensate its readers with some new vistas on these difficult and fascinating Old English poems.

Thanks . . .
To my friend and mentor Michael Cherniss, whose sure direc-

tion fanned the first sparks from which this book has grown. To his colleagues George Wedge, Donald Watkins, Stephen Goldman, and Ernst Dick, whose judgments both merciful and stern can still be traced in my work. Steve's question to me—"What makes Anglo-Saxon literature uniquely Anglo-Saxon?"—left unanswered nearly a decade ago, gets, I hope, a better response here at last.

To my overseas colleagues Hans Schabram, A. Grinda, G. Berghaus, and Roland Torkar, who in true academic brotherhood led me toward clearer light about *Wulf and Eadwacer* than I might ever have found on my own. To my colleagues at Vanderbilt University—Emerson Brown, Mary Jane Doherty, Gwendolyn Layne, John Plummer, Jim Crenshaw, Jim Kilroy, and Jack Aden—who read, questioned, or listened with patience and grace while I wrestled with the ideas in this book. They have suggested much and taught me even more.

To Martin Green, who helped me publish my work on *Riddle 1* in a different form; and to Patrick Conner, who has given freely his own learning and encouragement. His friendship is a gift too rich to be repaid. To Dorothy Bethurum Loomis, whose deep wisdom, healthy skepticism, infectious enthusiasm, and gentle wit have kept me at work during those times when it snowed on my spirit from the north.

To my wife and three children, who have waited patiently for me to return to the twentieth century during those long years when I lived too much in the tenth.

To the Research Council of Vanderbilt University, which twice gave me treasure toward the writing and publication.

To these friends and influences I owe many of the strengths of this book, but none of its many weaknesses. Success or not, the quest between these covers has been my own.

*Nashville, Tennessee*                                    JAMES E. ANDERSON

# ABOUT THE OLD ENGLISH TEXTS AND THE TRANSLATIONS

My main authority for the Exeter Book poems in this book is the photofacsimile edition of the manuscript by R. W. Chambers, Max Förster, and Robin Flower (1933). All spellings, necessary manuscript punctuation such as raised points, and descriptions of ornamentation have been adopted from that volume and checked against its splendid introductory material. The discussion and line drawing of the drypoint figure on folio 123, related to the text of *The Husband's Message*, are based on my inspection of the manuscript of the Exeter Book itself.

Among other authorities I have referred most to the edition of the Exeter Book by George Philip Krapp and Elliott Van Kirk Dobbie in the Anglo-Saxon Poetic Records (1936). For certain special difficulties, such as determining as accurately as possible the vacant letter spaces in the damaged poems after folio 118, I have mainly compared the judgments of Krapp and Dobbie with those of W. S. Mackie in the Early English Text Society edition of the Exeter Book; Roy F. Leslie, in his *Three Old English Elegies*; and John C. Pope, in his experimental restoration of *The Husband's Message* in the festschrift for N. R. Ker (1978). The missing letters are represented by the dots of the ellipses in the Old English texts. In those rare cases where my count of letter spaces does not agree with that of my authorities, I have made my own count, at my own peril, from the photofacsimile.

In a few instances, such as in *The Husband's Message*, where damaged lines can sometimes be partly restored on fairly secure paleographical or thematic grounds, I have kept the original number of damaged letter spaces in the Old English and offered or explained a partial restoration in the textual notes. From the corresponding Modern English line I have subtracted from the damage the number of restored Old English letters, and I have also translated the (hypothetically) restored word. For example, line 93 of *The Descent into Hell* reads

bimengdes . . . . . . . . . . . . . . . gust ealra cyninga,

with approximately sixteen letters missing from the manuscript. If, as I believe, the off verse once read *modigust ealra cyninga*, then the certain grammatical restoration of bimengdes[t] and the probable restoration of *modi-* to the line suggests the translation

> (you) deigned to consort . . . . . . . . . . . of all kings
>     most [? dauntless],

with eleven missing Old English letters instead of sixteen. Such places, relatively rare in this edition, give at least a crude impression of the good effects of judicious textual restoration. For a truly startling experience of those effects every interested reader should see John C. Pope's full paleographical restoration of the damaged lines of *The Husband's Message*, a scholarly tour de force on which much of my discussion of that poem depends.

A few words are missing from the Easter Riddle, in Part Two, for a different reason. Perhaps because Exeter Book poetry runs continuously across the page as if it were prose, either the Exeter Book scribe or his unknown source has omitted part of a line of poetry on four occasions: at *The Wife's Lament* 24a, *Judgment Day I* 39a, *Resignation* 99, and *The Husband's Message* 9a. In each of the first three instances an approximately correct portion of the incomplete line is left blank in both the Old English text and the translation. In the fourth instance the metrically defective verse is filled out by compounding a simplex word in the manuscript. For thematic reasons advanced in this book the hypothetical compound word most often adopted in older scholarship still seems to be the best possible emendation. All manuscript irregularities, whether from physical damage or scribal error, are treated fully in the textual notes. The notes and Works Cited provide complete information on the many authorities I have consulted in making the present edition.

In the Old English texts given here the following standard manuscript abbreviations have been silently expanded: 7 to *ond*; barred thorn þ to *þaet* (as conjunction); occasional abbreviated inflections, such as *on þissū life*, *The Wife's Lament* 41b, to their spelled-out forms: *on þissum life*.

Manuscript spellings in þ and ð are everywhere retained, but manuscript wyn ƿ is consistently spelled *w*. For the manuscript runes of *The Husband's Message* and *The Ruin*, I have with much regret substituted the letter values. Readers who wish to see for themselves the calculated visual mystery of the runes on these pages should consult the photofacsimile.

Necessary emendations, such as for corrections of obvious or probable scribal errors or for restorations of damaged text, are enclosed in brackets. A question mark shows doubtful emendations or restorations as well as doubtful translations based on them. At some places in the damaged poems of *The Easter Riddle*, letters or words missing from the Old English text can be restored with varying degrees of thematic or paleographical certainty. Nevertheless, I have restored the damaged Old English texts conservatively, without attempting to fill in what is actually missing from the manuscript. Damaged but readable letters or traces of letters appear inside brackets. Thus the Old English texts represent the manuscript itself as faithfully as present conditions allow. In the facing translations, however, where I have felt less obligation to conservatism, the bracketed passages sometimes include fairly certain or conjectural restorations which are further described in the discussions or Textual Notes. In the Textual Notes, too, the reader will find many conjectural restorations of Old English words and parts of words, both by me and by other editors. Most of this material does not appear in the Old English texts themselves but is nevertheless essential for any worthy attempt at a full description of the poems.

Word division and punctuation for syntax follow standard editorial practices rather than the manuscript, which has very little, if any, syntactical punctuation. In a few places, such as in the final passage of *The Wife's Lament*, my punctuation represents my own understanding of syntax and therefore differs from former treatments. My rare solitary judgments in matters of versification and emendation are explained in the discussions and notes.

For convenient reference the page divisions of the manuscript are indicated in the Old English texts of the poems with a virgule (/) at the exact point of division and the number of the new folio page at the left of the affected line. Recto and verso pages are designated *a* and *b* respectively throughout.

Finally, for both riddlic journeys in this book, Old English texts are given their most widely used editorial titles in brackets. The common editorial titles of individual poems are also given in brackets above the facing-page translations. All these titles are the conveniences of modern scholarship; the Exeter Book itself contains no titles.

The facing-page translations of the poems attempt, for better or worse, to retain some of the effect of the alliteration in Old English poetry. Like all other alliterative translations of Old English poems, these sometimes show more tension between form and meaning than one would wish. As much as my decision for an alliterative translation would allow, I have intended to be everywhere literal and grammatically faithful to the original poems. I have made no attempt to reproduce Old English meter. For the benefit of the nonspecialized reader the translations follow their originals line for line as closely as the syntactical differences between Old and Modern English will permit. To some specialized readers my translations will sometimes appear to force the Old English texts to fit my own reading of them. Since it is precisely the riddle solver's task to wrest concealed meaning from a reluctant text, I make no general apology for this feature of my work, however much I may regret any specific errors. Although these translations thus represent considerable labor, they do not pretend to accomplished bardship; indeed, they are perhaps best where the Old English poetry, too, is prosaic. To such truly superb poetry as *The Ruin* my rendering may well do some additional damage. Luckily it is the sort of damage that all worthy poetry manages to survive.

Citations from Scripture are from the New American Bible except for those one or two instances where I have cited some especially well-known King James phrasing. As these few exceptions are intended to show, it is a source of instant pleasure to recognize certain familiar and cherished Bible verses at the heart of otherwise strange and elaborate riddling. In thus deriving comfort from the familiar, the tenth-century riddle solver and the twentieth-century reader would no doubt find close intellectual kinship if they could bridge the millennium of time that divides them.

# ABBREVIATIONS USED IN THIS BOOK

| | |
|---|---|
| *AN&Q* | *American Notes and Queries* |
| *AnM* | *Annuale Medievale* |
| *ASD* | Joseph Bosworth, *An Anglo-Saxon Dictionary*, ed. T. Northcote Toller |
| ASPR | Anglo-Saxon Poetic Records |
| *ChauR* | *Chaucer Review* |
| E | English |
| EETS | Early English Text Society |
| *ELH* | *Journal of English Literary History* |
| *ELN* | *English Language Notes* |
| *ES* | *English Studies* |
| G | German |
| Goth | Gothic |
| *Hist. eccl.* | Bede, *Historia ecclesiastica gentis Anglorum* |
| *JEGP* | *Journal of English and Germanic Philology* |
| L | Latin |
| *LeedsSe* | *Leeds Studies in English* |
| *MÆ* | *Medium Ævum* |
| *MED* | Hans Kurath, Sherman M. Kuhn, and John Reidy, eds. *Middle English Dictionary* |
| MHG | Middle High German |
| *MLN* | *Modern Language Notes* |
| *MLR* | *Modern Language Review* |
| MLS | Modern Language Society |
| Mod | Modern |
| *MP* | *Modern Philology* |
| *MScan* | *Mediaeval Scandinavia* |
| *Neophil* | *Neophilologus* |
| *NM* | *Neuphilologische Mitteilungen* |
| *N&Q* | *Notes and Queries* |
| n.s. | new series |
| NYU | New York University |
| OE | Old English |
| *OED* | Sir James A. H. Murray et al., eds., *Oxford English Dictionary* |

| | |
|---|---|
| OFris | Old Frisian |
| OHG | Old High German |
| ON | Old Norse |
| o.s. | old series |
| OSax | Old Saxon |
| *PELL* | *Papers on English Language and Literature* |
| *PMLA* | *Publications of the Modern Language Association of America* |
| *PQ* | *Philological Quarterly* |
| *RES* | *Review of English Studies* |
| Scand | Scandinavian |
| *SN* | *Studia Neophilologica* |
| *SP* | *Studies in Philology* |
| SUNY | State University of New York |
| Swed | Swedish |
| *TSL* | *Tennessee Studies in Literature* |
| *ZdA* | *Zeitschrift für deutsches Altertum und Deutsche Literatur* |

Two Literary Riddles in the Exeter Book

# INTRODUCTION
# THE JOURNEY TO WISDOM:
# ON RIDDLING AND THE RIDDLE SEQUENCE

The intention of this book, besides providing an edition and translation of 788 lines of Exeter Book poetry found in two groups in the manuscript, is to suggest a new reading of this poetry without casting unnecessary doubt on already widely accepted readings. In Part One the three untitled manuscript poems known to modern readers as *Soul and Body I* or *The Soul's Address to Its Body* (here called *The Soul's Address*), *Deor*, and *Wulf and Eadwacer* (folios 98a–101a) are considered not only as separate texts but also as interlocked parts of an allegory on the wasted life. In Part Two the eleven poems from *The Wife's Lament* through *The Ruin* (folios 115a–124b) are viewed as another tandem compilation, this time on the events of the Easter triduum and their celestial meaning. Both of these groups of poems have texts of pronounced "Germanic" character; that is, *Deor*, *Wulf and Eadwacer*, *The Wife's Lament*, *Riddle 30b*, *The Husband's Message*, and to some extent *The Ruin* are built on native imagery, themes, and landscapes. But in these pre-Christian settings the eighth-century intellectual heritage of the Anglo-Saxon conversion works silently away. Playfully following the spirit of Pope Gregory's famous advice to Augustine of Kent and Bishop Mellitus of London, the "old poetry" ostensibly preserves traditional ideas and stories and remembers ancient customs and places in order to insinuate parallel truths of Christianity—its moral discriminations; its Scriptures; its liturgy; its sacraments of marriage, penance, and the Eucharist; and its hope of heaven. Then, two centuries after the probable composition of these unspoken allegories on native subjects, some late-tenth-century teacher, seeing a new use for the surviving poetry of a former age, married it to the penitential and liturgical poetry of his own time of energetic monastic revival and church reform. These, in hypothesis, are the widely distant intellectual movements

3

which produced the two great Exeter Book sequences that I call *Riddle 1* and *The Easter Riddle*.

The anonymous arranger of the sequences—the Exeter Book riddler or (in Part Two) the Easter riddler—could well have been mainly a derivative rather than an original genius. That is, he could have borrowed reasonably whole both the younger devotional poems of his groupings and the cherished "Germanic" masterpieces with which he framed his unique art. For to fit the newer poems with the old he needed not so much the gift of poetry as a firm understanding of his native literary traditions. Above all, he had to see clearly how the poets of his own day were still following their eighth-century predecessors' habit of adapting the thought and diction of the old heroic poetry to witty expressions of the new Christian faith. And while no one can guarantee that the riddler did not himself write all or part of the newer texts in his sequences, our few likely samples of his own work are not very accomplished poetry. There are, for instance, some oddly placed lines in *Resignation B*, on the unattainable desire for (figurative) seafaring, which seem to bridge thematically *The Wife's Lament* and *The Husband's Message* with rough and perhaps even unfinished patchwork. Similarly, such defective poetry as *is nu    swa hit no waere / freondscipe uncer* (*The Wife's Lament* 24–25a) may be the riddler's prosaic touch rather than, as we generally assume, the fault of the scribe. Thus the Exeter Book riddler might have attained to poetry in an unusual—indeed, something of a riddlic—way.

His carefully arranged poems are here defined as riddles, in essence if not always in appearance, on internal and contextual grounds. The dense obscurity especially of the "Germanic" texts, arguably the most troublesome poems in Old English, greatly fades as their implicit parallels in Scripture or in Christian ideology occur to the reader. The celebrated ambiguity of these pieces in fact consists of double reference, and therefore of double meaning, half of which, as in all other riddling, lies well concealed. Moreover, both groups of poems, despite their outward variety of themes and genres, appear to have been consciously placed in or next to the Old English riddles of the codex.

*Wulf and Eadwacer*, once thought to begin the riddle collection even though it defied solution, seems best read in thematic and formal conjunction with *Deor*, which in turn has thematic and perhaps even visual connections with *The Soul's Address*. Between *Wulf and Eadwacer*, the end of our first group of poems, and *The Wife's Lament*, which begins the second group, lie fifty-eight relatively brief riddles of native English inspiration on natural phenomena, plants and animals, and tools and objects of military and domestic life, with the occasional obscenities found in every collection of genuine folk riddling.[1] Within the second set of texts, between *The Wife's Lament* and *The Ruin*, occur the dialogue and folk riddles known as *Pharaoh* and *Riddle 30b* and the first seventeen lines of *The Husband's Message*, of folk-riddle form and origin and still widely known as "Riddle 60." Immediately after the end of *The Ruin*, on folio 124b, the short folk or folk-inspired riddles resume and continue uninterrupted (except by a lost manuscript leaf) to folio 130b, the apparent end of the Exeter Book. Difficult as they are, and situated next to or mixed among the folk riddles of the codex, the two poetic sequences examined here have been kept hidden not only by the absence of any obvious paleographical marking but also by our general modern neglect of the complex literary riddle.[2]

In our time, which relegates riddling largely to the simple word games of the nursery or of children's books, it is hard to remember how seriously riddles were once taken or how intri-

---

[1] Archer Taylor, *The Literary Riddle Before 1600*, pp. 9–10, defined the folk riddle according to Frederick Tupper, *The Riddles of the Exeter Book*, pp. xvi–xvii: a "scanty framework," quick introduction of the key clue, naïve description, a sudden interruption of the movement toward a solution, and a final summation.

[2] Taylor, *The Literary Riddle*, defines the literary riddle as "a long series of assertions and contradictions . . . often put in the form of a speech . . . by the [riddle] object" (p. 3) and as a frequent sacrifice of conceptual unity in favor of wealth of details (p. 7). These fundamental distinctions between the usually brief, quick-moving, and thematically unified folk riddle and the more leisurely, slower-moving, more learned and intricate, and sometimes apparently disunified literary riddle are central to my introductory argument and to the methods of this book.

cately they could be devised.[3] Yet only a few generations ago Goethe recaptured some of the magic of the riddler's ancient art in these lines from "Alexis und Dora":

> Thus poses the poet his riddle,
> Deftly, locked in with words, many times in his listeners' ears;
> The rare binding of delicate images gladdens each hearer.
> Yet still is missed the one word that encloses the meaning.
> But if stubborn Discovery comes, then every spirit is lifted,
> And sees in his poem a doubly gladdening sense.[4]

These few brief lines superbly describe the riddler and his relationship with his audience, on whose perceptions the solution depends. In that tense time between the posing of a riddle and the sudden finding of the answer, the riddling game is a kind of combat, a contest of wits between riddler and solver. The apparent simplicity of the game can be deceptive indeed. While all true riddles are essentially fair contests containing a system of double-meaning clues sufficient to lead to the answer, they do not have to be easy. Like the tendrils of a climbing vine hidden in other dense foliage, the clues of a riddle—at once the avenues and the obstructions to its meanings—may be thoroughly concealed in a thicket of words and as hard to trace to the right solution as the vine to its stem. Some riddles, notably the obscene ones, are conceived as double-tracked metaphors, with a true and a false spur for simultaneous trains of analytical thought. Thus obscene riddles lead to an innocent solution and to entrapment in an obscenity at the same time. A handy example of this sort of riddle is *Riddle 25* from the Exeter Book:

> I am a wondrous wight, a pleasure to women,
> of use among neighbors; no one I injure
> of the citizenry, except for one slayer.

---

[3] Mathilde Hain, *Rätsel*, p. 53, observes the low esteem generally accorded the riddle today: "Today the riddle is generally dismissed to the nursery and the school primer." The translation is mine.

[4] Quoted in ibid., p. 49. The translation is mine. Goethe's emphasis on the pictorial aspect of riddling is already found in Aristotle's *Rhetoric*.

My stem is straight up; I stand in a bed,
hirsute somewhere below. Now and then chances
some quite charming churl's daughter,
a bold-minded maid, to grasp onto me,
race toward my redness, ravage my head,
guide me into a cell. Soon enough
she who squeezes me feels my gathering,
the twisted-haired woman. Wet is the eye.[5]

The reader who has guessed the answer "penis" is, of course, correct. Betrayed, however, by his own impurity of mind, he might well wince inwardly when he is told the equally good (but perhaps less conspicuous) answer "onion." There is, perhaps, a certain hostile "fun" but little enough of Goethe's "joy" in a discovery like this.

The psychological combativeness of riddling appears to have its physical counterpart in heroic cultures, where much more than just the solver's pride is sometimes at stake. Riddlic tasks or adventures which try the powers of the mind are as sacred to heroic societies as the martial tests of a young man's courage and strength.[6] These trials of mind and knowledge may be posed either singly or in series, and the hero's very neck may be the price of defeat.[7] One benevolent social purpose of such "neck riddling" is to eliminate pretenders from contention for the throne—to try to see whether God, or the gods, will take the side of the future king. Hence the many riddling trolls and monsters of folktales, against whose threatening enigmas the young hero, and sometimes heroine, must wager life itself. In the grisly

[5] The translation is mine. The most available OE text is still found in George Philip Krapp and Elliott Van Kirk Dobbie, eds., *The Exeter Book*, ASPR 3:1936; hereafter cited throughout as ASPR 3.

[6] See the discussions of protoliterary and biblical riddling in S. H. Blank, "Riddle," in *The Interpreter's Dictionary of the Bible*; and James L. Crenshaw, "Riddle," in the *Supplementary Volume* of the same work (1976).

[7] As Hain, *Rätsel*, p. 50, observes, André Jolles, *Einfache Formen*, thinks of all riddling as neck riddling in its essence. Here, however, I take the psychological and physical combativeness of riddling as two separate (though sometimes related) ingredients of the form.

*Kindermärchen* "Rumpelstilzchen" a young mother must discover her dwarfish tormentor's name, a riddle connected with his appearance (*Stilzchen* 'little wooden leg') and behavior (*Rumpel* 'rubbish, lumber, junk'; also *rumpeln* 'to rumble, jolt, stomp'), at the implied cost of her own baby's flesh if she fails. When she succeeds by the pure chance of overhearing the unguessable name in the forest, Rumpelstilzchen meets a fate which his name has concealed even from himself: in rage he stomps his wooden leg immovably into the earth and perishes by starvation.[8]

An even more terrible and famous riddle, perhaps of very ancient folk origins, underlies Sophocles' *Oedipus Rex*. The play begins with the Sphinx's neck riddle, whose solution has destroyed the poser and made Oedipus's name "famous," as he boasts. But the Sphinx's riddle is really only a trap, for it leads Oedipus unawares into an even more dangerous sequence of riddle questions. Who killed King Laios? I, Oedipus. Who then am I, Oedipus? A man of singular and incomprehensible destiny, both riddle solver and riddle, monster and hero. For audiences through the ages a still more unanswerable question, perhaps the secret of the play's spell over so many centuries, is implied: If this great man is both solver and riddle, what, then, is Man? By contrast, some of the hidden possibilities of Oedipus's fate become only too clear. To begin with, the Sphinx's riddle has perhaps not been as completely answered as Oedipus thought. It seems to deal secretly with the geometrical laws which govern points in a plane and is therefore of potentially great irony if applied to the "figure" of Oedipus himself. He would then become the two-legged hero who is most unstable in the plane of earth just when he seems to stand most proudly; the man of unique destiny who, with pinned ankles in the "morning" of his babyhood, was never really four-footed at all; and in his blind and ruined old age, tapping out his exile with a cane, at last the three-pointed figure, stable only in the hindsight of his suffer-

---

[8] This is a brief analysis of the original "Rumpelstilzchen" collected and retold in Jacob and Wilhelm Grimm, *Kinder und Hausmärchen*. Hain, *Rätsel*, p. 37, thinks of such riddlic folktales as ultimately related to the Greek myth of the Sphinx.

ing.[9] The well-known pun on 'swollen (foot)' and 'knowledge' in his name comes to haunt both him and us, who watch helplessly as the sudden knowledge of his swollen feet plays decisively in his own destruction.

In English literature, among the best literary expansions of a neck riddle into a major narrative work is the fourteenth-century romance *Sir Gawain and the Green Knight*. The poet wages Gawain's neck in a contest of ax blows and then withholds from him (though not from the reader) the identity of his host and his challenger, who are one and the same. The clues to this secret reside in a series of temptations alternated with a series of hunting scenes, in which Gawain is implicitly compared to the nature of the hunter's various prey. Another handy medieval English example of a literary neck riddle is Chaucer's *Wife of Bath's Tale*, in which a condemned knight barely escapes (with supernatural aid and his own spiritual wisdom) his riddlic death sentence, the apparently unanswerable question "What do women most of all desire?"

Such lethal riddling does not, however, exclude the sense of joy in Goethe's description of the riddle game. Solving a riddle and then winning the game can indeed exhilarate the senses and enlarge the understanding; therefore, in various cultures riddles have appeared as banqueting entertainment for guests, in public contests at carnivals and fairs, in the making of marriage contracts or even at weddings themselves, in children's games, or as ritual questioning in catechetical form.[10] As "questions which demand answers," riddles make natural vehicles not only for religious catechism but also for the time-honored dialogue method of teaching natural and philosophical wisdom.[11]

---

[9] That Sophocles, in fifth-century Athens, could have had access to the idea of (Pythagorean) mathematical wit may be reasonably concluded from the presence of such wit even in Pythagorean-based architecture in sixth-century Italy. See Ned Nabers and Susan Ford Wiltshire, "The Athena Temple at Paestum and Pythagorean Theory," *Greek, Roman, and Byzantine Studies* 21 (1980): 207–15.

[10] Hain, *Rätsel*, p. 1; Taylor, *The Literary Riddle*, pp. 31, 54.

[11] The words in quotation paraphrase André Jolles, "Rätsel und Mythos," in *Germanica: Festschrift für Eduard Sievers*, pp. 632–45, who sees the riddle as an

The most famous early-medieval dialogue riddles, from an eighth-century manuscript of Saint Gall, are the *Joca monachorum* ("Simple Games of the Monks"), probably copied for instruction as well as entertainment. In this collection there is an exegetical question on the strength of the Egyptian army that drowned in the Red Sea. The composer of the little dialogue poem *Pharaoh*, midway in *The Easter Riddle*, is thought to have borrowed the question and the dialogue form from the *Joca*, though the English poem would then seem to be avoiding the strictly numerical answer in the Continential manuscript in favor of a more oblique response. The fanciful *Altercatio Hadriani Augusti et Epicteti Philosophi* ("Disputation of the emperor Hadrian and the scholar Epictetus"), preserved for us in a tenth-century manuscript, was once known in much earlier versions, if a latter-day association of its tradition with Bede has any merit.[12] A popular work, many times recopied and expanded after the tenth century, the *Altercatio* has a number of questions with riddlic features and meaning. Once, for example, the teacher asks, *Quid est in exilium?* ('What thing is in exile?'), to which the student answers, "The whole world." In this little exchange an echo from Old English exile poetry is not unthinkable, for English influence can be traced in other Continental riddle books, such as the Rhenish "Lorsch Riddles" of the ninth century and the "Strasbourg Riddle Book" of the early sixteenth.[13] In the intervening centuries, one supposes, a number of other Continental riddle books now lost were indebted in some part to English models.

This supposition is founded mainly on the remaining riddle monuments of the seventh and eighth centuries, which, except for one seventh-century collection from the library of Bobbio, in Lombardy, and the vernacular riddles of the Exeter Book, are the work of distinguished Anglo-Latin writers. The earliest

_____

inversion of myth, wherein an answer has been devised to a deeply felt but unexpressed question. See also Hain, *Rätsel*, p. 48.

[12] Hain, *Rätsel*, p. 3.

[13] Ibid.; Taylor, *The Literary Riddle*, pp. 63, 73.

known English riddler is none other than Aldhelm of Malmes-
bury, of the late seventh century. In the early eighth century
Archbishop Tatwine of Canterbury left forty Latin riddles as evi-
dence of his interest and skill in the art. Probably on the influ-
ence of Symphosius, a late-fifth-century author of one hundred
folk-inspired poetic riddles, the pseudonymous Englishman
"Eusebius," perhaps Abbot Hwaetberht of Wearmouth, added
sixty riddles to Tatwine's forty to make a "century" of Anglo-
Latin texts.[14] Late in the eighth century the great Carolingian
scholar Alcuin of York wrote mathematical riddles, perhaps
modeled on a lost *Altercatio* or on its suggested second- or third-
century neo-Pythagorean source, which he collected under the
title *Disputatio regalis iuvenis Pippini cum Albino.* But Alcuin's only
express debt, which sometimes extends even to paraphrase, is to
Symphosius.[15]

Among teachers, scholars, and clerics of such caliber the op-
portunity for allegory and spiritual instruction in riddles was
not lost. A collection of Latin prose riddles attributed to Bede
poses questions on biblical themes. The great missionary Boni-
face wrote twenty riddles, some of them with acrostic answers,
on the ten virtues and vices. In at least one critical estimation
these are "awkward and difficult allegories," so crowded with lit-
erary embellishments that as riddles they nearly fail.[16] A "diffi-
cult liturgical riddle" is found in an eleventh-century pontifical
of Nevers, but the present liturgical reading of certain poems in
*The Easter Riddle* (*Homiletic Fragment II, Riddle 30b,* and *The Hus-
band's Message*) would mean, if it is right, that English literature
boasts much earlier examples.[17] The allegorical thrust of medi-
eval riddlic texts also seems to have been widely perceived by
their readers, for such lexical glosses as there are in the riddle

---

[14] Tupper, *Riddles*, pp. xxxiv–xxxvi; Taylor, *The Literary Riddle*, p. 53.

[15] Hain, *Rätsel*, pp. 10–11.

[16] The critical judgment in quotation marks is by Taylor, *The Literary Riddle*,
pp. 62–63.

[17] Taylor, ibid., pp. 67–68, translates, answers as "(liturgical) book," and dis-
cusses this little-studied Continental text.

collections often ignore the literal meaning of words and supply their allegorical significance instead.[18]

In short, the century which, in most scholarly opinions, produced the Exeter Book riddles and the "elegies" located among them seems to have been a markedly, perhaps even predominantly, English riddling age. From earlier ages it inherited its fascination with riddling, and from its guiding spirit, Pope Gregory himself, it could also have taken a love of wordplay employed for the glory of God. In Bede's famous anecdote Gregory once observed, in a string of spiritual witticisms, that heathen Anglian slave boys from the province of Deira were indeed "angelic faces" to be rescued *de ira* 'from wrath' and that their king Ælle should one day be made to sing alleluia.[19] Worthy English scholars between Gregory's time and Alcuin's could hardly have overlooked the useful kinship between the allegory of the church fathers and the double meaning of the riddles. The historical evidence, circumstantial but also fairly strong, suggests that the Exeter Book still contains all but a few of an original century of vernacular riddles, most of which seem to be folk-inspired. The same evidence does not exclude a sly intrusion into this folk collection of two long literary riddles on allegorical conceptions.[20] These sequential riddles would seem to inherit their tandem structure from the serial riddlic tasks along a hero's way to wisdom. But in postconversion England such tours de force of antiquarian and modern learning would have answered the deep need for instruction in Christian wisdom. The designation of

[18] Ibid., p. 70.

[19] *Hist. eccl.* 2.1.

[20] Indeed, the Exeter Book may contain in the *Maxims* some unacknowledged (because truncated) riddle material. Taylor, *The Literary Riddle*, p. 16, quotes from early Vedic dialogue riddles in which the questions occur in stanzaic groups followed by corresponding groups of answers. Questions: "Who is the friend of the traveler?" "Who is the friend of him who remains at home?" "Who is the friend of the sick?" "Who is the friend of the dying?" Answers: "A caravan is the friend of the traveler." "The wife is the friend of him who remains at home." "The doctor is the friend of the sick." "Charity is the friend of the dying." The Exeter and Cotton *Maxims* strongly resemble a group of such brief riddle answers for which the questions have been lost.

*Riddle 1* and *The Easter Riddle* as "journeys to wisdom" tries to account for the combined pagan and Christian inspiration in their design, for they appear to me to follow that brilliant cultural compromise that shaped the Anglo-Saxon conversion.

Nothing is known about the anonymous tenth-century compiler-poet of such intricate and arduous riddlic journeys as these. To have challenged and instructed his readers in such fashion he must have been brilliant, and perhaps a little arrogant as well. These features of his personality and his intellectual interests encourage a guess at his identity. The ancient saga material of *Deor*, and probably also of *Wulf and Eadwacer*, seem to mark him as an avid antiquarian, yet the middle poems of *The Easter Riddle* leave little doubt that he was a monk or cleric deeply committed to the liturgical and other reform activities of his own time. In fact, *The Husband's Message*, the eucharistic poem in *The Easter Riddle*, is an extended runic pun inspired by a meditation on the Eucharist as *mysterium* (OE *geryne*), as a passage in the Old English translation of the reformed Benedictine office makes clear. Earlier in *The Easter Riddle* the first lines of *The Descent Into Hell* focus on the first Easter visit to the Holy Sepulcher. The lines remind us that the Exeter Book (variously dated from about 950 to about 990) and the first known English liturgical *quem quæritis*, in the *Regularis Concordia* of Winchester Cathedral (ca. 975), are almost contemporary productions.

Scanty as they are, such facts at least do not deny some possible links between *The Easter Riddle* and the late-tenth-century Benedictine reform. And even though *The Ruin* (like the other heroic and elegiac framework poems of our texts) is probably of eighth-century composition, the Roman ruins at Bath, the most likely literal basis for the poem, commanded repeated attention in later Anglo-Saxon times.[21] The ruined baths much interested Saint Dunstan's "Saxon" biographer of the early eleventh century, who particularly mentioned the hot springs that also ap-

---

[21] For a cogent summary of linguistic and archaeological arguments that date *The Ruin* in the eighth century, see R. F. Leslie, *Three Old English Elegies: The Wife's Lament, The Husband's Message, The Ruin*, pp. 26–28, 34–36.

pear in the poem.[22] Without straining for proof where only con-
jecture is possible, one can nevertheless imagine how contriving
hidden wisdom from diverse old and new poetry might have en-
gaged a peculiar genius like Dunstan's own. A scholar of notable
gifts and a chief exponent of the Benedictine Reform, Dunstan
(ca. 925–88) eventually rose to be archbishop of Canterbury
and political adviser of great influence especially on King Edgar
(944–75). From his earliest school days at Glastonbury, Dunstan's
wit, which was said to be remarkably brilliant, was sometimes
attended by a haughtiness that stirred the envy and malice of
his fellows. He was a keen lover and collector of old poetry, and
his famous classbook, preserved in the Bodleian Library, seems
to show, among wide-ranging interests, a youthful fascination
with runes.[23] Sometime before his death in 988, Dunstan had
turned to recounting skillfully the deeds of sacred heroes, as
the great Benedictine teacher Abbo of Fleury (945?–1004) per-
sonally remembered.[24] In 973, at the height of his power and
influence in the realm, Archbishop Dunstan prepared the order
of coronation for his friend Edgar in a great national ceremony
held at Bath. There cannot be much doubt that Dunstan went to
Bath and performed the crowning himself, though his presence
there is nowhere specifically recorded.[25] The final passage of *The
Ruin*, badly damaged but noticeably repetitious in the surviving

[22] Ibid., p. 23 & n.5.

[23] The remarks on Saint Dunstan's high intelligence, youthful promise, and en-
thusiasm for old poetry are in R. W. Hunt, Introduction, *St. Dunstan's Classbook
from Glastonbury*. Folio 20a of this photofacsimile of the *Classbook* has a runic al-
phabet of a rather fantastical form.

[24] Abbo's *Passio Sancti Eadmundi*, on the martyrdom of King Edmund of East
Anglia in 869, is dedicated to Dunstan and based on the story as Dunstan
claimed to have heard it from King Æthelstan, who had learned it from an aged
eyewitness of the martyrdom, Edmund's own armor-bearer. Dunstan was still
telling the story in his old age when Abbo heard it at Ramsey sometime between
985 and 987. Abbo's *Passio* and its dedication are in Thomas Arnold, ed., *Memori-
als of St. Edmund's Abbey*, pp. 3–25. See also G. I. Needham, ed., *Ælfric, Lives
of Three English Saints*, pp. 18–19, 43–59, a vernacular version of Edmund's
martyrdom.

[25] William Stubbs, "Memorials of St. Dunstan, Archbishop of Canterbury," in
*Historical Introduction to the Rolls Series*, pp. 20–21, notes that the anonymous

words and theme, was perhaps a spliced ending rather like the ungainly allegorical application that concludes *The Seafarer*. If the words *þæt is cynelic þing* (*Ruin* 48) play on 'kingly thing' and royal 'assembly,' as Old English *þing* can mean especially elsewhere in the Exeter Book, then the allegory of *The Ruin* may have been playfully inverted at the end to include a topical allusion to the great ceremony at Bath.[26]

In short, the secretly joined poems of *Riddle 1* and *The Easter Riddle*, from the heroic legends of *Deor* and the runic lore of *The Husband's Message* to the concealed vision of eternal bliss in *The Ruin*, might be suspected to fit more than just the general spirit of Dunstan's times. In *Riddle 1* and *The Easter Riddle* the Exeter Book scribe could have been at relatively fresh work, copying poems arranged into spiritual lessons by Dunstan himself or, at the very least, by someone from Dunstan's time and circle, a contemporary Benedictine with a mind as learned and agile as his own. If a recent opinion of an original Glastonbury provenance for the Exeter Book is right, perhaps *Riddle 1* and *The Easter Riddle* were copied at Dunstan's old school as monuments either to or of his literary interests.[27] This circumstantial evidence for Dunstan's influence in the two great sequences is, of course, too weak for anything more than speculation, though future work on other Exeter Book poetry may someday make a stronger case.

The foregoing thoughts on the riddler's method of compo-

---

Saxon priest who wrote Dunstan's first biography tells little of Edgar's reign and does not mention his successors at all. Another source, however, mentions that Dunstan himself anointed and crowned both Edward and Æthelred even though the political influence he had enjoyed under Edgar had waned. It is therefore unlikely that anyone other than Dunstan would have officiated at Bath in 973. For still another treatment of Saint Dunstan's life, including the full texts of the medieval biographies of him, see Stubbs, *Memorials of St. Dunstan, Archbishop of Canterbury*, Rolls Series 63.

[26] C. W. M. Grein, *Sprachschatz der angelsächsischen Dichter*, 2d ed., gives *þing* 2. 'Versammlung, Gerichtsversammlung,' and cites *Christ* 927, *Exeter Maxims* 18, and (noted with ? as uncertain) *Christ* 25. This meaning may have been borrowed from ON: in Mod Scand, *thing* means 'parliament.'

[27] Patrick W. Conner, "A Contextual Study of the Old English Exeter Book" (Ph.D. diss., University of Maryland, 1975), chap. 1, suggests a Glastonbury ori-

sition, the venerability of and peculiar English interest in his genre, his hidden spiritual purpose, and his Benedictine identity all bear on the remaining question of his particular audience. If *Riddle 1* and *The Easter Riddle* were conceived at Glastonbury but copied into the Exeter Book, as some scholars believe, at Crediton, then these poems once attained more than local popularity. Their pronounced Benedictine spirituality notwithstanding, they are, perhaps before all else, word games, and therefore likely to have been perceived as entertainment in a monastic community. Together *Beowulf* and Bede's story of Caedmon (*Hist. eccl.* 4.24) suggest that for the Englishman, whether monk or warrior, vernacular poetry and feasting went together, no doubt still in the tenth century as they had in the eighth. All of these premises point to the colloquium, the time after the evening meal which the monks set aside for conversation and fellowship, as a likely occasion for communal riddle solving on spiritual themes. In such an atmosphere *Riddle 1* and *The Easter Riddle* might become both written and oral productions delivered by a reader to his brethren at table. Especially if (let us suppose) a night's reading consisted of a single poem from initial to initial in the manuscript, the hearers would have been challenged not only to solve each single text but also to find the larger plan concealed over several days. Since in the Exeter Book the great tandem riddles have no obvious paleographical boundaries, their great single answers would have appeared to reader and hearers alike as vivid allegories of the divine secrets which all faithful Christians wait to know.

---

gin for the probable lost exemplar of the present MS, to which a probable origin at Crediton sometime later than 965 is assigned. Such estimated date and origin would not exclude the possibility that the final lines of *The Ruin* might contain a reference to the coronation of Edgar at Bath. Conner divides the poems of the Exeter Book into two generic groupings, a "native group" and a "church group," and argues the thesis that these groups are not demonstrably interrelated in the MS, which he continues to see as a miscellany according to prevailing scholarly opinion to date. His generic distinction is a useful one unless, as is the thesis of this book, the MS contains some innovative riddling which mixes and combines native and church poems into new texts.

# PART ONE

# *Riddle 1*: A Grim Opening Lesson

*Deor*

*Wulf and Eadwacer*

*The Soul's Address*

The end of *The Soul's Address* and *Deor*, lines 1–22, folio 100a of the Exeter Book, showing the only stanzaic decoration and layout of the entire codex. Photograph by Ron Benedict.

# INTRODUCTION

The group of three adjacent Exeter Book poems which I call *Riddle 1* is discussed here out of manuscript order. *Deor* and *Wulf and Eadwacer*, the second and third poems in the group, must first be understood as a double riddle on a well-known Germanic heroic subject: marriage by abduction, with its attendant feuding and bloodshed. Only then does the previous manuscript poem, here called *The Soul's Address*, complete the spiritual vision of *Riddle 1*. Like the earthly lovers in the two refrain poems to come, the sinful soul and body have also let a deceitful marriage lead them to a fearful disaster. The texts and translations of the three poems of *Riddle 1* are arranged as they appear in the Exeter Book.

### *Deor* and *Wulf and Eadwacer*: Fatal Marriage on Earth

Of the eight Exeter Book poems which we call elegies, the two briefest—*Deor* and *Wulf and Eadwacer* (folios 100a–101a)—are in many ways also the most obscure. The forty-two poetic lines of *Deor* seem to tell the full story of a dispossessed minstrel's lament, yet an echo of Boethian consolation seems to jar against the famous heroic stories on the minstrel's mind. As a whole, therefore, his song has a puzzling dual effect. His old heroic tales themselves also present some curious difficulties of vocabulary, names, images, and manuscript readings. The opening line of the poem, about Weland the Smith, is strangely abrupt. The third stanza tells a story whose very identity is uncertain. Worst of all, perhaps, we cannot solve these problems by obvious comparisons, since no minstrel called Deor appears anywhere else in Germanic literature.

The next nineteen lines of poetry in the manuscript, generally called *Wulf and Eadwacer* from what seem to be two men's names in the text, only magnify the uncertainties of *Deor*. The feminine nominal appositive in *ic reotugu* 'I, the wailing one' (from *reotan*, line 10) and the feminine ending on *seoce* (line 14) confirm that a woman is speaking. But the outburst *Gehyrest þu, eadwacer* at line 16, along with the shift to direct address and bitter tone and the question whether *eadwacer* and *wulf* (line 17) are proper names, might almost imply a different speaker or even a separate poem. For the unity of these nineteen lines, then, we rely heavily on the implicit word of the scribe, who copied them without a break at line 16. Moreover, since the word *eadwacer* has plausibly been read as an epithet rather than a name, the number of male figures in the poem and also the title *Wulf and Eadwacer* are open to some debate.[1] The speaker's tone has been variously assumed or described as respectful, ironic, sarcastic, jocular, and bitterly resigned.[2] But if the last lines end the story bitterly, the first line seems to put the reader even more awkwardly in medias res than does the beginning of *Deor*.

From these shadowy appearances *Wulf and Eadwacer* might be either fragmentary or complete, heroic or elegiac, or perhaps a woman's song taken as a set piece from a longer heroic work.[3] It

[1] See John F. Adams, "'Wulf and Eadwacer': An Interpretation," *MLN* 73 (1958): 5; *ASD* under *eadwacer* 'watcher of property.'

[2] For a sampling of the diverse opinions on the theme, genre, tone, and number of male figures in the poem, see Adams, "'Wulf and Eadwacer,'" pp. 1–5; Gustav Budjuhn, "Leodum is minum—ein ae. Dialog," *Anglia* 40 (1916): 256–59; Alain Renoir, "'Wulf and Eadwacer': A Non-Interpretation," in Jess B. Bessinger, Jr., and Robert P. Creed, eds., *Franciplegius: Medieval and Linguistic Studies in Honor of Francis Peabody Magoun*, pp. 147–63; Neil D. Issacs, *Structural Principles in Old English Poetry*, pp. 114–17; A. C. Bouman, *Patterns in Old English and Old Icelandic Literature*, pp. 95–106; Norman E. Eliason, "On Wulf and Eadwacer," in Robert B. Burlin and Edward B. Irving, Jr. eds., *Old English Studies in Honour of John C. Pope*, pp. 225–34; Donald K. Fry, "Wulf and Eadwacer: A Wen Charm," *ChauR* 5 (1970): 247–63; Emily Doris Grubl, *Studien zu den angelsächsischen Elegien*, pp. 163–67, 174–75, hereafter cited as *Elegien*; Charles W. Kennedy, *The Earliest English Poetry*, pp. 48–52; Marijane Osborn, "The Text and Context of *Wulf and Eadwacer*," in Martin Green, ed., *The Old English Elegies: New Essays in Criticism and Research*, pp. 174–89.

[3] The view of *Wulf and Eadwacer* as an elegy descends mainly from the opinions of Henry Bradley, in *Academy* 33 (1888): 197–98; and Levin L. Schücking,

has an unusual concentration of hapax legomena, rare words, and obscure images, far more even than in *Deor*. Its crude or irregular verse and alliteration so perplexed its first modern editor, Benjamin Thorpe, that he chose merely to print the untranslated words, of which he could neither "make . . . sense, nor . . . arrange the verses."[4] Long since arranged, the verses have received aesthetic judgments at opposite extremes. Levin L. Schücking once described the half line *Wulf, min Wulf* (line 13a) as a dramatic outcry of unmatched intensity, and indeed it appears to be a sample of the woman's wailing. But another German scholar—in an annoyed tone of voice—has called the same words "a nonverse in my view."[5] Finally, if *Deor*'s name is unfortunately unique, the woman who follows him is utterly anonymous. Every question raised in *Deor* becomes in *Wulf and Eadwacer* an agony of scholarly doubt.

In 1962, P. J. Frankis conjectured that some of our doubt might come from reading the two poems separately.[6] Except for a charm or two whose refrains stem from reiterative magic, *Deor* and *Wulf and Eadwacer* are, as Frankis noted, our only two sur-

---

*Kleines angelsächsisches Dichterbuch*, pp. 16–19, hereafter cited as *Dichterbuch*. Identifications of *Wulf and Eadwacer* with various heroic legends or poems stem from Schücking, *Dichterbuch*; W. H. Schofield, "Signy's Lament," *PMLA* 17 (1902): 262–95; and Rudolf Imelmann's books: *Die altenglische Odoaker-Dichtung*; *Wanderer und Seefahrer im Rahmen der altenglischen Odoaker-Dichtung*; *Zeugnisse zur altenglischen Odoaker-Dichtung*; and the best-known *Forschungen zur altenglischen Poesie*. The possibility that *Wulf and Eadwacer* might be an elegiac set piece from a heroic poem or cycle is proposed by Schücking.

[4] Benjamin Thorpe, ed. and trans., *Codex exoniensis: A Collection of Anglo-Saxon Poetry, etc.*, p. 527.

[5] Schücking, *Dichterbuch*, p. 17. Clifford Davidson, "Erotic 'Women's Songs' in Anglo-Saxon England," *Neophil* 59 (1975): 459 & n.2, calls *Wulf and Eadwacer* "one of the summits of Anglo-Saxon poetry" because of the presumed emotional force of its outcries. Imelmann, *Forschungen*, p. 91, attempts to emend line 13a for the sake of metrical regularity, but Ernst Sieper, *Die altenglische Elegie*, argues against emendation. I do not know whether the vocal annoyance I once heard has ever been expressed in writing.

[6] P. J. Frankis, "*Deor* and *Wulf and Eadwacer*: Some Conjectures," *MÆ* 31 (1962): 161–75.

viving Old English poems with purely literary refrains. Frankis therefore guessed that they had been deliberately placed together in the Exeter Book and supported his guess with a suggestion of cross-textual wordplay on *deor* 'beast' and *wulf*. From both texts together he deduced a hypothetical narrative, a story of thwarted love, abduction of a woman, and ensuing conflict. Even though they were not tested against every detail of the two poems, his conjectures were, I think, very nearly right. Pursued to their limits, however, Frankis's ideas suggest not his rather perfumed tragedy of wasted love but a double riddle based on a famous Germanic abduction story and full of the old heroic reek of blood and death. But the same wordplay that Frankis detected also extends beyond *Deor* and *Wulf and Eadwacer* into the preceding poem in the Exeter Book, *The Soul's Address*. From their many plays on words and themes these three texts appear to be not only distinct poems but also a long triple riddle which equates heroic abduction with spiritual death and exposes pagan heroism as bitterly unheroic in the end. In that event the Exeter Book riddles would not begin wtih *Wulf and Eadwacer*, as was once widely believed, or even with *Deor*. Possibly, though not certainly, the scribe also left some graphic clues in *Riddle 1*, whose affinities of theme begin with *The Soul's Address* on folio 98a.

To begin with, *Deor* and *Wulf and Eadwacer* share more than the simple fact of their refrains. Beneath the apparent vagueness of both refrains lies elusive rhetoric—the kind of language which defies guesses and paraphrases but seems to repay close thought. In *Deor* the refrain *þæs ofereode, þisses swa mæg* contains both uncertain pronoun reference and double meaning in the verb. *Ofereode* means not only 'passed away,' as it is often translated, but also 'went on, transferred,' especially with genitive objects such as *þæs* and *þisses*.[7] Because these pronouns are objects

---

[7] *ASD*, under *ofergan*; C. W. M. Grein, *Sprachschatz der angelsächsischen Dichter*, under *ofer-eode, ofer-gangan*; hereafter cited as *Sprachschatz*. Alternatively, Edward I. Condren, "Deor's Artistic Triumph," *SP* 78, no. 5 (1981): 65, solves *þæs* and *þisses* + verb in the refrain as "genitive of respect + imperative verb [of] common agreement" and gives the most frequent modern reading 'That passed

rather than subjects, the line seems best rendered in the passive voice: 'That was moved on; this can be, too.' The shift in tense from *ofereode* to *mæg* also hints of playfulness rather than merely clumsiness in the thought. In one sense 'that' becomes the story of each stanza which has just 'passed by' before the refrain, and 'this' becomes the next story, to which the argument of the poem can 'move on.' In the last line of *Deor*, 'that' looks backward to Deor's complaint of his own dispossession, while 'this' seems to squint ahead at *Wulf and Eadwacer*, whose refrain insists on unlikeness. Together, then, the two refrains have the aura of a riddler's wit, the same deceptive habit of mind that contrived more obvious double riddles elsewhere in the Exeter Book.

In *Riddle 42*, for one example, the scrambled rune names produce the anagrammatic solution *hana* 'cock' and *hæn* 'hen.' The remainder of the text, however, plays on widely distributed folklore motifs of the cock and hen as both fleshly and spiritual marriage partners.[8] The riddlic word *orþoncbendum* 'bonds of skillful thought' then links the copulating cock and hen in the implicit farmyard of *Riddle 42* to the nobler marriage of "body and soul," figuratively confined *in geardum*—that is, within the nature of Man—in *Riddle 43*. The scribe seems to have acknowledged the joint themes with a sly graphic trick of his own: he copied both riddles as one text but also "separated" them with a bold raised point and a somewhat elongated small capital in the middle of a manuscript line. For two later one-line fragments, *Riddles 75* and *76*, the cock and hen are again the probable solu-

---

away, so may this.' Morton Bloomfield, "The Form of *Deor*," *PMLA* 79 (1964): 535, estimates over one hundred different modern renderings of this difficult line.

    [8] Motifs of the cock (and hen) also known to the poet of *Riddles 42/43* are found in Pliny, *Natural History* 10.25; Stith Thompson, *Motif-Index of Folk-Literature*, B251.1.2; N543.2; V211.7.1; K2061.7; E732.3; Z32.1.1; Gertrude Jobes, *Dictionary of Mythology, Folklore, and Symbols*, vol. 1, under *cock* and *hen*; Hanns Bachtold-Stäubli, *Handwörterbuch des deutschen Aberglaubens*, vol. 3, under *Hahn* 3, 6, 11, and 12; vol. 4, under *Huhn*; Maria Leach and Jerome Fried, eds., *Funk and Wagnalls Standard Dictionary of Folklore, Mythology, and Legend*, under *cock*; and Beryl Rowland, *Birds with Human Souls*, pp. 20–21, 23–27.

tion. The swath maker of *Riddle 75* appears in runes as *DNLH*, feasibly deciphered as an inverted vowelless spelling of *HæLeND* 'Savior.' The riddlic creature seems to be the cock, a frequent symbol of Christ, pecking his way through scattered corn. This answer is partly urged by *Riddle 76*, which presents a single image of *ane . . . idese sittan* 'a lone lady sitting.' She might easily be a setting hen, perhaps made to stand for the brooding Church on earth.[9] These fairly certain paired riddles are good reasons for approaching *Deor* and *Wulf and Eadwacer* with a riddler's care.

To borrow a prominent motif from *Riddles 42/43* (the numbering of the Anglo-Saxon Poetic Records) a successful riddlic device is both lock and key to true meaning. Likewise, the ambiguous refrain of *Deor* both shows and conceals the true argument of the poem. At first the refrain connects the stanzas about Weland and Beadohild, which must be recognized as two sides of the same violent abduction story. The opening line of the poem says that Weland tried punishment on *him* 'them,' that is, the brothers of Beadohild. According to the old legend, Weland slaughtered them, and Deor mentions their death in the first line of stanza 2. In further accord with the legend, Deor recalls that Weland's revenge was bloody: the puzzling phrase *be wurman* (line 1) means 'with purple,' a poetic reference to blood which we know from Elizabethan speech. *Wurma* was also a dye extracted from snails, the familiar blood red of many a medieval book cover.[10] But the rest of the first stanza shows Weland as victim, whom Niðhad cruelly hobbles with *swoncre seonobende* 'thin sinew-bands' (line 6), a riddlic—indeed a skaldlike—conceit on Weland's severed hamstrings. This phrase begins a strain of Nordic touches throughout *Deor* and *Wulf and Eadwacer*: the promi-

---

[9] The possible solutions of the runes *DNLH* in *Riddle 75* as *hælend* and of *Riddle 76* as "hen" are by W. S. Mackie, ed., *The Exeter Book, Part II, Poems IX–XXXII*, p. 242. See also ASPR 3:371, n. on *Riddles 75* and *76*.

[10] *OED*, under *purple*, cites the meaning 'blood' from the 1590s. Perhaps because OE *wurma* 'purple' (dye made from a snail, etc.: see esp. Grein, *Sprachschatz*) did not survive, this OE instance of 'purple' meaning 'blood' has escaped general notice.

nent mention in *Deor* 36 of the Jutish *Heodeningas*, for example, or the strong formal resemblance of *Wulf and Eadwacer* to the Norse *ljoðhattrstrophe*.[11] But Deor's other old stories are not interrelated at all in Germanic legend. They appear together only in *Deor*, probably in some mutual connection with the singer's ambiguous refrain.

The first two stanzas of *Deor* allude to the suffering and revenge of a famous abductor and to the mental agony of his female victim. According to Frankis, *Deor* and *Wulf and Eadwacer* taken together also comprise an abduction story told alternately by a man and a woman. Deor the minstrel sketches old stories that somehow lead to a longer treatment of his own tale of woe. All of these structural clues suggest that his refrain is bound in yet divorced from narrative time. The refrain not only would look back at what has just been told and ahead to what comes next but also would draw timeless comparisons between each of Deor's old stories and his own trouble. In telling his misfortunes, however, Deor becomes a man with a grudge and a case to argue, against both his lord and the *leoðcræftig monn* 'man subtle in song' (line 40) who has taken his wealth and position. He should be slanting the old stories to favor his own case in the sixth part of the poem. If we proceed from these hypotheses, *Deor* shows a hidden coherence built around the minstrel himself.

Stanza 1 implies that Deor has sought a revenge like Weland's, apparently for the reason given in stanza 6: his *londryht* 'land rights' have been taken from him and given to another singer. Since this grievance is so much less than Weland's, violent retribution would be unjust, yet stanza 2 insinuates just such an outrage, namely, that Deor has avenged himself on a woman just as Weland did. But if Deor means to glorify Weland's deeds, and

[11] Grubl, *Elegien*, pp. 163–67; Ruth P. M. Lehmann, "The Metrics and Structure of 'Wulf and Eadwacer'," *PQ* 48 (1969): 151–65, esp. p. 163. Less successful attempts to identify *Wulf and Eadwacer* with specific Norse poems have been made by Imelmann and also by Bouman, *Patterns*, pp. 95–106. Condren, "Deor's Artistic Triumph," p. 66, briefly recounts the story of Weland's captivity, maiming, and revenge and gives its sources in full.

therefore by innuendo to exalt himself, then he would conveniently omit the more unheroic elements in the Weland story. In fact, he does not say, as the legend does, that Weland murdered his male enemies in their sleep; instead, the deaths of Beadohild's brothers are couched in riddlic language and told piecemeal across both stanzas. Stanza 1 gives five lines to Weland's suffering, but only the first line—by far the hardest—to his crimes. Stanza 2, again unlike the legend, focuses not upon the violation of a helpless woman but upon Beadohild's mental anguish afterward. The rape itself is concealed in a passing euphemism about her pregnancy, and her agony is ascribed to other causes—the deaths of her brothers, her increasing size, and worry about how a vague *þæt* 'it' (line 12) might end. Deor does not mention that Weland was the cause of all her grief.

As still further evidence for Frankis's argument, these omitted truths about Beadohild seem to appear from between the lines of the woman's narrative in *Wulf and Eadwacer*. In line 11 the woman complains that [*se beaducafa*] *mec . . . bogum bilegde* 'this man bold in war mounted me with his shoulders.' Her complaint suggests bestiality, for OE *bog* more precisely means 'shoulderbone of an animal,' and ModG *belegen* can still mean 'to mount (for sexual intercourse).' These images of brutish lovemaking belong to the main wordplay in the poem, on *Wulf* as both man and animal. Like Beadohild, the woman seems to have endured forcible rape, the probable source of her *lað* 'loathing, pain' (line 12b). Paradoxically, however, she also remembers *wyn* 'pleasure' (line 12a) and genuine anxiety and longing for Wulf during his long absences and *seldcymas* 'rare returnings' (line 14). In the Beadohild stanza of *Deor* there is no corresponding joy except, perhaps, for Beadohild's unborn child, the source of her greatest anguish. Deor, who seems so absorbed in himself, could be expected to miss the paradox of motherly love, which might then be left for the woman of *Wulf and Eadwacer* to express. But her *wyn* and *lað* also seem to riddle on the curse of Eve (Gen. 2:16), which Gregory the Great once explained (Bede, *Hist. eccl.* 1.27) as the pleasure of bodily union and the pain of childbirth.

Implicitly, then, if not quite expressly, the speaker of *Wulf and*

*Eadwacer* 12 appears to share both Beadohild's confused feel-
ings and their cause. The otherwise mysterious *hwelp* of *Wulf
and Eadwacer* would thus become a riddlic one—a child stolen
while still in the womb of its abducted mother. Of several pro-
posed emendations for *earne* (line 16), *ear[m]ne* best sustains the
riddlic theme of maternal grief: this woman seems to worry, as
Beadohild does, about the dark future of her 'poor whelp' con-
ceived in misfortune.[12] The unique compound *beaducafa* 'man
bold in war' (line 11) seems, then, to be a bitter and grief-laden
choice of words. It applies to Wulf's bestial embraces, not his
deeds, and probably insinuates that he is bold mainly at pressing
women. But perhaps also, in an unspoken parallel with Weland,
Wulf has "boldly" committed stealthy murders of his own before
taking flight. In her harder words and images Wulf's bride seeks
to compare him with Weland in most unflattering ways.[13]

[12] ASPR 3:320 reviews the various emendations of MS *earne* in older scholar-
ship. Many scholars, including Martin Lehnert, ed., *Poetry and Prose of the Anglo-
Saxons*, 1:24; and Lehmann, "Metrics and Structure," pp. 162, 164, emend to or
accept *ear[m]ne*. Possibly the poet had in mind a gnomic idea: *Wulf sceal in bearwe,
earm anhaga* (*Cotton Gnomes* 18). See also the discussion and n. 30 below.

[13] John M. Fanagan, "*Wulf and Eadwacer*: A Solution to the Critics' Riddle,"
*Neophil* 60 (1976): 132, interprets the words *beaducafa* and *eadwacer*, regardless of
their reference, to suggest "a tyrannously vigilant possessor" of the speaker.
Among the more recent interpretations of *Wulf* and *eadwacer* as ironic refer-
ences to the same person is Emily Jensen, "Narrative Voice in the Old English
*Wulf*," *ChauR* 13 (1979): 373–83. Jensen thinks of the last lines as the speaker's
objection to Wulf's insensitivity rather than as grim hints of his danger. Wesley S.
Mattox, "Encirclement and Sacrifice in *Wulf and Eadwacer*," *AnM* 16 (1975):
39–40, takes the broad resemblance of *Wulf and Eadwacer* to the Beadohild saga
as hints of the speaker's killing of her own child in revenge against her people
(line 1) for their impending crime against Wulf. Arnold E. Davidson, "Interpret-
ing *Wulf and Eadwacer*," *AnM* 16 (1975): 24–32, revives an old argument for
reading the poem as a love triangle. George K. Anderson, *The Literature of the
Anglo-Saxons*, p. 164, has objected to this reading on the grounds that love tri-
angles are otherwise unknown in Old English literature. Osborn, "The Text and
Context of *Wulf and Eadwacer*," p. 179, thinks of MS *eadwacer* as a proper noun
designating someone other than Wulf, and of the speaker of the poem as Wulf's
mother. This interpretation does not account for the apparent sexual innuendo
in the poem. In sum, the thoroughgoing ambiguity of the text, itemized by such

Deor, however, is also busy comparing himself with other famous avengers besides Weland. In stanza 4 the minstrel relives the glory of Theodoric of Verona, who returned after long exile to the wealth and power he had lost. The clue to Theodoric's identity lurks in the words *ahte . . . mæringa burg*, not a reference to a place or tribe but a skaldic conceit on exile. The word *mæring*, found only this once in poetry, denotes a medicinal herb or flower, perhaps basil, in Anglo-Saxon leechcraft. The declaration *Ðeodric ahte þritig wintra mæringa burg* would then become another skaldic touch, meaning 'Theodoric held for thirty winters a fortress of basil flowers,' i.e., lived in exile in open fields, an ironic "stronghold" indeed.[14] These thirty years of exile, which Theodoric of Verona overcame, Deor wrongly compares with his own lost minstrelsy and forfeited landholding privileges of *fela wintra* 'many winters' (line 38): the echo of *wintra* is the riddlic key for this larger argument. Deor's hope, expressed in the refrain, that like Theodoric's his own exile will pass, would perhaps be Boethian if only it made good sense. But whereas the Theodoric of legend was unjustly exiled, the Weland and Beadohild stories and their probable analogies in *Wulf and Eadwacer* already suggest that Deor is hardly innocent of crime. The falsity of his comparison undermines the hope of his refrain.

---

scholars as Davidson (above) and Peter S. Baker, "The Ambiguity of *Wulf and Eadwacer*," *SP* 78 (1981): 39–51, continues to generate and regenerate certain fundamental interpretive issues.

[14] *ASD* gives *mæring* as 'a plant name' but notes that Oswald Cockayne, ed., *Leechdoms, Wortcunning, and Starcraft of Early England*, 3 : 21, suggests 'sweet basil' from context in a medicinal recipe. Condren, "Deor's Artistic Triumph," pp. 72–73; and Kevin Kiernan, "*Deor*: The Consolation of an Anglo-Saxon Boethius," *NM* 79 (1978): 338, follow Frankis in reading MS *mæringa burg* as an allusion to Theodoric's fortress city of Ravenna. Alternatively, Kemp Malone, in his edition of *Deor* and in several articles (see n. 15 below), would identify stanza 4 not with Theodoris of Verona but with Theodoric the Frank. Joyce Hill, ed., *Old English Minor Heroic Poems*, p. 93, cites evidence from the ninth-century Rök runestone, Notker of Saint Gall's translation of Boethius's *De consolatione philosophiae*, and Procopius's history of the Gothic wars of *Mæring* as a possible place-name or tribal name. The question whether *mæringa* in *Deor 14* is a common noun or a proper noun must therefore remain open.

Nevertheless, the refrain also "moves on" to stanza 5 and Eormanric, Theodoric's lord in legend though not in history. This legendary connection, which is not exploited in stanzas 4 and 5, is perhaps a deliberately false trail. Indeed, stanza 5 is only superficially about Eormanric, the cruelest tyrant of Germanic song and story, in Deor's words a man of *wylfenne geþoht* and a *grim cyning* (lines 22–23). The second half of the stanza is given to Deor's real purpose, not Eormanric himself but his oppressed subjects, who sat *sorgum gebunden* 'bound in sorrows' (line 24) and wished for the tyrant's downfall. Deor's ulterior motive for telling their side of the story is revealed, again with a sly lexical echo, as the minstrel begins his own complaint in stanza 6. He, too, knows how a man *siteð sorgcearig* 'sits full of sorrow' (line 28) when his luck turns bad. By comparing himself with the persecuted Goths of old, Deor begs the other side of the question with a liberal dash of self-pity: his own lord, who has cruelly cast him out, is Eormanric's match in tyranny and injustice. The suggested parallel between Deor and the Goths, both secret malefactors of their lords, is cunningly left unwrought.

The obscure and much-discussed third stanza begins with the claim that 'we . . . many have heard' its legend, and the mention of sleeplessness and *sorglufu* 'sorrowful love' (line 16) implies a love story both tragic and famous. If this tale is as celebrated as all the others, *mæð hilde* (line 14) probably does not contain the otherwise unknown and phonologically unlikely name Mæðhild.[15] But if the name is *Hild* instead, and if *Geates* (line 15)

---

[15] Condren, "Deor's Artistic Triumph," p. 71, derives MS *mæð hilde* from OHG *Mathilt*. But T. Northcote Toller, *Supplement to An Anglo-Saxon Dictionary* (hereafter cited as *Supplement*) under *Mæðhild*, takes sound phonetic objection to such a derivation. The widely various readings and emendations of MS *mæð hilde* may be traced in Grein, *Sprachschatz*, under *mæð*, and also in *Bibliothek der angelsächsischen Poesie*, 1:250; Mackie, ed., *The Exeter Book, Part II*, pp. 82–83; Sieper, *Elegie*, pp. 125, 156–57; Kemp Malone, "On *Deor* 14–17," in *Studies in Heroic Legend and in Current Speech by Kemp Malone*, ed. Stefan Einarsson and Norman E. Eliason, pp. 142–58; Kemp Malone, ed., *Deor*, pp. 8–9, 37 n. 1; Kemp Malone, "An Anglo-Latin Version of the Hjaðningavig," *Speculum* 39 (1964): 35–44; Kemp Malone, "The Tale of Geat and Mæðhild," *ES* 19 (1937): 193–99;

hides a riddlic eponym *Geat* 'Jute,' spelled as in *Anno 449* of *The Anglo-Saxon Chronicle*, then the lines call to mind a widely told tale of abduction which Saxo Grammaticus knew as Jutish. This is the story of the eternal fight of the Heodenings. In four separate Scandinavian versions including Saxo's, Hild is stolen by Heoden and pursued by her angry father to an island supposedly in either the North Sea or the Baltic.[16] Instead of making peace between Heoden and Hagena and their battle-poised armies, Hild falsely tells each general that his enemy will fight to the death. A prominent feature of the legend is a ring which Heoden offers as a bridal price to effect the truce, and perhaps Hild originally took offense at the cheap offer. But in the extant versions her treachery goes unexplained and only redoubles her Valkyrian mystery and power. Each night after the fighting, she ranges the battlefield and rouses the slain with her magic, so that the warfare over her is forever resumed at daybreak. All the contested details of lines 14–17 in *Deor* can be read as riddlic traces of this story.

If we can judge from spellings found in Anglo-Saxon law, the word *frige* (line 15) is a variant plural of *freo* 'freeman, soldier.'[17]

---

Kemp Malone, "Mæðhild," *ELH* 3 (1966); 253–56; F. Norman, "Deor: A Criticism and an Interpretation," *MLR* 22 (1937): 374–81; F. Norman, "Deor and Modern Scandinavian Ballads," *London Mediaeval Studies* 1, no. 2 (1937–39): 165–78; Thorpe, ed. and trans., *Codex exoniensis*, p. 378; R. K. Gordon, trans., *Anglo-Saxon Poetry*, rev. ed., p. 71; R. W. Chambers, *Widsith: A Study in Old English Heroic Legend*, pp. 21 ff.; R. M. Wilson, *The Lost Literature of Medieval England*, p. 25; Michael Alexander, trans., *The Earliest English Poems*, rev. ed., p. 36; Constance B. Hieatt, trans., *Beowulf and Other Old English Poems*, rev. ed., p. 85 and n. 2; and numerous other places. Condren, "Deor's Artistic Triumph," and also Kiernan, "*Deor*: The Consolation," p. 338, accept Malone's reported discovery of a Geat-Mæðhild story outside *Deor*. Kiernan, working from the occurrence of some Germanic names assigned to characters in the Alfredian Boethius, seeks to identify Geat and Mæðhild as Orpheus and Eurydice. But the Orpheus-Eurydice interlude, an Alfredian revision of the story in Boethius's *Consolatio*, shows itself no trace of the names Geat or Mæðhild.
[16] See Chambers, *Widsith*, pp. 101, 104; Malone, "An Anglo-Latin Version of the Hjaðningavíg," pp. 36–38.
[17] Felix Liebermann, *Die Gesetze der Angelsachsen*, 2:1, 80–81, under *freo*; and

*Geates frige* would refer not to 'Geat's love,' as it is usually rendered, but rather to 'the Jute's [i.e., Hagena's] troops'—a riddlic clue to the armies of the Heodening myth. If line 14 is understood to name Hild, then *þæt mæð* could only designate the neuter OE cognate of OHG *mad*, MHG *mat* 'harvest, mowing.'[18] Probably, then, the poet intended another skaldic conceit here, this time on mowing. Hild's destructive "harvest" consists not of hay but of Geat's men, who become *grundlease* 'loose from the ground' like hay when it is mown. The metaphor implies a mental picture of Hild gathering up the slain like hay from their resting places. Abruptly shifting his metaphor, however, the poet expresses this reaping, in grammar more like OSax than OE, as 'rob[bing] them all [i.e., the dead] of their sleep.'[19] Behind the shift perhaps lies some riddlic wordplay whereby the Anglo-Saxon reader was challenged to leap from *binom* 'robbed' (line 16) to the synonymous *bireafde*, then to an unspoken pun on *ripan* 'to reap.'

Probably because it was an abduction story belonging to Deor's own people, the *Heodeningas* (line 36), and therefore closest to the riddlic center of his narrative, this middle stanza was also carefully infused with more riddlic obstacles than any other discrete part of *Deor*. But perhaps there is some even keener craftiness of Deor's part. As in stanza 5, where he appears to insinuate that his lord is like Eormanric, so stanza 3 might attempt to pass blame on a woman who has acted like Hild. For the present it

1:128 ("Ælfred und Guthrum" 5). Sieper, *Elegie*, pp. 157–58, follows older scholarship in reading *frige* of *Deor* 15 as 'Freien,' *homines liberi, viri ingenui, proceres*—i.e., freeman of some kind rather than 'loves, affections,' etc. The legal meaning of *frige* then perfectly fits *Deor* as a riddle word.

[18] Malone, "On *Deor* 14–17," pp. 146–47, rightly finds no evidence for Grein's and Mackie's assumption of a neuter OE noun corresponding to ON *meiða*. But *ASD* and Toller, *Supplement*, give OE and MHG authority for a neuter noun *mæð* 'mowing, hay-harvest.' Thomas Tuggle, "The Structure of *Deor*," *SP* 74 (1977): 232–33, also notes that MS *þæt mæð* can only mean 'hay harvest' and that *mæð hilde* would therefore mean 'harvest of battle,' but he does not try to fit this reading into the larger context of the stanza or the poem.

[19] On the peculiar grammar of *Deor* 16 the best brief review is still ASPR 3:319 n.

would be hard to imagine how Deor's rival Heorrenda, or even the wittiest of Norse skalds, could be more *leoðcræftig* 'subtle in song' (line 40) than the wily minstrel himself.

Woven among his artful old stories, Deor's real complaint appears to be his best-guarded secret, to be pieced together from what he does not say at least as much as from what he says. Like Weland he has brooded over an injustice and apparently exacted bloody revenge for it. From stanza 2, about Beadohild, we might guess that he has abducted and impregnated a woman, perhaps after also killing someone in her family. In stanza 3 he refers darkly to the most famous abduction story of his own people, a great mythical drama which he has perhaps hoped to restage. He seems here to have a dual purpose: to glorify his violent deeds while also excusing them as crimes, by the simple device of blaming others for provoking and betraying him. Stanza 4 suggests that, like Theodoric, he has been exiled. In stanza 5 he claims to resent his lord as justly as Eormanric's subjects resented their tyrant-king. Matched against the old legend, this last comparison is clearly overblown. Whereas Eormanric was cruel enough to have his own wife drawn apart by horses on mere suspicion of infidelity, Deor's only substantial complaint is that his own lord has seized his wealth and position and given them to another singer. His suffering, then, also falls far short of the imprisonment and maiming that Weland endured, and, unlike Theodoric, he has probably caused his own exile. Even his attempt to discredit his rival as *leoðcræftig* only seems to recoil upon himself, for the word shows his own craftiness, especially at self-delusion, but involuntarily praises Heorrenda as 'skillful in song.' Instead of achieving a fame like Heoden's, Deor seems to become, like Unferð in *Beowulf*, a braggart and would-be hero who cannot get his stories straight.

Like all other such falseness, Deor's seems to begin in the refusal of wisdom. In lines 31–34 he remembers, as Boethius also knew all too well, that the favor of this world is changeable. But rather than consolation, Deor's last refrain seems to imply a foolish hope built on the fickleness of princes: as his lord's disfavor came over him, so it can pass, too. In this quite un-Boethian self-deception he shows himself to be both a lesser hero than Heoden and a lesser minstrel than Heorrenda. Worse still, the other meaning of the double-edged refrain—its suggestion of onward movement into the next poem—stands to unmask Deor to the world. With Frankis I believe that *Wulf and Eadwacer* takes up the abducted bride's part of the story. The many ambiguities of the woman's song would then need to be solved not only internally but also as riddlic rebuttals to the folly in *Deor*.[20] From a love turned to bitterness she now looks back to proclaim her unlikeness to the cunning minstrel, whom she calls *Wulf* either in truth or in riddlic wordplay on his rapacity or his deceptiveness or both. *Ungelic(e) is us*, she says: 'For us it is unlike.' But the unwritten 'it' of the OE will also prove to be a riddle that embraces far more than one unlikeness.

Most obviously, perhaps, the foolish braggadocio of *Deor* is unlike the bitter tone of *Wulf and Eadwacer*. Even as the minstrel flatters, excuses, pities, and deludes himself, the woman is contriving grim riddles of her own on his desperate plight. The stark reality is summed up in her final words, which Frankis and others have recognized as a biting turn on the words of the marriage promise. Insofar as the word *giedd* can mean 'formal speech, vow,' *uncer giedd geador* 'our vow together,' the woman declares, was never joined, and *mon eape tosliteð* 'is easily rent asunder' (lines 19a, 18a). Her use of *toslitan* 'to rend, tear, or bite to pieces' extends a dominant theme of wolfish rapacity in the poem.[21] With the entire thought the sense of her earlier lines

[20] All but one or two of the internal solutions for the obscurities of the poem in Peter S. Baker, "The Ambiguity of *Wulf and Eadwacer*" (see n. 13 above) are nevertheless accepted here. Fanagan, "*Wulf and Eadwacer*: A Solution," p. 133, notes the contrast between the "generalized, moralizing tone" of the refrain of *Deor* and the specificity of the refrain in *Wulf and Eadwacer*. If the two refrain poems are read together, this difference makes the woman's song seem all the more like harsh rebuttal of Deor's.

[21] James B. Spamer, "The Marriage Concept in *Wulf and Eadwacer*," *Neophil* 62 (1978): 143–44, notes a gloss of the Vulgate *separet* of Matt. 19:6 with OE *to-slitan* in the Lindisfarne Gospels, and suggests that *to-slitan* might therefore have been a natural and unemphatic rendering of the idea 'put asunder.' However

agrees: their marriage in the wilderness has been only a pre-
carious togetherness, full of pain and weeping and long periods
of separation and now subject to a violent end. This dramatic
disparity between Deor's and the woman's tone also seems to have
a technical cause which the poet has hidden in the ambiguous
word *giedd*. Besides 'vow, formal speech,' *giedd* also means 'song,
poem,' and thus carries the innuendo of two songs—that is, *Deor*
and *Wulf and Eadwacer*—whose marriage has been an uneasy
one at best. By inference the two poems themselves make a
strange and unlikely pair, perhaps a union of heroic and elegiac
song. No one, it seems, had ever joined them, until their tenuous
partnership was made with a riddler's wit. Thus, I think, the
woman's last lines twist the meaning of the unlikeness which she
has already twice asserted in her refrain.

In the story created by the dual texts, she is unlike Wulf, or
Deor-Wulf, first because of her knowledge of his peril. Her song
closes with a chilling hint of easy separation by bestial violence
(line 18), an echo of the explicit theme in the opening lines. In
the puzzling first line she seems to see Wulf as an easy victim of
*leodum . . . minum*, that is, of members of her own family or clan.
She implies that he is about to become a *lac*, a word that means
'gift,' sometimes with the innuendo of 'sacrifice, [sacrificial] vic-
tim.'[22] The resulting image would be as skaldic as the conceits of

---

true this guess might be for OE generally, the poet can hardly have overlooked
the fortunate wordplay in the word *to-slitan* in the special context of *Wulf and
Eadwacer*.

[22] Baker, "Ambiguity," pp. 40–41, argues soundly from context and philologi-
cal evidence for 'gift,' but the larger context of *Riddle 1* would imply that *lac*, even
used with *giefan*, could be sarcastic here. The difficulties which line 1 (and the
poem as a whole) has presented in scholarship can also be deduced from Imel-
mann, *Forschungen*, pp. 100–105; Lehmann, "Metrics and Structure," p. 157;
and from comparisons of several full translations: by Henry Bradley, given in
full in Kennedy, *The Earliest English Poetry*, p. 49; Kemp Malone, "Two English
Frauenlieder," in Stanley B. Greenfield, ed., *Studies in Old English Literature in
Honor of Arthur G. Brodeur*, p. 108 (prose); Kemp Malone, *Ten Old English Poems
Put into Modern English Alliterative Verse*, p. 21 (poetry); Mackie, ed., *The Exeter
Book, Part II*, p. 87; Adams, "'Wulf and Eadwacer': An Interpretation," p. 5; Bur-
ton Raffel, *Poems from the Old English*, 2d ed., p. 64; Bouman, *Patterns*, p. 105;

*Deor*, since it calls to mind the heathen sacrifices of wolves and men together which so repulsed Adam of Bremen on his visit to the sacred groves of Old Uppsala. In *Wulf and Eadwacer* itself the line seems to make an ironic skaldic hit at Deor-Wulf, who cannot see for himself how much he resembles the impotent victims of Hild. The next line, which assumes special urgency as part of the refrain, also hints that Wulf's enemies have the advantage of surprise. The unique word *aþecgan* probably adds some trenchant irony of its own. With its perfective prefix, its causative relationship to *þicgan* 'to consume food or drink,' and its resemblance to the words *geþecgan* 'to be consumed (by thirst)' and *ofþecgan* 'to be slain (by the sword),' *aþecgan* seems to mean not merely 'kill' but 'consume completely,' or, in the context of wordplay on *Wulf*, 'eat up.'[23] Taking *þreat* to mean 'troop, crowd, pack

---

Gordon, *Anglo-Saxon Poetry*, rev. ed., p. 81; Sieper, *Elegie*, pp. 179–82 passim, 275; Lehmann, "Metrics and Structure," p. 164; Alexander, *The Earliest English Poems*, p. 85. A strong case for reading *lac* in the sense of 'sacrifice,' with reference to Bede's testimony on pagan sacrifices of animals, is made by Mattox, "Encirclement and Sacrifice," pp. 35–37. Osborn, "Text and Context," p. 179, suggests that by the last lines the speaker has realized that Wulf is the predator rather than the victim she had thought of in line 1. This reading could help explain the speaker's change in tone as the poem progresses, a shift also noticed by Mattox, "Encirclement"; Renoir, "A Non-Interpretation"; and others. But I suspect that the apparent shift of tone in *Wulf and Eadwacer* can be explained instead as the female speaker's clever deception throughout the poem.

[23] On *aþecgan*, see Baker, "Ambiguities," pp. 42–45 passim, who cites linguistic and internal evidence for the generic meaning 'kill.' Although it is probably correct, the generic meaning also seems to miss the likely specific wordplay on the theme of ravenous beasts. The wordplay can be deduced from the various dictionary entries for (*a-*)*þecgan*, *geþecgan*, *ofþecgan*, the similar word *ofþyrsted* in *The Soul's Address* 37, and the rare poetical contexts of all these words. The causative relationship of *þecgan* to *þicgan* is also a helpful clue. For the considerable difficulty presented by the word, see the various renderings in the translations (n. 22 above); Imelmann, *Forschungen*, pp. 82–85; Schofield, "Signy's Lament," p. 266; Lehmann, "Metrics and Structure," p. 158. A long line of scholars, most recently represented by Osborn, "Text and Context," p. 177, takes the repeated line (2 and 8) containing *aþecgan* as a question. My reading of the line as a statement assumes that deliberate (i.e., riddlic) ambiguity, rather than uncertainty, is the prevailing mood of the poem.

[? of wolves],' I think line 2 forebodes tragedy with a tinge of black humor: "They'll eat him up if he comes to the pack." While Deor absurdly hopes for reconciliation with his estranged lord, the woman sees her Wulf in danger of being chewed up himself. In the next line she might even be gloating a bit to be "unlike" him.

Wulf's bride sees his military situation, which is the riddlic matter of the next few lines, from a safe distance, for they are separated from one another on two islands. In line 5 the woman knows that Wulf's island is *fæst* and *fenne biworpen*, 'fast' and 'encircled by fen.' To judge from the theme of impending slaughter in line 1, however, *fæst* is probably a riddlic word, not 'secure,' as it is usually understood, but rather 'made fast, sealed off' against Wulf's escape. A picture then emerges of a man surrounded, caught between impassable marshes and men who are *wælreowe* (line 6), perhaps not so much bloodthirsty in general as "eager for blood," specifically Wulf's. They now appear to be the woman's own angry people, with whom she abruptly began her song. From all the riddlic clues the drama in the first lines of the poem seems clear: Wulf's angry pursuers have "unjoined" the lovers on two islands, have stealthily encircled the unwatchful Wulf on one of them, and need only play the waiting game to make their easy kill. Joined together with *Deor*, the situation so far would be full of ironic unlikenesses: Deor sings of Weland's imprisonment but seems not to know of his own entrapment; he thinks in terms of deeds known to many, yet he seems to be outnumbered and even alone. His predicament is not heroic but miserable and desperate, and the woman's knowledge, compared with his ignorance, is terrible indeed.

The bride's suffering, as unlike Deor-Wulf's as Beadohild's misery was unlike Weland's, is recounted in the past tense in *Wulf and Eadwacer* 9–15. In some part her superior knowledge of the threat against her abductor proceeds from the very nature of a woman's lament, which can complain of suffering without heroic delusions—without, say, the Wanderer's fleeting impulse to keep his heroic silence (*Wanderer* 11b–14). In this middle passage the speaker recalls her exile with Wulf in the elegiac manner, with images of sadness in which even the "rainy weather" cooperates (line 10), loneliness and sickness and uncertainty of Wulf's rare visits to her in the wilderness (lines 13–15a), and her agony of joy and loathing at his rough embraces (lines 11–12). *Nales meteliste* 'not at all lack of meat' (line 15b) at first suggests that her anguish has been psychological rather than physical and seems to commend her abductor as a good forager and hunter, like his namesake the wolf. But I think the verse is really an indelicate riddle on her final parallel with Beadohild: from the ambivalent joy and suffering of her carnal union with Wulf she still has "no lack of meat," for she now hides a *hwelp* in her womb and between the lines of her song. The faint sarcasm of a riddlic likeness to Beadohild would in some measure belie her elegiac voice.

If Wulf's bride could thus be closing her memories on a false note, it would especially behoove us to know how her sad reverie begins. But line 9 is arguably the most difficult of the entire poem, since its preterite verb *dogode* is a hapax legomenon of uncertain meaning. It is sometimes identified with OSax *adogian*, unfortunately also a hapax, which seems in its only recorded instance to mean 'endure,' in which case the woman would be saying *Wulfes ic mines widlastum . . . dogode* 'I endured my Wulf's tracks of exile.' But this is an illogical way of introducing her own wandering unless she is purposely speaking in an impossibly hard riddle. Moreover, even in a poem of such unusual verse as *Wulf and Eadwacer*, the rare but regular b verse of a short stem vowel *dogode* appears to eclipse the otherwise unknown versification which *dōgode*, from OE *\*(a-)dōgian*, would require. From the pervasive wordplay on *Wulf*, a *hwelp*, and carnivorous activity such as devouring, tearing, and carrying off meat, I think the disputed word is *dogode*, the preterite of OE *\*dogian* 'to dog,' with dative object grammar like its probable synonym *folgian* 'to follow.' The noun *docga* 'dog' occurs only once in Old English, as a gloss for L *canis* in a figure of speech about just such cruel and rapacious men as Wulf and his wolfish attackers.[24] From the

---

[24] For the type of (rare) versification perhaps involved in *Wulf and Eadwacer* 9b, see, for example, A. J. Bliss, *An Introduction to Old English Metre*, pp. 15–16, 30.

noun, probably a pejorative word, the riddling poet of *Wulf and Eadwacer* might even have invented his verb. The inconsistent medial consonant of *docga/dogode* might derive from a Celtic origin, as parallel spellings of early ME *hogge, hoge* 'hog,' a confirmed Celtic loanword, would seem to attest.[25] The whole of line 9 thus appears to say that the woman 'dogged' Wulf's tracks in exile *wenum* 'with thought,' or 'with deliberation' i.e., deliberately or voluntarily. But *dogode*, if it means 'dogged,' would also have overtones of cunning or malice, and *wenum* would then seem to mean 'by design.' If so, the speaker's words suggest elopement, the typical behavior of women in Germanic abduction stories; yet in line 11 her use of animal imagery hints of forcible rape.[26]

---

In disagreement with Baker, "Ambiguity," pp. 46–47, who accepts the emendation to *hogode* as argued by Alfred Bammesberger, *Beiträge zu einem etymologischen Wörterbuch des Altenglischen*, p. 37, I do not find *\*dogian* to be an entirely "supposititious" verb. *MED* has *dogged, doggedli, doggedlice*, all possible evidence of an unrecorded verb *dogge(n)* from OE *\*do(c)gian*. For early-sixteenth-century citations of 'to dog' as 'to follow or pursue' (usually with stealth or malicious intent), see *OED*, under *dog* v. On the single occurrence of OE *docgena*, gen. pl. of *docga* used figuratively in a gloss for evil and vicious men of the kind who also inhabit *Wulf and Eadwacer*, see Herbert D. Meritt, *Fact and Lore About Old English Words*, p. 123, par. 4. For the long history of the argument over the emendation of MS *dogode* to *hogode*, see also Imelmann, *Forschungen*, p. 86; *ASD*, reversed by Toller, *Supplement*, and Alistair Campbell, *Addenda and Corrigenda to An Anglo-Saxon Dictionary*. Mattox, "Encirclement and Sacrifice," p. 37, accepts MS *dogode*, possibly as an obscure reference to encirclement. Osborn, "Text and Context," p. 182, also thinks of MS *dogode* as the verb 'to dog' and cautiously translates 'to follow.' If MS *dogode* is retained as our earliest recorded instance of 'dogged, followed [in stealth or malice],' a meaning which would fit perfectly the context and wordplay of *Wulf and Eadwacer*, then *ic [wulfes widlastum] wenum dogode* 'I deliberately dogged [Wulf's tracks]' might ultimately be more of the double-talk and excuse making of which I am already accusing Deor and his bride. On the strength of such eminently possible wordplay on *wolf/dog* and on the thematic bestiality of the poem, I have retained the MS reading of line 9.

[25] Max Förster, *Keltisches Wortgut im Englischen*, p. 18 (ae *hogg* oder *\*hocg*), documents ME variants *hogge, hoge* and suggests that *dog*, like *hog*, was originally a Celtic loanword. See also Thomas Wright, *Old English Vocabularies*, 1:698, 36–37; 758, 18–19; 611, 35, for ME spellings *hoge, hoggeshere*.

[26] Johannes Hoops, *Reallexikon der germanischen Altertumskunde*, 3:460ff. ("Raubehe"), finds only elopements—no forcible rapes—as Germanic literary themes.

Given the relative powerlessness of Germanic women even in the late times of codified law, we cannot presume that women's elopements were not also brutally forced; indeed, they probably sometimes were.[27] But in *Wulf and Eadwacer* the speaker uses the word *wenum*, a hint of acquiescence, at least, in her own exile. She cries out *Wulf, min Wulf*, as to a lover whose long absences made her sick, and she remembers their life in exile as a time of mixed joy and pain. In a plain word, her argument somehow does not add up.

As before, this imbalance of theme in *Wulf and Eadwacer* should perhaps be weighed against some unresolved innuendo in *Deor*. One such possibility remains: the minstrel's elusive suggestion, near the heart of his scheme, of yet another woman as treacherous and ferocious as Hild. Like the Weland and Beadohild stories, the Hild stanza of *Deor* seems to answer a veiled duplicity in the lament of Wulf's captive bride. This duality is already reflected in the intuition of those many scholars who agree to name the poem *Wulf and Eadwacer* because it seems to address two different men. The two islands of line 4 are a likely riddlic

---

Thus Deor's bride, much like Deor himself and like the false soul in *The Soul's Address*, seems to be talking deceitfully: on the one hand she loved Wulf, and followed him willingly; on the other (to excuse herself now that she is apparently caught) she dogged him deliberately, with the malicious intention of entrapping him.

[27] Germanic sources themselves do not entirely sustain Tacitus's (or some modern scholars') enthusiasm for the dignity and respect allegedly given to Germanic women. Cf. the laws of Æthelberht of Kent, which provide monetary compensations and fines for injuries done to women by beating, seduction, and possibly also rape but do not expressly forbid such treatment. See Liebermann, *Gesetze*, 2:2 ("Eheschliessung") for review of women's elaborately defined (but also thereby elaborately restricted) freedoms in the English marriage codes. Two other important studies on the question of Germanic women's status are Gerda Merschberger, *Die Rechtsstellung der germanischen Frau*; and Reinhold Bruder, *Die germanische Frau im Lichte der Runeninschriften und der antiken Historiographie*. For enthusiastic modern acceptance of Tacitus's view of respected Germanic women and their "companionable" marriages, see Hilda Ellis Davidson, *Gods and Myths of Northern Europe*, p. 10; but for equally overstated opposition to Tacitus's view see John Thrupp, *The Anglo-Saxon Home: A History of the Domestic Institutions and Customs of England, from the Fifth to the Eleventh Century*, p. 21.

clue that *Wulf* and *eadwacer* are not the same person and that the last lines of the poem, beginning with *Gehyrest þu, eadwacer?* (line 16a), are not spoken to Wulf, who seems to appear in third person as the figurative beast in line 17. I think the question (or exclamation) is spoken to one of the speaker's angry clan, someone called *wælreowe* in the earlier lines.

The word *eadwacer* 'wealthwatcher' seems to me to be a sarcastic epithet, immediately reversed by a reminder of the stolen *ear[m]ne hwelp* 'poor whelp,' who stands to disgrace the family. Her last lines would then incite *eadwacer* to make quick work of Wulf and of her own nonmarriage—in other words, to take the "gift" of easy slaughter in her opening line. Pursued, like Hild, and perhaps also caught by her family, she seems now to turn on Deor-Wulf with the treachery of Hild and the ferocity of Norse saga heroines who urge their menfolk on to bloody revenge. Small clues of her two-facedness even seem to occupy her refrain. The plural, not dual, pronoun *us* in *Ungelic is us* (line 3) seems to designate more people than just Wulf and the bride herself: 'For us [Wulf and me and someone else?] it is unlike.' The line seems to declare the woman's arrogant presumption of her own safety. Even more vague and uncertain, the grammar of *Ungelice is us* (line 8) hints at plural things, i.e., vague conditions, and perhaps also a hidden shift of reference: 'For us [my people and me?] the situation is unlike [all of Wulf's dangers].[28] Simi-

---

[28] Baker, "Ambiguity," pp. 45–46, discusses the grammatical dual-plural ambiguity of *us* in the refrain, concluding from internal evidence that "the speaker unwillingly finds herself on both sides of the battle." In terms of purely Germanic themes this judgment is probably correct. In the larger scheme of *Riddle 1*, however, the falseness and duplicity of the soul, Deor, and possibly also his bride would suggest that her ambiguity is a deliberate attempt to conceal her own acquiescence in her abduction. Much, of course, depends on one's reading of the difficult and perhaps even riddlic word *wenum* in line 9. Jensen, "Narrative Voice," p. 375, thinks of *us* as a reference to the speaker and her lover, different from the rest of the lovers in the world. This reading has the support of *The Wife's Lament* 35–37, where such a sentiment is plainly expressed, but it does not explain why the speaker in *Wulf and Eadwacer* does not use the dual form *unc* rather than the plural *us*. Moreover, the variant forms *ungelic* and *ungelice* could

larly, the woman would abandon her false outcry to Wulf (lines 13–15) to divert *eadwacer's* lust for vengeance from herself. The small and perhaps secret variation in her refrain should therefore be given more attention than it customarily receives, for its grammar seems to link *eadwacer* with *leodum . . . minum* 'my people' of line 1. The woman's entire song as I read it would be a cunning abandonment of the man she also pretends to love, a deception much like the poem of the shifty minstrel whom she professes to be 'unlike.' But her riddle is even harder than Deor's, perhaps because she is even more ominously *leoðcræftig* than he.

*Deor* and *Wulf and Eadwacer* together appear to hide not one but four *leoðcræftige* singers: Heorrenda, the minstrel who calls himself Deor, the woman who calls him Wulf, and most of all the riddler who has joined these two unjoinable poems. The heroic source of his double riddle, for example, might seem hopelessly well concealed; indeed, his confession that his song "never was joined" might mean that he composed his story himself from stereotypical features of good tales of abduction. But the skaldic touches in both poems suggest that he borrowed or even translated snatches of a known heroic story and 'joined' them into a new form. The names Heodeninga and Heorrenda, which Deor connects intimately with himself, also imply that the riddler had a particular heroic story in mind. Deor's rival Heorrenda is almost certainly Horant, the skillful singer of the MHG poem *Kudrun.* Were it not so loaded with self-pity, Deor's word *leoðcræftig* would describe Horant perfectly. He comes as a stranger to Hagen's kingdom, enters the conspiracy to steal Hilde, and distracts the king from the plot with wonderful music. Charmed into carelessness, the fierce old king gives Horant rich gifts and a distinguished vassalage, perhaps the same *folgað tilne* 'high office' and *londryht* which Deor complains of losing.[29] Although the *Kudrun*

---

be hiding different references in the refrain of *Wulf and Eadwacer*, a possibility that no previous reading has fully considered.

[29] For passing notice of the word *folgað* in *The Wife's Lament* as a legalism, see Leslie, *Three Old English Elegies*, p. 7. Cf. Liebermann, *Gesetze*, 2:2, 425

poet does not say that Hagen dismisses his own singer to make room for Horant, a gulled king as in *Kudrun* could perhaps be the missing motive for Deor's complaint and revenge. Possibly the poet of *Deor* and *Wulf and Eadwacer* used an otherwise unpreserved tale of Hagen's cheated minstrel, who bitterly resented Horant's success but hoped it would not last. Later events in *Kudrun* prove Horant's luck to be fleeting.

Although they were composed as much as three and a half centuries apart, the English *Deor* and the German *Kudrun* might confirm one another even beyond their coincidence of names. In *Kudrun*, Hagen himself is carried off in infancy by an eagle that sets him down in the foreign kingdom he will grow up to rule. His tyrannical rule then generates two abductions, Hilde's and Kudrun's, from his own family. The eagle episode therefore seems to name abduction as the perpetual evil of Hagen's house. In Scandinavia his legendary inheritance was not an endless series of abductions but a single abduction resulting in eternal strife. Deor alludes to this famous northern version in stanza 3, but in essence the clues of his own story markedly resemble the second abduction in *Kudrun*. He compares his lord, who might be Hagen of the Heodenings, to the tyrant Eormanric; but to the embittered woman of *Wulf and Eadwacer*, who seems to correspond partly to Kudrun, this bungling minstrel must pay the whole debt of their failure together.

Just as Deor proudly links himself to the Heodenings and to the legend of Hild, so his bride appears to borrow her lethal rhetoric from the Heodening cycle. She pictures him as a cornered wolf, brought to bay on one of two islands, whose memory the *Kudrun* poet might have preserved as two names—Wülpensand and Wülpenwert—for the spot where the great battle over Kudrun takes place. Furthermore, a woman of wolfish mind occupies all three of our stories. In the northern version the rapacious

---

("Gefolge" 9b); 1:165 (*II Æthelstan* 25.1); 2:107n.3. On *londryht* see Murray F. Markland, "*Deor: þæs ofereode, þisses swa mæg*," *AN&Q* 11, no. 3 (1972): 35; Grein, *Sprachschatz*; and Liebermann, *Gesetze*, 2:1, 131. By picking a few legal words, Deor is perhaps grasping for a legal basis for his complaint.

woman is Hild, as Deor also knows. In *Kudrun*, Gerlind, the mother of Hartmut, Kudrun's abductor, is several times called *diu wülpinne*: her prototype might originally have spoken those last savage and sarcastic taunts to a kinsman jeered as *eadwacer*. In that case the English riddler would have "joined" the speech of two different women into a single treacherous personality, much as *Riddles 42/43* and *46/47* appear to be conflated from previously distinct texts. For reasons which emerge only after some reflection on *The Soul's Address*, a composite speaker of *Wulf and Eadwacer*, who would belong to the things that "never were joined" before, would be taunting *eadwacer* and teasing the reader with a sly allusion to the greatness of Hagen: this time not an eagle but only a mere skulking wolf carries an infant away. A modern reading of *earne hwelp* (*Wulf and Eadwacer* 16) as 'eagle's whelp' might seem attractive despite the mixed metaphor if the poem riddled about eagles. But since the riddling is on *wulf*, some choice among several published emendations must probably be made, and *ear[m]ne* seems to be the best of these from the standpoint of theme.[30]

By riddlic logic the speaker of *Wulf and Eadwacer*, whether or not assembled from prototypes of Kudrun and Gerlind, would have been conceived to act with the wolfishness of yet another Hild. Her behavior would then comprise a riddlic match to *Deor* in two ways, first to Hild's celebrated treachery and then, more

---

[30] Adams, "'Wulf and Eadwacer': An Interpretation," p. 5, takes MS *earne hwelp* as 'eaglet,' without explanation and with no apparent concern for the mixed metaphor of an 'eagle's whelp.' If, as I have suggested, there is concealed sarcasm in the rhetorical contrast of *eadwacer* and *ear[m]ne*, i.e. (essentially), "you watch riches but let my poor whelp escape to the wood," then possibly the source of such play is the alliterative legalism *earm ond eadig: dives et pauper* (Liebermann, *Gesetze*, 2:1, 57, under *eadig* 3). See also n. 12, above, for a possible gnomic reference for *ear[m]ne*. On the other hand, Baker, "Ambiguity," p. 50, prefers the emendation *ear[g]ne* 'cowardly, vile,' which has strong merits given the skulking nature of the wolf and the sarcastic innuendo of *beaducafa*, line 11. I prefer *ear[m]ne* because the phrase *earm ond eadig* supplies a likely (formulaic) source of wordplay and because the word *ear[m]ne* would seem to add veiled sarcasm, not compassion, as Baker assumes, to the text.

cunningly, to Deor's own. I suggest that we have failed to discover the names Deor, Wulf, and Eadwacer in known heroic sources for the best of reasons: they simply are not there. The appellations Deor and Wulf seem to come from Boethius's *De consolatione philosophiae* 4, pr. 3, where unnatural men are likened to beasts and the avaricious man who seizes the property of others is the wolf. The refrain poet thus seems to have allegorized his heroic sources, partly retelling, partly inventing a heroic story from an eternal wellspring, the endless rapes of the Heodenings. Scrupulously logical, he seems to have understood this "eternal" source as the mother of his own invention. For from the cyclical misfortune of the Heodenings one might easily join together a new antiheroic story by unjoining the lovers in an old tale.

### *The Soul's Address*: Bad Marriage as Spiritual Death

The riddler's method in *Deor* and *Wulf and Eadwacer* gives no visible hint of his purpose. To turn the feats of old heroes into the invented foolishness of invented imitators would be contagious madness unless it had a point. This impasse is removed, I think, by a tenth-century compiler who takes us backward in the Exeter Book, from the cross-textual punning on *deor*, *wulf*, *wylfenne geþoht*, and vicious bestiality of *Deor* and *Wulf and Eadwacer* to more talk of beasts, exile, and violent separation in the longer poem just preceding *Deor* in the manuscript. Since this third poem is not a soul-and-body dialogue, its widely used title *Soul and Body II*, from the Anglo-Saxon Poetic Records, is not entirely accurate. I prefer to call it *The Soul's Address*.

Unlike either *Deor* or *Wulf and Eadwacer*, *The Soul's Address* has no signs of double-talk or playfulness, and none of the more obvious devices of riddling. Its tone is serious, its ostensible purpose didactic, its main concern the relationship of body and soul. Yet it is not a debate, for the soul rants after death at a vacant body that endures the abuse in silence. The main dramatic interest of the poem comes from the soul's monologue of eighty lines; yet the poem is not exactly a dramatic monologue either.

The soul's speech comes between sixteen introductory lines of grim warning and twenty-five closing lines of macabre graveyard imagery. The exordium is in a sense conventionally didactic, a moralizing plea in third person for spiritual reflection in this life, before death comes. After death it will be too late to examine the state of the soul, whose reward will then be *swa wite swa wuldor* 'just such griefs, or else glory,' as it has earned by its conduct in mortal life (lines 7b–8). The poet speaks of eternity in threatening understatement: *Long bið sippan* 'It will be long thereafter [death]' (line 5b) that the spirit receives its due from God himself. Several lines (9–14) then paint dreadful images of the soul *gehþum hremig* 'crying out for relief.' After seven nights' journey beyond death it will find the body, *butan ær wyrce ece Dryhten, ælmihtig God, ende worlde* 'unless almighty God, the Lord everlasting, should work before then the end of the world.' Thus the poet subordinates the theme of the imminent Apocalypse, as if perhaps he were merely satisfying a convention of didactic poetry.

Finally, the Exeter Book does not contain the fullest version of *The Soul's Address*. The same poem, despite numerous lexical and dialectal variations, appears with forty-four additional lines in the Vercelli Book. Outwardly, then, the Exeter Book text of this rather dry poem has comparatively little merit of its own. Expediently, if not justly, scholars have not given it very much separate attention.

The vocabulary of the opening lines, however, suggests that perhaps *The Soul's Address* should not be considered alone at all. The poet begins by urging *hæleþa æghwylc* 'every man' to prepare himself for the moment *þonne se deað cymeð* 'when death comes.' Death *asundrað þa sibbe, þa þe ær somud wæron, lic ond sawle* 'sunders the siblings which once were joined, body and soul.' The lexical parallels to *Wulf and Eadwacer* are striking enough to suggest thematic correspondences as well: death will come unexpected, even more surely than to the unwatchful Wulf *gif he on þreat cymeð* 'if he comes upon the pack.' It will sunder body from soul just as Wulf and his bride, who are *sib* 'kin' in conjugal flesh, are separated on two islands and by the looming threat of the minstrel's death. Besides these smaller coincidences of word and theme, a touch of the same falsity and self-delusion found in *Deor* and *Wulf and Eadwacer* appears even before the soul begins its address. In a passing subordinate clause the poet declares that the soul will again encounter the body *þa heo ær longe wæg* 'which it had long carried about.' These words appear to make the soul the governing principle which drives the body about in this life. The soul therefore ought to be mainly responsible for earthly conduct; yet it addresses the body with *cealdan reorde* 'cold speech' (line 15b). It calls out *grimlice* 'grimly' to the flesh, *swa cearful* 'as follows, filled with grief' (lines 17–22):

> "Hwæt drug þu, dreorga?   To hwon dreahtest þu me,
> ...........................................
> lames gelicnes?   Lyt þu geþohtes
> to won þinre sawle sið   siþþan wurde,
> siþþan heo of lichoman   læded wære!
>    Hwæt wite þu me, werga!"

Since OE *wearg* means both 'exile' as a substantive and 'wretched, accursed' as an adjective, it is possible to read these lines as the soul's first condemnation of its erstwhile partner as an outlaw, in riddlic anticipation of the trapped abductor in *Wulf and Eadwacer*:[1]

> "Villain, what have you done? Why have you vexed me,
> ...........................................
> you clump like clay? Little you thought
> about what the state of your soul would become
> after it should be freed from the flesh!
> How you do rack me, you wretched thing!"

Unaware that the poet of the exordium has already stolen its thunder, the soul violently denies its spiritual custody and heaps

---

[1] *ASD*, under *wearg*. C. W. M. Grein, *Sprachschatz der angelsächsischen Dichter*, under *wearg, wearh, werg*, also gives 1. Wolf; 2. geächteter friedloser Verbrecher. The form *werga* is to be taken as the weak substantive adjective of direct address: '(You) damned one, wretched one.' There does not seem to be any wordplay on the meaning 'wolf' here unless by association of the wolf with the outlawed man, as in the *Exeter Maxims* 146–47, where, incidentally, the word *sliteð* also appears.

names and dire accusations upon the body instead. But as the governing creature whom the body could only follow through life, the soul inadvertently curses itself with its own words. It tries mightily to escape, mentioning itself sometimes in the first person, at other times in the third, writhing to avoid its own part in the blame. Its rhetorical antics broadly resemble the shifting pronouns and double-dealing argument of *Wulf and Eadwacer*. In the end, however, the soul is caught in its own guilt and snatched away to *secan helle grund* 'seek the bottom of hell' (line 98a), for its belated and false complaint does not divert the awful scrutiny of God.

The last forty-four lines of the Vercelli Book text show *se halga sawl* 'the holy soul' as it comforts the worm-riddled body with assurances of their glorious reunion. In the Exeter Book version, without these lines, the soul only berates itself. Death has struck the body deaf and dumb; it cannot answer the soul's insults, accusations, or threats of damnation. Rave or dissemble as it will, the soul must encounter even with its rhetoric the spiritual facts of its own falseness and punishment. With tricky logic it tricks itself. Its reasoning crumbles, for example, just before it departs to hell (lines 93b–96), where it addresses the body as *þu* but simultaneously lapses into dual pronouns. The argument is a classic study in duplicity:

> "Ac hwæt do wit unc
> þonne he unc hafað geedbyrded    oþre siþe?
> Sculon wit þonne ætsomne    siþþan brucan
> swylcra yrmþa    swa þu unc ær scrife."

> "But what shall we do for ourselves
> when he has begotten us yet once again?
> We shall then bear together just such griefs
> as you already ordained for us."

With this hostile answer to its own pretended question the soul disappears from sight and mind to seek the pit of hell. At line 99b the poet turns to the earthly grave, where the helpless body lies in a different state. Here, then, the separate natures of body and soul implicitly belie the soul's parting thoughts.

Though the onslaught of the worms is luridly described, the corpse cannot feel its horrors, which will end when the greedy worms have divided and eaten it. The soul, on the other hand, will know its own agony forever. Thus the body's demolition by worms and the soul's punishment in hell are different in every way. In the soul's insulting words the body is *lames gelicnes* 'the likeness of clay' (line 19), an inferior being worthy only of contempt. Yet as the soul is the far higher creature, so the poet is silent about its inexpressible torments: *swa wite swa wuldor*, either torment or glory, as he has said. The horror of the soul's squandered life on earth is still intangible, however—best grasped by comparison with more familiar suffering. So the poet seems to use the closing admonition of *The Soul's Address* as a riddlic *gemyndum* 'reminder.' To *æghwylcum men . . . modsnotterra* 'each man among wise men' the suffering of Deor-Wulf and his bride can serve to recall the agonies of the hapless body and the unhappy soul.

*Deor* and *Wulf and Eadwacer* would thus operate as a kind of riddlic parable whose spiritual meaning lies in *The Soul's Address*. Deor does not know his peril, but his bride now laments her chosen life of fear and pain. Like the soul, who tries to feign thirty thousand winters of unwilling captivity in the body, the woman now protests, perhaps to a third party included in the plural (as opposed to dual) pronoun *us*, that her marriage to Wulf was never really joined. Suddenly she and Wulf are as different as soul from body: *Ungelic is us* 'It [Wulf's danger] is not like that for us'. Her argument, that she only followed the wolf who carried off their whelp, is internally false, like the soul's attempt to blame the body for their tragedy. The woman's invective and the soul's name-calling are much alike: *werga* in *The Soul's Address*, sarcastic play on the name and concept of *wulf* in *Wulf and Eadwacer*. Similar anticipatory wordplay also occurs at *The Soul's Address* 77–78a, where the soul says that the body should far rather have been created *on westenne wildra deora þæt grimmeste* 'of wild beasts in the wilderness the grimmest of all' than ever to have become a baptized man. The imagery of wolves and beasts, beginning with *werga/deora* in *The Soul's Address*, extends to *deor/wylfenne* in *Deor* and culminates in the many resounding plays on *Wulf* and the frequent predatory rending and eating in *Wulf and Eadwacer*. In *Deor* and *Wulf and Eadwacer* the would-be hero is exposed as the skulking outlaw beast of the wood. Moreover, he is the sacrificial criminal, both human and animal, of the pagan North. In the contrasting "English" poetry of *The Soul's Address*, the soul has outlawed itself from the spiritual heroism into which it was baptized. All of these analogies are signs of riddlic *orþoncbendum* 'bonds of skillful thought' which, in my reading, bind together *The Soul's Address*, *Deor*, and *Wulf and Eadwacer* into a secret parable not unlike some of Christ's own, but in riddlic order, preceded rather than followed by the application.

The explicit idea of *orþoncbend*, a lexical hint of a secret connection, comes from the joined *Riddles 42/43*, which closely resemble our longer triple riddle in many ways. In only thirty-two lines the double riddle transforms the farmyard cock and hen into the body and soul as traveling companions through mortal life. In the threefold riddle the earthly life is also a pilgrimage jointly undertaken by flesh and spirit, as the soul's arguments often imply and the woman in *Wulf and Eadwacer* obscurely states when she recalls following Wulf into exile. In *Riddle 43* the soul and body travel as a noble guest and its lower *esne* 'fellow,' enclosed together *in geardum*, that is, in the figurative 'yard' of Man. Together they can find bliss among numberless kindred in their home, i.e., the angels and saints; or else they can find *care*, *gif se esne his hlaford hyreð yfle, frean on fore* 'sorrow, if the fellow serves his lord evilly, his master on the journey' (lines 8b–10a). Neither *The Soul's Address* nor *Riddle 43* leaves any doubt about who must lead and who must serve. By comparison with *Riddle 43*, *The Soul's Address* seems grim and gloomy because it warns relentlessly against the evil journey but says little of the happier one. Yet the good journey is at least implied at the beginning and end of *The Soul's Address*, too. The poem begins *Huru þæs behofaþ hæleþa æghwylc* 'In truth, of this every man has need' to examine deeply the state of his soul before death. By such reflection every man can join the fraternity of *modsnotterra* 'wise men' in the last verses. They are, by implicit contrast with the fallen soul, the spiritual heroes in the poet's scheme. It is they who can guide the riddle solver on his own journey. But the thoughtless soul which casts away its own redemption will endure worse torment than the worm-ravaged body, and worse pain and anguish than the false heroes of pagan legend.

The estranged body and soul in *The Soul's Address* and the "unlike" hero and heroine of *Deor* and *Wulf and Eadwacer* have similar miseries, described with the same themes or even in the same words. In *Wulf and Eadwacer* the speaker knows Wulf's enemies as *wælreowe* 'eager for blood.' They will eat Wulf alive, as the ironic refrain word *aþecgan* tells. The bestial innuendo of *tosliteð* (line 18) reveals their intention to separate the lovers with wolfish savagery. In *The Soul's Address* the same word + *slitan* tells how grim and greedy beasts, here worms rather than wolves, will rend the dead body: *beslitan seonwum*, line 57a; *seonowum beslitan*, line 68a; *goman toslitene, seonwe beoð asogene . . .* , lines 104–105a. The OE *asogene* 'sucked dry, consumed' uses the same prefix as *aþecgan* in *Wulf and Eadwacer* and has virtually the same thematic effect. The grisly insistence on parted sinews corresponds with Weland's riddlic *seonobende*, that is, his severed hamstrings, in the gory first stanza of *Deor*.

Like Weland and the other heroes and heroines of Deor's old stories, and also like Wulf and his bride, the soul suffers both exile and imprisonment. Like the minstrel and the woman, too, it blames all of its trouble on someone else. In various language all three poems seize on the themes of chains, hunger and thirst, and the captivity which brings such torments. The soul complains of being 'bound with hard hunger and pent up in the pains of hell' by the tyrannical body: *þu me . . . hungre gebunde ond gehæftnadest    helle witum* (lines 28–29). In lines 36–38 the body is accused of being *wines sæd* 'sated with wine,' so that the soul *ofþyrsted wæs Godes lichoman, gæstes drinces* 'was athirst for the body of God and the spirit's drink," where *ofþyrsted* may be the lexical parallel of *aþecgan* 'consume by eating, eat up' in *Wulf and Eadwacer*. But the soul's charge is as false as Wulf's bride's efforts to blame him for a disastrous journey which, as she admits, she freely undertook. Her confession that she had *nales meteliste* 'no lack of meat at all' (line 15) seems to be a bitter jest on coition and pregnancy in *Wulf and Eadwacer*, but in the larger riddle it also shatters the soul's flimsy alibis about spiritual thirst and starvation. Thus the soul, like the woman, speaks with cunning falsehood. Its adversary the body, if it could speak, might bring even more plainly ridiculous charges, like Deor's, against its lord. The Exeter riddler, however, does not need to exhaust this analogy, which demonstrates fallen human nature clearly enough as it is. The reader's imagination is wisely left to finish the job.

Although it might have been borrowed wholesale, or nearly so, to fit a riddler's plan, the matter of *Deor* and *Wulf and Eadwacer* would also have been picked for its insistence on the violence, agony, and sorrow of enslaved heroes. The tyrants Niðhad and Eormanric once bound their prisoners in woe and torment (*on nede legde, seonobende, Deor* 4–5; *sorgum gebunden, Deor* 24). Weland knew *sorge ond longaþ* and the miseries that belong to elegiac winter, *wintercealde wræce*; and the love of Hild and Heoden turned to *sorglufu* 'sorrowful love.' Deor himself seems oblivious to all the sorrow in the tales he has chosen, but of his own sorrow he sounds a bit more evasive, preferring to say that 'one' *siteð sorgcearig, sælum bidæled* 'sits full of sorrow, cut off from the good times' (line 28). There is a hint here of the soul's wily but illogical third-person reference to itself as *þin* [i.e., the body's] *sawl* (*The Soul's Address* 57).

Moreover, in all three poems of *Riddle 1* the speakers' perils arise from their self-deceptions. When the minstrel finally speaks in the first person (*Deor* 35ff.), he shows ignorance of the nonsense in his own complaint. It takes the woman, whose blindness seems more willful than Deor's, to show in spite of herself how closely their *renig weder* 'rainy weather' matches Weland's wintry torments, or how their *widlast*, their track of exile, answers to Theodoric's 'fortress' built only of basil flowers. As it reviles the body, the hypocritical soul pretends that its rightful submission to the flesh has ended in the 'sorrow' so often found in *Deor*. It declares itself *synnum gesargad* 'sorrow-laden with the body's sins' (line 62), and its taunt *ne sindan þine dreamas wiht* 'your joys are not worth a jot' (line 60) helps suggest the irony of *Wulf and Eadwacer* 12: *Wæs me wyn to þon, wæs me hwæþre eac lað* 'It was thus far my pleasure, that it still was my pain.' Like the woman, too, the soul feigns a long-standing wish for deliverance from its captor: *Hwæt ic uncres gedales gebad* 'How I have awaited our parting!' (*The Soul's Address* 34). But like the earthly antagonists in the following two poems, the soul may dodge the blame as it will: it can escape neither its own guilt nor its terrible doom.

As it stops speaking, the soul perches upon the brink of hell, from which, as the poet now teaches, it *sceal . . . secan helle grund, nales heofondreamas, dædum gedrefed* 'shall . . . seek the bottom of hell, not at all heaven's joys, vexed by its deeds' (lines 97–99a). Its lot is eternal banishment to *helle grund*, as shelterless as Theodoric's absent stronghold and as *grundleas* as the eternal victims of Hild's anger. The pit of hell and the earthly bed of worms now become the two loci for the unhappily parted soul and body, just as in *Wulf and Eadwacer* the doomed lovers are trapped on separate islands. Like the misguided minstrel and even more like his bride, the dissembling soul tries to glorify and excuse itself all at once *þonne se dead cymed* 'when his death comes.' But the similar intrigue of all three poems ends similarly, too, in self-mockery and destruction. Like Deor, who perhaps hopes that his exile will end, like Theodoric's, after *þritig wintra*, the soul has let itself be fooled by time: *Þæt me þuhte ful oft þæt wære þritig þusend wintra to þinum deaðdæge* 'Very often it seemed to me to be thirty thousand winters until your deathday' (lines 32b–34a).

From all these and many more analogies of word and theme it is possible to see an enormous riddlic comparison of wasted spiritual and heroic life. The final forty-four lines of the longer Vercelli Book *Soul's Address*, a portrait of *se halga sawl*, the soul in a state of holiness, appear to have been left out of the Exeter Book so that only a vision of fire and brimstone would remain. The Vercelli Book *Soul's Address* thus helps show how the three poems of *Riddle 1* were fitted together—partly by original writing, but even more by astonishingly clever joining of what had never before been joined. The matter of *Deor* and *Wulf and Eadwacer*, with its strong Scandinavian affinities, might have been acquired in a time and place of uncommon access to Danish heroic poetry and allegorized in especially bitter memory of Danish adventurism in England. One thinks, albeit tentatively, of ninth- or early-tenth-century East Anglia, after the Viking devastation and Danish settlements there; and the words *fenne biworpen* 'encircled by fen' in *Wulf and Eadwacer* 5, though perhaps a meaningless coincidence, might preserve an East Anglian touch in what already looks to some scholars like the translation of a Continental poem.[2]

By scholarly consent, however, the Exeter Book was probably copied in a southwestern scriptorium, perhaps at Crediton, in the late tenth century, quite far in time and place from Viking East Anglia. But even if the Exeter Book shows occasional signs of derivation from another manuscript now lost, the anonymous arranger of the riddlic journeys and the Exeter Book scribe were probably near contemporaries. Sometimes, as in the spliced *Riddles 42/43* and *46/47*, the copyist seems to show faithfulness to, if not actual complicity in, the riddler's witty remaking of old texts. In these paired riddles the midline junctures, which have been interpreted simply as mistakes, appear instead to be scribal responses to the *orþoncbendum*, or secret word and theme linkages, of the texts.[3] Although the decorations of the Exeter Book

[2] See, for example, Ruth P. Lehmann, "The Metrics and Structure of 'Wulf and Eadwacer,'" *PQ* 48 (1909): 151–65, who perceives strong formal and rhetorical similarities between *Wulf and Eadwacer* and the Norse *ljoðhattrstrophe*. I am now working on some other possible East Anglian narrative connections in the Exeter Book. From an anthropological study of Germanic kinships, Janemarie Luecke, "*Wulf and Eadwacer*: Hints for Reading from *Beowulf* and Anthropology," in Martin Green, ed., *The Old English Elegies: New Essays in Criticism and Research*, p. 197, also concludes that the story matter of *Wulf and Eadwacer* is very old and that the poem conceals a killing between its lines.

[3] Craig Williamson, ed., *The Old English Riddles of the Exeter Book*, p. 276, thinks (apparently along with all other editors to date) that *Riddles 42/43* and *46/47* were joined by "a similar [scribal] mistake." For reasons advanced here and elaborated in "Two Spliced Riddles of the Exeter Book," *In Geardagum* 5 (June, 1983): 57–75, I think that both of these paired texts were deliberately rather than mistakenly joined. As I unfortunately did not say in that article, there is even scriptural authority for the joining of *Riddle 46* ("bookmoth") with *Riddle 47*

are generally spare and without obvious order, the relatively numerous initials and capitals and the unique marginal decorations of folios 98a–100b, also uniquely proximate to one another in the manuscript, could perhaps have been drawn with an extra measure of care.

The large sweeping initial *H* that begins *The Soul's Address* on folio 98a is followed by a full manuscript line of block capitals, as generally in eight other major divisions in the Exeter Book. Only two folio pages later, on folio 100a, the initial *W* of *Deor* closely matches the initial of *The Soul's Address* in size and decoration, though *Deor* has only an enlarged *e* following its initial rather than a capitalized first line. The five remaining stanzas of *Deor*, four old heroic misfortunes and Deor's own longer complaint, have bold initials of relatively modest size. Of these five letters the initials of the Beadohild and Deor stanzas seem plainest, little if anything more than block capitals in form. Their plainness is matched by the solitary initial *L* of *Wulf and Eadwacer* (folio 100b), which, however, is noticeably larger than they. It is possible, if not immediately likely, that the scribe was hinting at interrelationships and subordinations of themes within *Riddle 1* by the various ornamentation and the relative proportions of these letters. But his method, if there was one, would seem to have been a riddle of its own, designed to operate as do the poems themselves, offering suspicion rather than tangible proof.[4]

---

("illuminated holy book") in Luke 12 : 33–34, where Christ speaks of the Word as divine gift to the heart, the treasure that neither thief can steal nor moth destroy. Both the word *orponcbendum* in *Riddle 42* 15 and the reference to Weland's *seonobende* in *Deor* 6 appear to serve as riddlic "bonds" for the joining of once independent texts.

[4]I have provided a fuller (if also too confident) discussion of the ornament and proportions of letters in *Riddle 1* in *"The Soul's Address, Deor*, and *Wulf and Eadwacer*: How and Where the Exeter Book Riddles Begin," in Green, ed., *The Old English Elegies*, pp. 225–26. In this germinal version of the present discussion the paleographical observations are useful for showing how some scribe, either of the Exeter Book or of a lost exemplar, might have conceived the decoration of these poems. Marijane Osborn, "The Text and Context of *Wulf and Edwacer*," in Green, ed., *The Old English Elegies*, p. 187, also thinks (in an argu-

The Hild, Theodoric, and Eormanric stanzas of *Deor* also have small serifed crosses at the left of their initials in the margin of folio 100a. These bold decorations, whether by the Exeter Book scribe's hand or by some later one, are drawn with noticeable care. Perhaps, of course, they are nothing more than neat doodling. But they are also unique in the whole manuscript, strange in their juxtaposition to heathen stories and therefore possibly some kind of graphic fun. Whether they are supposed to match what might be three small crosses in both the initial *H* of *The Soul's Address* and the initial *W* of *Deor*, I cannot tell. Coincidentally or not, *Riddle 1* has three poems, within which the Hild, Theodoric, and Eormanric stories feature the three major themes of abduction, exile, and wolfish cruelty that underlie the entire Christian parable of the careless body and soul. Stanzas 1 and 2 of *Deor*, on the heathen stories of Weland and Beadohild, are not signed with crosses even though the margin has ample room. This absence of crosses may have been deliberate, perhaps to insinuate the male-female relationship that not only typifies body and soul but also marries *Wulf and Eadwacer* into the riddler's grand scheme. At any rate, the marginal crosses of *Deor*, and also the surrounding initials and capitals, further disturb the eye with suspicions already in the mind—that after the unique minuscule word *finit* at the end of *Physiologus* the riddles of the Exeter Book begin with an even subtler thematic grouping of *The Soul's Address*, *Deor*, and *Wulf and Eadwacer*.

These three poems have as their ancient ancestor the riddle journey and as their Christian inspiration the parable set in reverse. Together the poems can be read to compare the *visibilia* of wasted lives in this world to the *invisibilia* of eternal grief in the

---

ment which does not go as far as the present one) that the Exeter Book compiler saw a general thematic likeness in *The Soul's Address*, *Deor*, and *Wulf and Eadwacer* and therefore arranged them together in the MS. In a return to much nineteenth-century opinion, Osborn reads the modest initial *L* of *Wulf and Eadwacer*, rather than the major ornamental division on fol. 98a, as the beginning of the Exeter Book riddles. The older designation of *Wulf and Eadwacer* as *Riddle 1* survives prominently in *ASD*.

next. As separate works the texts might seem dull, fragmentary, or obscure; but when they are joined according to their riddlic potential, they suggest a hidden path of contemplative discovery. They may arguably be called *Riddle 1*, though their traditional and accurate separate editorial names should not be thereby discarded.

A truly finished description of *Riddle 1* would seem to require a few words about one last faint sign in the manuscript. This is an unserifed cross drawn in pencil in a modern hand, one of two or three such hasty penciled crosses in the codex. It lies at the right of the bold capitalized word *behofaþ*, *The Soul's Address* 1, folio 98a. Possibly it is one of the less famous pencil marks of the "mighty scholar" George Hickes, made in Queen Anne's time to guide his remarkable copyist Humphrey Wanley to chosen passages in the Exeter Book.[5] Could Hickes, or someone else after him, have responded faintly to the three crosses in the margin of *Deor* and thus blazed a previous trail through the craftily joined poems of *Riddle 1*? It is at once humbling and exciting to dog that trail to an end, there to confront the possibility of a silent and forgotten predecessor.

[5] R. W. Chambers, "Modern Study of the Poetry of the Exeter Book," in R. W. Chambers, Max Förster, and Robin Flower, eds., *The Exeter Book of Old English Poetry* (photofacsimile edition), p. 34. The words "mighty scholar" are Chambers's. Chambers also discusses and lists the eight runic passages which Hickes is known to have marked in pencil for Wanley to copy; see p. 34 and n. 9. One of the copied passages, which I have seen in the Exeter Cathedral Library, is an astonishingly good counterfeit of the original. The suggestion that the penciled cross of fol. 98a, like the still unexplained penciled boxes and number codes that mark the runic riddles, could be Hickes's I owe to Mrs. Audrey Erskine, of the University of Exeter and Exeter Cathedral Library.

# The Texts

*The Soul's Address*
*Deor*
*Wulf and Eadwacer*

# [THE SOUL'S ADDRESS]

    Huru Ðæs behofaþ    hæleþa æghwylc
þæt he his sawle sið    sylfa bewitige,
hu þæt bið deoplic    þonne se dead cymeð,
asundrað þa sibbe,    þa þe ær somud wæron,
5    lic ond sawl[e]!    Long bið siþþan
þæt se gæst nimeð    æt Gode sylfum
swa wite swa wuldor,    swa him in worulde ær
efne þæt eorðfæt    ær geworhte.
    Sceal se gæst cuman    gehþum hremig,
10    symle ymb seofon niht    sawle findan
þone lichoman    þe heo ær longe wæg,
þreo hund wintra,
butan ær wyrce    ece dryhten,
ælmihtig God,    ende worlde.
15    Cleopað þonne swa cearful    caldan reorde,
*98b*    spriceð grimlice    gæst to / þam duste:
"Hwæt drug þu, dreorga?    To hwon dreahtest þu me,
eorþan fylnes    eal forweornast,

---

    Note: for convenient reference to scholarship, the established titles of the three poems in *Riddle 1* have been kept as bracketed headings in both the original and the translation and the translation given independent line numbering.

    1: After the word *finit*, ending *Physiologus* in the MS, there is an empty ruled line for extra spacing. The initial *H* of *Huru*, beginning *The Soul's Address*, has no color but is very large and gracefully curved, with spare but effective ornamentation. The words *Huru þæs behofað* are in large, bold block capitals that take up the entire first MS line of the poem. At the right of the word *behofað*, and raised slightly above it, is a penciled cross in an anonymous hand, possibly Hickes's.

    5: *sawl[e]*. MS *sawl*, generally emended to *sawle* on the authority of the Vercelli Book text of the poem.

    9: *Sceal*. The MS has a period followed by a prominent small capital *S*. I suspect that this capital and similar capitals at lines 15, 22, 49, 54, 71 (? see note),

# [THE SOUL'S ADDRESS]

In truth, of this every man has need,
himself to reflect on the state of his soul,
how dark it will be when his death comes
and sunders the siblings which once were joined,
5    body and soul! Long thereafter it will be
that the spirit receives from God himself
just such grief, or else glory, as in this world
its vessel of clay once accomplished for it.
     The spirit shall come crying out for relief;
10   after seven nights shall the soul always meet
the corpse it had long carried about,
wait three hundred winters
unless almighty God, the Lord everlasting,
should work before then the end of the world.
15     Then full of cares it will call with cold speech.
The spirit thus grimly will speak to the dust:
"Villain, what have you done? Why have you vexed me,
you foulness of earth all withered away,

---

86, and 111 may be rhetorical divisions. I have made them the basis for paragraphing in both text and translation.

    12: *þreo hund wintra.* The MS has no off verse. The difficulty might be either faulty copying or faulty memory, since the Vercelli Book text has "þreo hund wintra, butan ær þeodcyning, / ælmihtig God,   ende worulde / wyrcan wille,   weoruda dryhten" (lines 12–14).

    15: *Cleopað.* MS **.** *Cleopað*, another possible rhetorical division. The argument seems to turn from general remarks on the fate of the soul and body to the speech of the soul itself.

    17: *drug þu.* MS *druguþu.* ASPR 3:317 suggests a possible error for *druge þu* and the question 'What hast thou done?' Thus I interpret this and the following clause, ending at line 19a, as questions. ASPR 3, following the Vercelli Book reading *druh þu*, suggests that the reading "more probably" should be *drug þu* 'thou dust.' But at line 22 another period and small capital suggest to me a turn from questions of pretended outrage to foregone conclusions.

lames gelicnes?    Lyt þu geþohtes
20    to won þinre sawle sið    siþþan wurde
siþþan heo of lichoman    læded wære!
        Hwæt wite þu me, werga!    Hwæt, þu huru wyrma gifl
lyt geþohtes    hu þis is long hider,
ond þe þurh engel    ufan of roderum
25    sawle onsende    þurh his sylfes hond,
meotud ælmihtig,    of his mægenþrymme,
ond þe þa gebohte    blode þy halgan;
ond þu me þy heardan    hungre gebunde
ond gehæftnadest    helle witum!
30    [Eardode] ic þe in innan.    No ic þe of meahte,
flæsce bifongen,    ond me firenlustas
þine geþrungon.    Þæt me þuhte ful oft
þæt wære þritig    þusend wintra
to þinum deaðdæge.    Hwæt ic uncres gedales bad
35    earfoðlice!    Nis nu se ende to god!
Wære þu þe wiste wlonc    ond wines sæd;
þrymful þunedest,    ond ic ofþyrsted wæs
Godes lichoman,    gæstes drinces.
Þær þu þonne hogode    her on life
40    þenden ic þe in worulde    wunian sceolde,
þæt þu wære þurh flæsc    ond þurh firenlustas
strong[e] gestyred,    ond gestaþelad þurh mec,
ond ic wæs gæst on þe    from Gode sended,
næfre þu me swa heardra    helle wita
45    ne[d] gearwode    þurh þinra neoda lust.
Scealt þu nu hwæþre minra gescenta    scome þrowian
on þam miclan dæge    þonne monna cynn

19: ASPR 3 punctuates the clause ending at 19a as an exclamation. I take
this and the previous clause as questions (see note on line 17). But the poet's in-
tention here is not certain.

22: *Hwæt*. MS . *Hwæt*, perhaps marking another shift in the argument.
See note on line 16.

30: [*Eardode*]. Not in MS, but supplied by both W. S. Mackie, ed., *The Ex-
eter Book, Part II, Poems IX–XXXII* (hereafter cited as Mackie), and ASPR 3 from
the Vercelli Book text.

    you likeness of clay? Little you thought

20    about what the state of your soul would become
    after it should be freed from the flesh!
       How you do rack me, you wretched thing! Yes, you bait
         for worms,
    precious little you heeded how long this hereafter is,
    or that by angels from the heavens above,

25    by his very own hand, with his splendid strength,
    the almighty judge sent you a soul,
    and bought you then with his holy blood;
    but instead you have bound me with hard hunger
    and pent me up in the pains of hell!

30    I [was seated] inside of you.    I could not get out of you;
    the flesh confined me, and your filthy lusts
    pressed upon me.    Very often it seemed to me
    to be thirty thousand winters
    until your deathday.    How I have awaited

35    our parting!    Now the end is not too good!
    You were too full of pride in your feasting, and sated
       with wine.
    You thumped about in your glory while I was athirst
    for the body of God and the spirit's beverage.
    If you had given heed then to this life here,

40    while I had to abide in you in the world,
    reflected that you were by flesh and foul lusts
    strongly drawn, but steadied through me,
    that I was the soul in you, sent from God,
    you'd nver have set me up with the need

45    of such hard hell pain through the lust of your urges.
    Yet for my chagrin you'll now bear shame
    on that great day when the only-begotten one

---

42: *strong[e] gestyred.* MS *strong gestyred*; cf. the Vercelli Book reading *strange gestyrned*, which is the basis for the emendation. *Gestyrned* appears to be a mistake in the Vercelli Book, however. *The Soul's Address* might have been a widely known, but not always carefully transmitted, literary favorite.

99a    se / ancenda ealle gegædrað.
       Ne eart þu nu þon leofre    nængum lifgendra,
50   menn to gemæccan,   ne medder ne fæder,
     ne nængum gesibbra,   þonne se swearta hrefn,
     siþþan ic ana of þe   ut siþade
     þurh þæs sylfes hond   þe ic ær onsended wæs.
       Ne magon þe nu heonan adon   hyrste þa readan,
55   ne gold ne sylfor   ne þinra goda nan;
     ac her sculon abidan   ban bireafod,
     besliten seonwum,   ond þe þin sawl sceal
     minum unwillan   oft gesecan,
     wemman mid wordum,   swa þu worhtest to me.
60   Eart þu dumb ond deaf,   ne sindan þine dreamas wiht.
     Sceal ic þe nihtes seþeah   nyde gesecan,
     synnum gesargad,   ond eft sona from ðe
     hweorfan on honcred,   þonne halege menn
     Gode lifgendum   lofsong doð,
65   secan þa hamas   þe þu me ær scrife,
     ond þa arleasan   eardungstowe;
     ond þe sculon moldwyrmas   monige ceowan,
     seonowum beslitan,   swearte wihte
     gifre ond grædge.   Ne sindon þine geahþe wiht,
70   þa þu her on moldan   monnum eawdest.
       Forþon þe wære selle   swiþe micle
     þonne þe wæran ealle   eorþan spede
     (butan þu hy gedælde   dryhtne sylfum),
     þær þu wurde æt frumsceafte fugel   oþþe fisc on sæ,
75   oððe eorþan neat   ætes tiolode,
     feldgongende   feoh butan snyttro,

     48: *ancenda*. MS *acenda* with superlinear addition of *n* by the Exeter Book scribe's hand.

     49: *Ne*. MS . *Ne*, another possible rhetorical division, beginning a description of the body's supposed privations, here of kinsmen and comrades.

     54: *Ne*. MS . *Ne*. Here the body is told that its earthly wealth cannot buy its freedom from death. In this passage the soul also betrays early knowledge of its own punishment and thus also shows the falseness of its helplessness and outrage. See esp. lines 61–66.

gathers together the whole race of men.
    By none of the living are you now loved,
50  no comrade to kinsmen, not to mother or father,
    no more beloved than is the black raven,
    after I alone went out of you
    by the selfsame hand by which I was sent.
        Nor can those red trinkets take you away from here,
55  nor gold nor silver, and none of your goods;
    but here your plundered bones must abide,
    torn from their sinews, and your soul must
    visit you often, to my great aversion,
    rack you with words, as you wrought upon me.
60  You are deaf and dumb, your joys not worth a jot.
    Yet I'll be compelled, sorrow-laden with sins,
    to find you by night, and flee from you straightway
    again at cockcrow, when holy men
    to the living God lift songs of praise.
65  I'll withdraw to the regions you'd destined for me,
    and to abodes without honor;
    and many a mold worm shall chew on you,
    tear at your sinews, swarthy creatures,
    grasping and greedy. Your follies are nothing
70  which here in the dust you displayed to men.
        Thus it had been very much better for you
    than that all the blessings of earth were yours
    (unless you would give them to God himself),
    that you'd been conceived as a bird at Creation,
75  or a fish in the sea, or a goat gathering food,
    an earth-ranging animal void of all wit,

---

54, 57, 67: *þe*. For *þe* in these places the MS originally had *þec*. The shadows of all the erased *c*'s are visible.

71: *Forþon*. The MS line contains a period, followed by what might be a small capital *F* on *Forþon*, since the top of the letter appears somewhat higher than some minuscule *f*'s nearby. A riddlic division is possible, since the next few lines contain some of the central lexical clues to *Deor* and *Wulf and Eadwacer*.

ge on westenne     wildra deora
þæt grimmeste,     þær swa God wolde,
ge þeah þu wære wyrmcynna     þæt wyrreste,
80  þonne þu æfre / on moldan     mon gewurde,
99b oþþe æfre fulwihte     onfon sceolde.
Þonne þu for unc bu     ondwyrdan scealt
on þam miclan dæge     þonne eallum monnum beoð
wunde onwrigene,     þa þe in worulde ær
85  firenfulle menn     fyrn geworhton.
    Ðonne wile dryhten sylf     dæda gehyran,
æt ealra monna gehwam     muþes reorde,
wunde wiþerlean.     Ac hwæt wilt þu þær
on domdæge     dryhtne secgan?
90  Þonne ne bið nænig to þæs lytel lið     on lime geweaxen,
þæt þu ne scyle for æghwylc     anra onsundran
ryht agieldan.     Ðonne reþe bið
dryhten æt dome.     Ac hwæt do wit unc
þonne he unc hafað geedbyrded     oþre siþe?
95  Sculon wit þonne ætsomne     siþþan brucan
swylcra yrmþa,     swa þu unc ær scrife."
Firenaþ þus þæt flæschord,     sceal þonne feran on weg,
secan helle grund,     nales heofondreamas,
dædum gedrefed.     Ligeð dust þær hit wæs,
100 ne mæg him ondsware     ænige secgan,
ne þær edringe     ænge gehatan
gæste geomrum,     geoce oþþe frofre.
Biþ þæt heafod tohliden,     honda tohleoþode,
geaflas toginene,     goman toslitene,
105 seonwe beoð asogene,     sweora bicowen;

86: Ðonne. MS . ðonne, with the largest and most prominent small capital of the poem. Here the soul seems to turn from berating the body to imagining God at the Judgment. The vision leads to a last desperate rhetorical question (lines 93b–94).

95–96: These lines might also be read as a question, but as an answer to the question just asked they would seem to emphasize the hypocrisy of the soul's argument. Thus I have adopted here the punctuation of both Mackie and ASPR 3.

yes, even of wild beasts in the wilderness
the grimmest of all, wherever God wanted you,
lo! even though you were the worst kind of worm,
80    than that ever you became man on the earth,
or were ever bound to receive the baptismal sign.
For you'll have to answer for both of us
on that mighty day when to all men will be
opened the wounds, the ones that men full of wickedness
85    made in the world since remotest ages.
    Then the Lord himself will listen to deeds
in speech from the mouth of every last man,
and requite their crimes. But what will you
say to the Lord there, on the day of doom?
90    Then no link will be grown so small on your limbs
that you should not pay for each one apart
its reckoning. For the Lord will be ruthless
at passing sentence. But what shall we do for ourselves
when he has begotten us yet once again?
95    We shall then bear together just such griefs
as you already ordained for us."
Thus reviling the flesh heap, it shall hasten away,
seek the bottom of hell, not at all heaven's joys,
vexed by its deeds. The dust will lie where it was,
100   nor will be able to offer an answer,
nor promise any easing there
to the saddened spirit, any solace or help.
The head will be broken, the hands split apart,
the jaws gaping open, the gums torn away,
105   the sinews sucked out, the neck gnawed apart.

---

101: *edringe*. A hapax. C. W. M. Grein, *Sprachschatz der angelsächsischen Dichter*, vol. 1, suggests L *refugium* by comparison with OE *e(o)dor*, and *ASD* follows Grein. T. Northcote Toller, *Supplement to an Anglo-Saxon Dictionary*, suggests *i(e)ðrung* 'amelioration, a making easier,' and cites Max Förster, *Englische Studien* 36 (1906): 326. J. R. Clark Hall, *A Concise Anglo-Saxon Dictionary*, 4th ed., enters both suggestions but compares *ieðrung* with *ieðrian*. This seems the more likely reading, and I translate *edringe* accordingly as 'easing.'

rib reafiað    reþe wyrmas,
drincað hloþum hra,    heolfres þurstge.
Bið seo tunge totogen    on tyn healfe
hungrum to hroþor.    Forþon heo ne mæg horsclice
110  wordum wrixlan    wið þone wergan gæst.
*100a*    ᵹifer hatte se wyrm,    þam þa geaflas / beoð
nædle scearpran.    Se geneþeð to
ærest ealra    on þam eorðscræfe.
He þa tungan totyhð    ond þa toþas þurhsmyhð,
115  ond to ætwelan    oþrum gerymeð,
ond þa ea[g]an þurhiteð    ufon on þæt heafod,
wyrmum to wiste,    þonne biþ þæt werge
lic acolad,    þæt he longe ær
werede mid wædum.    Bið þonne wyrmes giefl,
120  æt on eorþan.    Þæt mæg æghwylcum
men to gemyndum    modsnotterra.

111: *ᵹifer*. MS . *ᵹifer*, with a very prominent small capital. There is perhaps a momentary turn in the argument here, from the gory particulars of the grave worm's attack to general observations of its ravenous behavior. But at line 114 the poem returns to macabre details.

115–16: Mackie reverses these two lines, on the authority of the Vercelli Book text, for better rhetorical sense. I follow ASPR 3, where they are left as they appear in the Exeter Book. As I punctuate and translate them here, the lines make especially gruesome sense, in particular lines 116–17: when they penetrate the head, the source of man's nobility as a mortal creature, the worms achieve their own highest joy. Possibly, then, this passage was deliberately re-ordered for greater shock effect in the Exeter Book.

116: *ea[g]an*. MS *eaxan*, emended to *eagan*, which obviously agrees with *ufon on þæt heafod*, on the authority of the Vercelli Book text.

118: *he*. The word has no antecedent and does not appear in the Vercelli Book text. ASPR 2 includes it in the Vercelli Book to supply a subject for the clause beginning with *þæt* and takes *he* as a reference to "man in general." There are several other possibilities, all conjectural: (1) *he* is an error for the reflexive pronoun, so that the clause would read '(the body) that had long defended itself with clothing'; (2) *he* should be ignored as a confused attempt to "improve" the passage, and *þæt* should be treated as the relative-pronoun subject of its clause.

Voracious worms will ravage the ribs;
in bloodthirsty hordes they will drink the corpse dry.
The tongue will be pulled into ten pieces
to delight hungry feeders. It will have no force
110   to trade words wisely with the spiteful spirit.
     The worm has been called glutton whose gorge is
sharper than needles. It ventures forth first
of all things into the earthen grave.
It carves up the tongue and works through the teeth,
115   and clears for others the way to rich eating,
and eats through the eyes up into the head
to the worms' great joy, once the worn-out corpse
has grown cold, that with clothing long
had made resistance. It is then the worm's meat,
120   its food on earth. For each man
among wise men that can be a reminder.

----

This expedient requires taking *werede* in the intransitive sense of 'resisted' and understanding the clause to mean '(the body) that had long resisted (the worm's onslaught) with clothing.' Such an ironic reference to the gossamer armor of clothing against the worm would seem to fit the powerful graveyard imagery of the poem as a whole. Thus I have translated *werede* as 'made resistance,' unfortunately without hard lexicographical support for the intransitive meaning; (3) a third option, taken by Grein, *Sprachschatz*, vol. 1, and *ASD*, requires *werede* to mean 'dressed, wore clothes,' etc. (cf. Goth *wasjan* instead of Goth *warjan* 'defend'). But a statement that the body merely 'long wore clothes' seems much too bland for the context. Whatever the nature or source of the textual confusion, I would guess that the clause implies the utter uselessness of clothing as a defense against the worms.

    121: *modsnotterra*. Looks like a comparative, but Grein, *Sprachschatz*, vol. 1, takes it as a gen. pl. 'of (i.e., among) wise-minded men' on the authority of *modsnotra* in the Vercelli Book text. Accordingly, the closing sentence would mean 'That can be a reminder to each man among men of wise mind.' Like certain other references to wise or learned men in the Exeter Book riddles, this seems to me to be the riddler's in-joke, a special tongue-in-cheek challenge to his own monastic brethren. See, for example, a similar challenge to *þam þe bec witan* 'those who know books' in *Riddle 42* 7.

# [DEOR]

Welund him be wurman    wræces cunnade,
anhydig eorl    earfoþa dreag,
hæfde him to gesiþþe    sorge ond longaþ,
wintercealde wræce;    wean oft onfond,
5  siþþan hine Niðhad on    nede legde,
swoncre seonobende    on syllan monn.
    Þæs ofereode,    þisses swa mæg.

Beadohilde ne wæs    hyre broþra deaþ
on sefan swa sar    swa hyre sylfre þing,
10  þæt heo gearolice    ongieten hæfde
þæt heo eacen wæs;    æfre ne meahte
þriste geþencan    hu ymb þæt sceolde.
    Þæs ofereode,    þisses swa mæg.

We þæt mæð Hilde    monge gefrugnon;
15  wurdon grundlease    Geates frige,
þæt hi seo sorglufu    slæp ealle binom.
    Þæs ofereode,    þisses swa mæg.

Ðeodric ahte    þritig wintra
mæringa burg;    þæt wæs monegum cuþ.
20      Þæs ofereode,    þisses swa mæg.

1, 8, 14, 18, 21, 28: *Deor* is the only Exeter Book poem with stanzaic divisions graphically marked. The initial wyn of *Weland* in line 1 is similar in size, boldness, and gracefulness to the initial *H* of *The Soul's Address* two folios earlier. The wyn is somewhat more elaborately ornamented than the initial *H* of folio 98a. There are three small contiguous flourishes filled with what may be three small crosses high on the vertical stem of the wyn. Whether these are a visual play on the large, bold, carefully made and serifed crosses at the left of the stanzaic capitals at lines 14, 18, and 21 is difficult to say, especially since some scholars attribute the larger crosses to a hand later than the original scribe's. The bold, oversized serifed *e* of *Welund* in line 1 and the various secondary capitals or ini-

# [DEOR]

Weland tried punishment on them with purple.
The stalwart earl endured much distress,
had as companions his sorrow and pining,
winter-cold cares; often bore woes
5  after Niðhad laid narrow chains on him,
thin sinew bands on the excellent man.
    That was moved on; this can be, too.

Her brothers' death lay on Beadohild's mind
not so sorely as her own state
10  (which she had perceived plainly enough),
that she was made big, and never could know
with any confidence how it would end.
    That was moved on; this can be, too.

We many have heard of the harvest of Hild.
15  The yeomen of Geat came loose from the ground,
so this sorrowful love robbed them all of their sleep.
    That was moved on; this can be, too.

Theodoric held for thirty winters
a fortress of basil flowers. That to many was known.
20      That was moved on; this can be, too.

---

tials at lines 8, 14, 18, and 21 make *Deor* only slightly less paleographically distin-
guished than *The Soul's Address*. Folio 100a is arguably one of the two or three
most paleographically interesting pages in the Exeter Book.

14: *mæð hilde*. Often read *Mæðhilde*, an otherwise unrecorded and phono-
logically improbable name. See Introduction to Part One and notes above.

19: *mæringa burg*. So the MS. Often read *Mæringa burg*, but *mæringa* seems
on the available evidence to be a common rather than a proper noun. Like *mæð
hilde* of line 14, *mæringa burg* appears to conceal a riddlic image akin to a Skaldic
conceit. See Introduction to Part One above.

We geascodan    Eormanrices
*100b* wylfenne geþoht;    ahte wide / folc
Gotena rices.    Þæt wæs grim cyning!
Sæt secg monig    sorgum gebunden,
25  wean on wenan,    wyscte geneahhe
þæt þæs cynerices    ofercumen wære.
    Þæs ofereode,    þisses swa mæg.


Siteð sorgcearig    sælum bidæled,
on sefan sweorceð,    sylfum þinceð
30  þæt sy endeleas    earfoða dæl.
Mæg þonne geþencan    þæt geond þas woruld
witig dryhten    wendeþ geneahhe;
eorle monegum    are gesceawað,
wislicne blæd,    sumum weana dæl.
35  Þæt ic bi me sylfum    secgan wille,
þæt ic hwile wæs    Heodeninga scop,
dryhtne dyre.    Me wæs deor noma.
Ahte ic fela wintra    folgað tilne,
holdne hlaford,    oþþæt Heorrenda nu,
40  leoðcræftig monn,    londryht geþah
þæt me eorla hleo    ær gesealde.
    Þæs ofereode,    þisses swa mæg.


28: Here Deor's story of his own troubles begins with the oversized plain
block capital S of *Siteð*. The letter is serifed but somewhat crudely made.

30: *earfoða*. MS *earfoda*, with omission of the cross stroke for ð.

32: *dryhten*. A play on *Dryhten*, as the surrounding language and my trans-
lation show. Deor pretends to be talking about God and Fate, but he insinuates
that his earthly lord is responsible for his woes.

We have heard of Eormanric's
wolfish mind. Wide regions he held
in the realm of the Goths. There was a grim king!
Many a man sat bound in sorrows,
25   his woes on his mind—wished often enough
that the might of the kingdom would be overcome.
     That was moved on; this can be, too.


One sits full of sorrow, cut off from the good times,
grows dark in his thoughts, thinks to himself
30   that of anguish his share must be endless.
Then he may well think that in this world of men
the Lord, who is wise, will change his ways often.
To many an earl he will show honor,
gifts wisely given, but grief's portion to some.
35   Thus of myself I desire to say
that I in time past was the Heodenings' poet,
loved by my lord. A beast was my name.
For many winters I had a high office
and loyal lord, until Heorrend now,
40   a man subtle in song, assumed the land rights
that the guardian of earls had once given me.
     That was moved on; this can be, too.

---

37: *deor*. So the MS, which except for initial capitals does not capitalize proper names: see MS *heodeninga*, line 36; *heorrenda*, line 39. Most editions and commentaries would read *Deor*; hence the established title of the poem. I have retained the MS reading to show the play on 'beast' and the name Wulf, which also plays on the common noun *wulf*, in the next poem.

# [WULF AND EADWACER]

Leodum is minum swylce him mon lac gife.
Willað hy hine aþecgan gif he on þreat cymeð.
 Ungelic is us.
Wulf is on iege, ic on oþerre.
5 Fæst is þæt eglond, fenne biworpen.
Sindon wælreowe weras þær on ige.
Willað hy hine aþecgan gif he on þreat cymeð.
 Ungelice is us.
Wulfes ic mines widlastum wenum dogode.
10 Þonne hit wæs renig weder ond ic reotugu sæt,
þonne mec se beaducafa bogum bilegde.
Wæs me wyn to þon, wæs me hwæþre eac lað.
Wulf, min Wulf, wena me þine
*101a* seoce gedydon, þine / seldcymas,
15 murnende mod, nales meteliste.
Gehyrest þu, eadwacer? Uncerne ear[m]ne hwelp
bireð Wulf to wuda.
Þæt mon eaþe tosliteð þætte næfre gesomnad wæs,
uncer giedd geador.

---

1: The *L* of *Leodum*, the first word of *Wulf and Eadwacer*, follows the last refrain of *Deor* without extra vertical spacing in the MS. Although larger than any of the secondary stanza capitals of *Deor*, this *L* is a plain, rather undistinguished serifed block capital. Thus fol. 100b has only the tail end of the striking decorative effect of fol. 100a.

16: *eadwacer*. So the MS, though most scholars have preferred *Eadwacer*. Following John F. Adams, "'Wulf and Eadwacer': An Interpretation," *MLN* 73 (1958): 1–5, I read *eadwacer* and interpret the word as a sarcastic epithet. See discussion and notes.

*earm[n]e*. MS *earne*, variously emended to *ear[h]ne*, *ear[g]ne*, *ear[o]ne*, *ear-[m]ne*, the last of which seems to make the best thematic sense. Possibly *earne* represents a phonetic spelling of suppressed /m/ before coarticulated /n/: see MS *hearne* for *heardne*, *Waldhere* 5, and the telltale superlinear correction *heaðo*

# [WULF AND EADWACER]

For my people it's as if someone sent them a victim.
They'll eat him up if he comes upon the pack.
   It's not like that for us.
Wulf's on an island, I'm on another.
5  That island's sealed off, encircled by fen.
Men eager for blood are there on the island.
They'll eat him up if he comes to the pack.
   Things are not like that for us.
I dogged by design my Wulf's footsteps in exile.
10  When the weather was rainy and I, wailing one, sat,
then this man bold in war mounted me with his
    shoulders.
It was thus far my pleasure, that it still was my pain.
Wulf, my Wulf, thoughts of you
made me sick—your rare returnings
15  and a mourning mind, not at all lack of meat.
Do you hear, wealth watcher? Wulf's bearing off
our poor whelp to the wood.
One soon tears asunder what never was joined,
our song together.

---

beardna, *Widsith* 49. I do not agree with Adams's implication, "'Wulf and Ead-
wacer,'" p. 5, that the riddler would literally have said *earne hwelp* 'eagle's whelp,'
i.e., 'eaglet.' Moreover, for reasons given in the discussion above (Introduc-
tion and n. 30), mention of an eagle, even in a figure of speech, seems unlikely in
this poem.

    18: As they stand, these verses do not alliterate. But rather than attempt to
deal with all the irregularities of alliteration and meter in *Wulf and Eadwacer* (see
ASPR 3:320–21), I have left the text unchanged except for *ear[m]ne* in line 16.
Possibly this poem is a translation from a Continental language and did not
fit smoothly into OE verse. In any case, the discussion and notes above argue
that good riddling sense emerges from all the apparent technical nonsense of
the verse.

The inverted dry-point drawing of the horse and rider which accompanie the text of *The Husband's Message*, fol. 123a of the Exeter Book. In the tem porary absence of the MS from the Exeter Cathedral Library, this photo graph was taken of the hand-engraved image from Copy No. 219 of the photofacsimile. Compare the line-drawing on p. 240. Photo by Ronald Bene dict, United Methodist Publishing House, Nashville, Tennessee.

# INTRODUCTION

*Riddle 1*, composed of *The Soul's Address*, *Deor*, and *Wulf and Eadwacer*, appears to be arranged in the manuscript as a riddlic journey into exile, whereby the false soul's departure from God is secretly likened to a false hero's banishment from the society of men. *Riddles 2* through *59* appear, at least, to be brief texts which derive from folk riddling, ". . . secular poems, robustly celebrating the familiar objects and natural world of eighth-century England."[1] But abruptly at folio 115a of the Exeter Book, fourteen leaves after the final ringing clue of *Wulf and Eadwacer*, the briefer riddles are interrupted by nearly ten manuscript pages of various poetry—elegiac, didactic, devotional, homiletic, and heroic.

Most of these poems, especially the longer ones, do not look riddlic at all and therefore seem to intrude upon the Exeter Book riddles. Among them, however, appear some shorter, plainly riddlic texts. *Riddle 30b* (folio 122b), somewhat broken by a large hole in the page, is nevertheless restorable by comparison with its undamaged variant, *Riddle 30a* (folio 108a). On the recto of folio 122 the little dialogue poem which editors traditionally call *Pharaoh* is also partly lost, but its brief riddlic challenge escaped almost whole, and the gist of a solver's hesitant answer can still be recognized. The first seventeen lines of *The Husband's Message* (folios 122b–23b) most often appear, even in recent studies, as a separate riddle.[2] On folio 124b, after *The Ruin*, the short riddles of the Exeter Book resume. They seem to continue without further interruption (except by increasingly heavy dam-

---

[1] Michael Alexander, trans., *Old English Riddles from the Exeter Book*, p. 7 and back cover.

[2] See Frederick Tupper, *The Riddles of the Exeter Book*, pp. 43–44 (*Riddle 61*); W. S. Mackie, ed., *The Exeter Book, Part II, Poems IX–XXXII* pp. 190–91 (*Riddle 60*); ASPR 3:225 (*Riddle 60*); Craig Williamson, ed., *The Old English Riddles of the Exeter Book*, p. 103 (*Riddle 58*).

age and at least one missing folio) through folio 130b, the apparent end of the codex.[3]

The poems from folios 115a to 124b would therefore seem misplaced indeed if they were not like the sequential *Riddle 1* in a number of tantalizing ways. Like *The Soul's Address*, *Deor*, and *Wulf and Eadwacer*, these later intrusions among the riddles are of mixed genres interspersed with riddling. Possibly they should be regarded as literary riddles of a very elaborate sort. Indeed, if *The Husband's Message* is a text of some seventy rather than fifty-three lines, a reading I shall later defend both graphically and thematically, then at least this once a riddle is attached to other genres in a single poem.

This apparent confusion of genres seems to play against a hidden unity of theme. As in the connected refrains and cross-textual wordplay of *Riddle 1*, *The Husband's Message* echoes some words and motifs of *The Wife's Lament* as if answering them: a banished wife's account of her husband's voyage into exile is balanced by a former exile's proposal to his wife to rejoin him across the sea. In a sense these two poems, like *Deor* and *Wulf and Eadwacer* in a somewhat different sense, have a journey into exile as a central theme; and, like *The Soul's Address*, the poems known as *Judgment Day I*, *Resignation*, *The Descent into Hell*, *Almsgiving*, and *Pharaoh* speak of or hint at a spiritual journey. With a riddlic scheme of its own, *The Descent into Hell* imagines, rather vividly in places, the two great Holy Saturday journeys into hell and out again made by Christ and by John the Baptist, whose identity as chief petitioner for deliverance from hell is wittily concealed. The last lines of *The Descent into Hell* comprise a theological riddle on the journey of purification by baptism, the other great Holy Saturday event which had already brought Christ and John

---

[3] John C. Pope, "An Unsuspected Lacuna in the Exeter Book: Divorce Proceedings for an Ill-matched Couple in the Old English Riddles," *Speculum* 49 (1974): 615–22; John C. Pope, "Palaeography and Poetry: Some Solved and Unsolved Problems in the Exeter Book," in M. B. Parkes and Andrew G. Watson, eds., *Medieval Scribes, Manuscripts & Libraries, Essays Presented to N. R. Ker*, pp. 28–29 and nn. 17–18.

together in earthly life. The next two poems, *Almsgiving* and *Pharaoh*, pursue the theme of baptism by scriptural and liturgical reference. *Pharaoh* especially, a conspicuously illogical little riddle which answers itself, treats of the miraculous escape of Israel through the Red Sea, a story typologically related to the saving waters of baptism and an obligatory Scripture lesson of the Easter Vigil from very early times.

Although it advances the spiritual waters of the previous poems, however, *Pharaoh* also presents some doubtful internal logic. Unlike the *Joca monachorum* and other dialogues on scriptural subjects which it partly resembles, *Pharaoh* answers itself, in violation of the basic form of the riddling it pretends to be.[4] The riddle of *Pharaoh* can hardly be the Bible story itself, which is well enough known from the question and which appears plainly even through the somewhat damaged text. Rather, *Pharaoh* seems to challenge the solver to find its whole reason for being, and the answer suggests a higher wisdom arranged in a series of texts with concealed boundaries far outside the little poem itself. As in *The Soul's Address*, *Deor*, and *Wulf and Eadwacer*, those boundaries and a larger design for the poems between them emerge from an exploration of similar words and themes.

*The Wife's Lament*, *The Husband's Message*, and *The Ruin*, for example, all address or imply the favorite Anglo-Saxon elegiac themes of strife, exile, suffering and sorrow, and the decay of men's mightiest creations.[5] But in these poems the treatment of "Germanic" subjects is also consciously ambiguous, heavily laden with scriptural references and meaning. On intervening folios of the Exeter Book, such poems as *The Descent into Hell*, *Pharaoh*,

---

[4] Joseph B. Trahern, Jr., "The *Ioca Monachorum* and the Old English *Pharaoh*," *ELN* 7 (1970): 165–68, notes that the eighth-century Saint Gall MS has the question *Quod milli Eqyptii persecuti sunt filiis Israel?* and the answer *Xdccc* (1,800), because each of the 600 chariots counted in Exod. 14 would have had three riders. But, as Trahern says, the answer in the Old English poem "is . . . not at all typical of the genre" (p. 166). As I shall argue below in the proper place, the ambiguous answer in *Pharaoh* seems to reply in kind to a deliberately ambiguous question.

[5] These three poems are admirably treated together as elegies in Roy F. Leslie, ed., *Three Old English Elegies: The Wife's Lament, The Husband's Message, The Ruin*.

*Homiletic Fragment II*, and *Riddle 30b* follow principal events in the Paschal liturgy. The runes of *The Husband's Message* proclaim in a riddle the mystery of the Eucharist, and that same proclamation is found, simple and direct and without riddling, in the reformed Benedictine office of vespers. Together *The Husband's Message* and *The Ruin* disguise the climactic drama of Easter, the reaffirmation of the New Covenant which fulfills the divine inheritance of Man. As has long been suspected, therefore, the balanced exiles and ocean voyages of *The Wife's Lament* and *The Husband's Message* enclose the Paschal journey, from Good Friday to Easter, that anticipates the promised celestial reunion of the Bridegroom with his Bride.[6] Ultimately the journey is a spiritual one, with a destination in a kingdom not of this world. Like *Riddle 1*, *The Easter Riddle* does not contradict or deny the scholarly readings of its separate poems, but neither can it be apprehended merely as the sum of these individual parts. Analogous to the divine secrets of Scripture that it teaches, the Easter Riddler's grand scheme challenges a "wisdom" whose beauty the reasoning mind can glimpse but never perfectly explain. The elusive shape of *The Easter Riddle* is perhaps best grasped by statement and restatement, first in brief, then poem by poem in fuller detail.

[6] See, for example, John Gardner, *The Construction of Christian Poetry in Old English*, pp. 52, 107. I would agree with Joseph Harris, "A Note on *eorðscræf/eorðsele* and Current Interpretations of *The Wife's Lament*," *ES* 58 (1977): 207–208, that their thematic similarities do not necessarily make *The Wife's Lament* and *The Husband's Message* fragments of one and the same original poem, though I also suspect that they originally were just that before they were separated and "joined" (to borrow the boastful suggestion of *Wulf and Eadwacer*) with the poems that come between them in the Exeter Book. At issue is the value to be placed on lexical and thematic echoes as signs of textual relationships. James P. Holoka, "The Oral Formula and the Anglo-Saxon Elegy: Some Misgivings," *Neophil* 60 (1976): 570–76; and Neil D. Isaacs, *Structural Principles in Old English Poetry*, are two of many scholars who doubt that such echoes are anything other than oral formulas, or, perhaps (Holoka), indicators of single authorship wherever they seem to point to recognizable style. This position does not entertain a fundamental hypothesis of this book, that in some instances, such as in the present texts, oral formulas are exactly the kind of device that stood to be exploited for allegory and riddling.

Like the Church in waiting, but also like every hopeful Christian reader, the female narrator of *The Wife's Lament* must endure bitter loneliness of exile in this life. But rather than grief and despair at her separation from her absent spouse, she must learn patience and submission to God along the meditative way described in *Judgment Day I* and *Resignation*. With the penitent wife thus restored to obedience, *The Descent into Hell* now follows the exiled Husband on his triumphant Holy Saturday journey into hell. There, in his third meeting with his kinsman John the Baptist, he begins to collect the riddlic wealth and following of which his envoy will later boast in *The Husband's Message*. In the riddlic figure of John the two great deliverances from sin, Christ's hell journey and Holy Saturday baptism, come to inhabit the same poem, and the final lines on baptism are spoken by a concealed second figure, the priest, by whom the cleansing waters of the Jordan have come to flow in all the world.

The next little poem, called *Almsgiving* by modern editors, catechizes the scriptural relation of alms to baptism, perhaps to riddle on a customary penitential practice, the necessary human acceptance of divine forgiveness and grace.[7] *Pharaoh*, as we have seen, deftly employs the centuries-old typology of baptism from the readings of the Easter Vigil; i.e., the human readiness shown by almsgiving elicits the divine rescue by water and the spirit as it was foreshadowed at the Red Sea. Thus the sustained riddlic theme of crossing the waters, presented as an ocean voyage in *The Wife's Lament* and *The Husband's Message* and as baptism in several poems in between, attains the allegorical meaning of both divine and human dying to new life. The victory over death through the Passion and Resurrection and the correspondent cleansing of human nature through baptism, the chief spiritual events of Eastertide, are also the invisible framework for the arranged poems of *The Easter Riddle*.

After *Pharaoh* comes *The Lord's Prayer I*, freely and expansively

---

[7] Allen J. Frantzen, *The Literature of Penance in Anglo-Saxon England*, pp. 180, 183, places *Almsgiving* in the literature of catechetical instruction associated with the English customs of penance.

paraphrased in the general manner of *The Lord's Prayer II* and *III* from the Old English Benedictine office. But the paraphrase of *The Lord's Prayer I* is incomplete since it has no petitions for divine and human forgiveness. All the more space and emphasis, therefore, are devoted to the hope for the arrival of the heavenly kingdom and the government of the divine will on earth. In the only riddlic departure from accurate paraphrase, the supplicant asks for our daily bread, *þone singalan* 'the eternal kind,' i.e., the Eucharist. This touch of allegory gives an early clue to the deeper meaning of *The Husband's Message*. Next, however, comes *Homiletic Fragment II*, which the Easter riddler may have made into a fragment if in fact he did not already inherit it as one. It is essentially a creedal poem, and together with *The Lord's Prayer I* it recalls the two main catechetical ingredients of penance.[8] But in *Homiletic Fragment II* the hidden references to all three Persons of the Trinity appear to comprise a false trail as least as much as a genuine clue. The final lines on the Second Person, which deviate from the order of the Persons in the Creed, riddle the more emphatically on the presence of Christ as the Light of the New Fire at the Easter Vigil. In answer to the thematic clue of the Eucharist embedded in *The Lord's Prayer I*, *Homiletic Fragment II* gives a liturgical sign that the climax of Easter is very near.

In *Riddle 30b* this liturgical preparation for the Eucharist continues: the first spark of the New Fire at the end of *Homiletic Fragment II* grows into a flame. The flame is then passed about, as in the candlelight service of the Easter Vigil, and, in a lexical riddle, "kissed" in its spiritual form, i.e., embraced in the hearts of the faithful by means of the ritual Pax Domini, or kiss of peace. In also borrowing almost wholesale a rite of Germanic oath swearing from *Riddle 30a*, *Riddle 30b* anticipates the thor-

[8]Ibid., pp. 161–64, 175, describes penance and penitential literature, so strongly associated with the Lenten season, as customary occasions for instruction in just such fundamental articles of faith as the Lord's Prayer and the Creed. Universal instruction in these two articles (probably largely through the vehicle of penance) was insisted on by Archbishop Wulfstan. Frantzen believes that *The Lord's Prayer I* and *Homiletic Fragment II* may reasonably be seen as literary expressions of such penitential instruction.

oughly legal tenor of *The Husband's Message*. In this poem, with its complex dual-voiced riddling, the Eucharist of Easter, risen Word of the New Covenant, arrives at last under cover of the language of Germanic oath swearing. As at the first mass on Easter Sunday, the living presence of the Husband resumes in a mystery known only by faith in his promise to his waiting wife. But the promise is also delivered by a human messenger, the mass priest, who witnesses the timeless moment when salvation history is restored. At this most dramatic of moments, as the runes of *The Husband's Message* are given to the silent wife, the mystery of the Eucharist as it is expressed at vespers in the Benedictine office echoes in the mind:

. . . on æfen-timan ure drihten offrode æt his æfen-gereorde and dælde his discipulum þurh [h]alig geryne hlaf and win for his sylfes lichaman and for his agen blod.

. . . at eventide our Lord made offering at his evening meal, and by holy runing (i.e., mystery making) gave his disciples bread and wine for his own body and his own blood.[9]

Its difficult last lines make all of *The Husband's Message* a punning literary riddle on runes and *geryne* 'mysterium.'

The Easter journey then ends with *The Ruin*, whose extreme poetic beauty shows even through rather heavy damage to the text. Perhaps, as has long been thought, the poem was inspired by the fallen glory of Bath or some other Roman city. But the ambiguous language of *The Ruin* also riddles on the three Old Testament narratives of temple building and rebuilding in Jerusalem. Finally, in thematic innuendoes of the celestial city of Revelation 21, *The Ruin* surveys the destruction of all earthly things at the end of time. As the "invisible" drypoint drawing in the margin of *The Husband's Message* reveals, *The Easter Riddle*, like the vision of Revelation, moves beyond Time itself, and the solver sees a distant glimmering of heavenly light.

Thus the long way from *The Wife's Lament* through *The Ruin*

[9] James M. Ure, ed., *The Benedictine Office: An Old English Text*, p. 98. The translation is mine.

may be read as a riddlic exercise in the divine mysteries which free men from the strife, decay, and wavering fortunes of this world. The passage through this great riddle is slow and devious, nearly without visible connections, full of clues and obstacles that transcend its individual texts. At the beginning, in *The Wife's Lament*, even the Germanic commonplace has been made strange and obscure, as the elaborate ambiguity of literary riddling demands. Then, with a cunning and firm purpose equal to his texts, the compiler of *The Easter Riddle* lures his solvers ever closer to the hidden presence of his God.

### *The Wife's Lament*: The Riddle of Exile

From several generations of scholarship has evolved, by long and arduous debate, an acceptable modern reading of the obscure poem called *The Wife's Lament*. The general narrative situation of the poem, if not its every particular, seems fairly clear: it is a Germanic woman's elegiac complaint of her husband's exile, precipitated by blood feuding. Yet she is complaining not so much for her husband's sake as for her own. His absence has in effect destroyed their old conjugal vows, and she must now yearn for him endlessly from some sacred, or perhaps unapproachable, place of heathen refuge. This lonely and forbidding spot the brooding husband himself had commanded her to occupy before he departed *ofer yþa gelac* 'over the tossing of waves' (line 7). To judge from possible hints of the grave in her speech, the abandoned wife thinks of her enforced solitude as exile in characteristic Germanic terms: she is suffering, in her own view, the next thing to death itself.[1]

---

[1] On the heathen background of the poem, especially the references to death, the grave, and cave dwelling as a means of refuge, see Karl P. Wentersdorf, "The Situation of the Narrator in the Old English *Wife's Lament*," *Speculum* 56 (1981): 492–516; A. C. Bouman, *Patterns in Old English and Old Icelandic Literature*, pp. 55, 87–88; Matti Rissanen, "The Theme of 'Exile' in *The Wife's Lament*," *NM* 70 (1969): 90–104; Joseph Harris, "A Note on *eorðscræf/eorðsele* and Current Interpretations of *The Wife's Lament*," *ES* 58 (1977): 204–208. Harris thinks not of

But this composite literal reading of *The Wife's Lament*, sound as it appears, does not quite explain why the poem ends in thoughts of endlessness, or why the wife's final gnomic wisdom suggests to some readers the virtue of fortitude, to others the bleakness of despair.[2] Indeed, such contradictions of thought and feeling cannot be entirely resolved by studying *The Wife's Lament* alone. They make adequate sense only as the poem is located among the arranged texts of *The Easter Riddle* and then read with the concealed allegory of Easter always in mind.

Even the most basic of assumptions about *The Wife's Lament*, the general persuasion of a female speaker, has not escaped repeated challenges. Essentially the challengers argue that the theme of cruel lord and mistreated subject better applies to the comitatus than to husband and wife.[3] To be sure, the narrator speaks of a severed *freondscipe* (line 25), an absent *frean* (line 33) and *hlaford* (line 6), and (with implied envy) of more fortunate

---

sepulchral language but of the archaeologically attested early Germanic *Grubenhaus* instead. This study suggests, however, that the poet has deliberately made the wife speak ambiguously of what the Seafarer more plainly calls *þis deade lif*.

[2] Wentersdorf, "The Situation of the Narrator," p. 516, sums up *The Wife's Lament* as "a moving *cri de coeur*, colored throughout by genuine passion and quiet but unflinching courage." But the final lines of the poem, especially in their proposed riddlic connection with the following poems in the MS, are seen in this study to project not courage but false despair.

[3] See, for example, Rudolph C. Bambas, "Another View of the Old English *Wife's Lament*," *JEGP* 62 (1963): 303–309, and opposing arguments for a female speaker by Angela M. Lucas, "The Narrator of *The Wife's Lament* Reconsidered," *NM* 70 (1969): 282–97. Levin L. Schücking, "Das angelsächsische Gedicht von der Klage der Frau," *ZdA* 48 (1906): 436–49, once entertained the idea of a male speaker, and was refuted by W. W. Lawrence, "The Banished Wife's Lament," *MP* 5 (1908): 387–405. Later (*Kleines angelsächsisches Dichterbuch*, pp. 18–19) Schücking reversed his earlier position. See Kemp Malone, "Two English *Frauenlieder*," in Stanley B. Greenfield, ed., *Studies in Old English Literature* in *Honor of Arthur G. Brodeur*, p. 112. Alain Renoir, "A Reading of *The Wife's Lament*," *ES* 58 (1977): 4–5 and n. 4; and Martin Stevens, "The Narrator of 'The Wife's Lament'," *NM* 69 (1968): 72–90, also provide good reviews of the long-standing debate about the speaker's sex. Ludwig Ettmüller, *Engla und Seaxna Scopas and Boceras*, pp. 214–15, first identified the speaker as female from the grammatical clues of the first lines.

*frynd* (line 33) who have remained together in this world; and in law most of these words apply to the male relationship of lord and retainer.[4] On the other hand, the ambivalence of these same words is well known. Even in law, OE *hlaford* means not only 'lord' but sometimes also 'husband,' as the modern phrase 'lord and master' for 'husband' still playfully attests.[5] Old English *freond* 'friend' descends from an ancient Germanic word stem which meant both 'loving one' and '[legal] protector,' the dual role of a husband toward his wife, and a dual meaning upon which the poet could easily have equivocated.[6] Theoretically, at least, a married man of high rank could have been *hlaford* and *freond* to his wife and his retainers alike.

If at times the narrator of *The Wife's Lament* seems to speak or act like a man, a far greater weight of textual evidence identifies a woman. Old English *sið* 'tale, journey, adventure' (line 2) is a masculine noun, so that the foregoing words *minre sylfre*, with their feminine endings, make grammatical sense only if they are rendered partitively in ModE: 'a tale [journey etc.] of my own.' The phrase *minre sylfre* would then be pronominal rather than adjectival, as though the poet were half-concealing its feminine gender. But if this grammar was riddlic here, then the poet has also given fair notice of the deception with the unambiguous feminine grammar of *be me ful geomorre* (line 1). In the larger design of *The Easter Riddle* the contrasting masculine grammar of

---

[4] *Frea* 'lord' is the only exclusively poetic word among them. But even though *frea* does not appear in law, it is etymologically related to the very common legal word *freond*.

[5] Roy F. Leslie, ed., *Three Old English Elegies: The Wife's Lament, The Husband's Message, The Ruin*, p. 5 and n. 1, comments on the legality of marriage and, therefore, the dual application of *hlaford*, both 'lord' and 'husband.' See also Michael D. Cherniss, *Ingeld and Christ. Heroic Concepts and Values in Old English poetry*, pp. 117–18. Wentersdorf, "The Situation of the Narrator," pp. 492–93, argues on the basis of internal narrative clues (which he does not acknowledge as riddlic) that all references to 'lord' are also the wife's husband.

[6] See Leslie, ed., *Three Old English Elegies*, p. 4 and n. 1; Felix Liebermann, *Die Gesetze der Angelsachsen*, 2:1, 81; Karl von Amira, *Grundriss des germanischen Rechts*, 3d ed., p. 171 and n. 1. On the word *gemæcne* of line 18, see Amira, *Grundriss*, p. 177 (OE *gemæca*, OHG *gimahho*, etc.).

the words *Godes sylfes sið, The Descent into Hell* 52, are of special interest. They would seem to betray a conceptual contrast of a female and a male traveler on separate journeys, the fundamental riddlic idea of the entire sequence of poems. The grammar and language of *The Wife's Lament* thus confirm its touches of feminine themes, such as the reference to a *me ful gemæcne monnan* 'man fully matched to me' (line 18) or the implicit jealousy felt against *frynd* who *leger weardiað* 'keep their couches' (lines 33–34). In short, the bulk of the evidence reveals the destroyed promises of lines 21–25 as marriage vows and the speaker of the poem as a banished wife. Yet she sometimes describes her relationship with a *hlaford* in a man's legal terms.

The wife appears to contradict herself in other ways as well. She is shut up in one *londstede* 'plot of land' (line 16) yet also obliged to suffer 'far and near' (line 25). Her banishment, her oak-forested wilderness, and her many legal words seem characteristically Germanic. Yet, unlike Deor, she has no literal identity of name, tribe, or companions and therefore no traceable connection with similar Norse or Celtic women's songs.[7] Her closest likeness, in fact, appears to be a scriptural one. In being punished through the *dyrne geþoht* 'secret scheming' of her husband's kinsmen (*þæs monnes magas*, lines 11–12), she resembles the apocryphal heroine Susanna of Daniel 13, an archetype of the abused Bride the Church. Susanna and this banished wife endure much the same misery.

A beautiful and righteous Jewish exile in Babylonia, Susanna is wrongly accused of adultery by two of her husband's closest companions, both elders and scholars of law. Her innocence, the injustice of the charge, and her husband's intimacy with her accusers are also the suggested theme of *The Wife's Lament* 11–12. Susanna arrives in court "with her parents, children, and all her relatives" (Dan. 13:30), and insofar as the word *folgað*, in *The*

---

[7] Formal and thematic parallels from other literatures are acknowledged in Ernst Sieper, *Die altenglische Elegie*, chaps. 3, 4; Leslie, ed., *Three Old English Elegies*, p. 11; Gareth W. Dunleavy, "Possible Irish Analogues for *The Wife's Lament*," *PQ* 35 (1956): 208–13. Such likenesses probably show not analogues but rather the universality, or even conventionality, of the wife's theme of exile.

*Wife's Lament* 9, means 'following,' perhaps it plays on that scriptural idea. In Anglo-Saxon law, however, *folgað* means 'district of [people's] legal jurisdiction' and (after the conversion) 'diocese.' The wife's repeated concern for her domicile, too, suggests that like Susanna she has been in court and that her word *folgað* means 'abode' or 'rightful place' with a hint of legal force.[8] Twice (lines 28 and 36) the wife mentions her lonely agony *under actreo*. The words seem to allude to the hard proof of Susanna's innocence, her second accuser's lie that she was found in adultery "under an oak" (Dan. 13:59). Like Susanna, who stands accused first by the two evil elders and then before all the people, so the wife seems to lament her persecution by both the narrower and the wider circles of Christ's kinsmen—first the Jews and then the whole flesh-and-blood brotherhood of Man.

For all the allegorical significance hinted by these likenesses to Susanna, the banished wife of *The Wife's Lament* is nonetheless also what she literally appears to be—a Germanic woman in Germanic exile.[9] Hers is a life-in-death as torturous, and apparently as final, as the death penalty first levied on Susanna. The oak tree of the poem, with its connection to the story of Susanna and

---

[8] Leslie, ed., *Three Old English Elegies*, p. 7, recognizes *folgað* as a legalism. For its full range of legal meanings, see Liebermann, *Gesetze*, 2:2, 425 ("Gefolge" 9b); 1:165 (*II Æthelstan* 25, 1 and translation); 3:107 n. 3 (where the translation given in 1:165 is corrected to 'Diözese'). F. L. Attenborough, *The Laws of the Earliest English Kings*, p. 141, translates *folgoþ* as 'diocese,' and the poet in *The Wife's Lament* might have expected his readers to hit upon this meaning. Wentersdorf, "The Situation of the Narrator," pp. 496–98, suggests a broad semantic range for *folgað*, to include 'protection, security,' or even (on the single instance of *exsulabat* in Bede, *Hist. eccl.* 5.11, rendered as *folgade*) 'exile, refuge, asylum.' These meanings, however, are speculative; the better-attested generic meaning of *folgað* is '[legal] district.'

[9] Suzanne S. Webb, "Imagery Patterns and Pagan Substructures: An Exploration of Structural Motifs in Five Old English Elegies" (Ph.D. diss. Washington State University, 1973), rightly observes that no imagery in *The Wife's Lament*, (or *The Husband's Message, Wulf and Eadwacer, Deor,* or *The Ruin*) is specifically Christian. This study argues however, that the absence of Christian reference in these poems is a deliberate obstacle to meaning in (probably eighth-century) allegorical riddling.

its implicit contrast to the biblical fig tree of life, in pagan Germania likewise suggested death by its association with the cult of Woden.[10] The wife's legal maneuvers, described in the early lines of her narrative, have coincidental scriptural and Germanic flavor as well. Her search for a *folgað*, which can mean a 'following' like Susanna's at court, perhaps also alludes to some such re-enfranchisement of lordless men as King Æthelstan provides for.[11] Almost certainly the narrator's self-description in line 10 as *wineleas wræca, for minre weaþearfe* has a ring not only of poetic but also of technical language. *Wræca* means 'outcast, exile, friendless person' in law and poetry alike. *Wineleas*, though a distinctly poetic word, has the legal synonym *freondleas*; and *þearf*, an element of *weaþearfe*, is the legal term for 'poverty, need.'[12] The first riddle of *The Wife's Lament*, then, is not the speaker's gender, which is unambiguously feminine, but her identity, which appears to be at once Germanic and scriptural. Similarly, the husband has two relationships, legal and marital, with his

[10] See, for example, Song of Songs 2:13 (the fig tree in connection with the Bride); Joel 1:12 (in connection with joy), Micah 4:4 (in connection with the New Israel), Matt. 24:32, Mark 13:28–29, Luke 21:29 (the parable of the fig tree), and the many appearances of the fig tree together with the vine as emblem of (sometimes withered) fertility. On the oak as the death-cult tree of Woden and a possible connection with *The Wife's Lament*, see especially Bouman, *Patterns*, pp. 87–88; and Wentersdorf, "The Situation of the Narrator," p. 503. Yet I also agree with Harris, "A Note on . . . Current Interpretations," who argues on textual and archaeological grounds that the wife of the poem need not be imagined to be dead herself.

[11] *II Æthelstan* 2 (Liebermann, *Gesetze*, 1:50–51) has: *Ond we cwædon be þam hlafordleasan mannum, ðe mon nan ryht ætbegytan ne mæg, þæt mon beode* [*bude* in two later MSS] *ðære mægðe, ðæt hi hine to folcryhte* [*ryht* in later MSS] *gehamette ond him hlaford finden on folcgemote*. Cf. the phrasing of *II Æthelstan* 8 (ibid., 1:154–55): *Ond we cwædon, gif hwylc londleas mon folgode on oþre scire ond eft his mægas gesece*, etc. For the legal usage of *secan*, see ibid., 2:1, 193 (*secan* 9 'jemanden angehn [a] um Rechtserlangung'). Heinrich Leo, *Angelsächsisches Glossar*, p. 53, lines 32–33, has "*secan*: eigentlich: machen, dasz etwas zur gerichtlichen Verhandlung kömmt [*sic*], vor Gericht suchen" ("in actuality: to see that a matter comes before a court, to argue before a court"). It is very likely that in *The Wife's Lament* the words *folgað secan* play on the attempt to find a legal patronage or 'following.'

[12] See Liebermann, *Gesetze*, 2:1, under *wræcca, freondleas, þearf*.

wife. His two kinds of lordship, which seem separately drawn, have deceived many a reader into thinking of two men in the wife's sad story. In riddlic truth, however, she is speaking of only one 'lord' in dual roles, and from multiple perspectives of time.

On the one hand, most of the several time words in the conventional prologue (*þæt* 'then, afterward,' line 2; *siþþan* 'since,' line 3; *nu* 'now,' line 4) stress the division of the wife's story into events of the dramatic past and present. The past events themselves are distinguished lexically by the time words *Ærest*, *ða*, *þæt*, *ða* (lines 6, 9, 11, 18), and paleographically by raised points and small capitals in the last three places. On the other hand, the wife's story, when interpreted chronologically, presents some rather untidy narrative difficulties. In some readings of the poem *ærest* of line 6 has meant 'first' in chronological time, and a strictly chronological arrangement of the time words in lines 6–18 would seem to designate the *hlaford* of line 6 and the *hlaford* of line 15 as two distinct persons, one of them the absent husband, the other a mystery variously identified. This is one widely published view of the dramatic situation in *The Wife's Lament*.[13] But if, as has recently been well argued, *ærest* means only that the husband's relatively fresh departure weighs 'first' on the speaker's mind, then all the events of lines 9–28 could have happened in the couple's troubled days before the husband's exile.[14]

---

[13] There is considerable debate in older scholarship whether the events of the poem are related in chronological or psychological order. See Leslie, ed., *Three Old English Elegies*, pp. 3–4, 6–7; Bouman, *Patterns*, pp. 49–60; Svetislav Stephanovic, "Das angelsächsische Gedicht 'Die Klage der Frau', *Anglia* 32 (1909): 399–433; Douglas D. Short, "The Old English Wife's Lament: An Interpretation," *NM* 71 (1970): 588ff.; Thomas M. Davis, "Another View of 'The Wife's Lament,'" *PELL* 1 (1965): 299–300. The best literal solution of the problem of narrative time is by Wentersdorf, "The Situation of the Narrator," who claims (pp. 494–96) that the past events of lines 7b–23 have taken place while the wedded pair were still together, before the husband's departure in lines 6–7a. Although Wentersdorf does not say so, this scheme of events is probably what the wife alludes to in the words *niwes oþþe ealdes*, line 4a. But as Susanna-Ecclesia the wife would also be speaking of liturgical time, therefore of timelessness, i.e., of a story *niwes oþþe ealdes, no ma þonne nu* (line 4).

[14] Wentersdorf, "The Situation of the Narrator," p. 496. This argument, and

In a psychological arrangement of the dramatic past *ærest*, which looks like a time word, would become a word of riddlic deception instead.

The elaborate problem of narrative time in *The Wife's Lament* has largely distracted the modern reader's attention from the word *A* 'always' of lines 5 and 42, the final time adverb both in the wife's prologue and in her poem as a whole. Though her sense of fleeting time is no doubt painful enough, the wife really begins and ends her story, and thereby frames all her thoughts, with a time word denoting timelessness. Thus she equivocates on time and timelessness together. Her past sorrows, dating from the very time she *up weox* 'grew up' (i.e., reached marriageable age, line 3), and her present solitude comprise her plural *wræcsiþa(s)* 'wanderings in exile' (lines 5, 38) 'in this life' (line 41b). But since at the end of her lament she is still waiting in gnomic and universal woe, she has also introduced the sad tale of her exiles as a ceaseless torment—one she will always know and presumably always sing. She is grieving, therefore, not so much at the loss of her husband as at her own suffering, and in a long middle passage (lines 15–28) she nearly succeeds in making her husband sound brooding and treacherous and his abandonment of her seem cruel.

From reflecting bitterly on many vows of a marriage which *is nu* * * * *swa hit no wære* 'is now as if it never had been' (lines 24–25), she is brought at midpoem to describe the place and mode of her present suffering. She spends her days sitting jailed in a deathlike place, a natural wilderness which she also describes in metaphors of civilization.[15] She paces inside her *eorðscræf*, a

---

the riddlic possibility that ultimately the wife's complaint is a culpable misunderstanding of the husband's old promises, suggests that her narrative is based on psychological rather than chronological past time and on a false belief in the misery of an endless present (i.e., a riddlic equivalency of *a* 'always' and *nu* 'now,' lines 4b–5a).

[15] ModG *sitzen* preserves in colloquial speech the ancient Germanic meaning 'to be imprisoned,' 'to sit in jail.' Jacob Grimm, Wilhelm Grimm, et al., *Deutsches Wörterbuch*, 10:1, *sitzen* 2n, gives 'im gefängnisse beschlossen sein' and cites the OE *Christ* 25–27; *þe we in carcerne sittað sorgende, sunnan wenað, hwonne us liffrea*

sepulchral cave which, like her oak tree, can double as both a heathen Germanic and a biblical emblem of death.[16] The forest grove of her confinement is surrounded by a landscape too expansive to be seen fully except in the mind's eye of a mourner who is *eal . . . oflongad* 'all worn out with longing' (line 29). In this imagined scene the dark valleys become plural, and the upthrusting hills seem like the briar-choked walls of *burgtunas* 'citadels' (line 31). The entire vast figurative countryside becomes for the narrator a *wic wynna leas* 'cheerless abode' (line 32), and the Germanic word *wic* overwhelmingly refers to all or various parts of a manmade, settled, sometimes defended place.[17] Such an odd prison as this, both localized and vast, natural and enclosed, shows the touch of the learned riddler. On the one hand, the hints of walls and civilization in the words *burgtunas* and *wic* suggest the biblical garden in which Susanna is first accosted by the evil elders and then wrongly placed in their false witness against her.[18] On the other hand, the wild and unsurveyable vastness of the wife's surroundings suggest the world which con-

---

*leoht ontyne*, etc. ON also preserves this meaning in the idiom *sitja inni* 'sidde i fængsel.' See Johan Fritzner, *Ordbog over det gamle norske Sprog*, vol. 3.

[16] Wentersdorf, "The Situation of the Narrator," pp. 498–503. But as Harris, "A Note on . . . Current Interpretations," argues, OE *eorðscræf* (and perhaps *sitta[n]* as well) may also allude to the *Grubenhaus* of early Germania, a type of construction linked to women and their traditional occupations, such as weaving. Harris argues with such evidence against recent allegorical readings of *The Wife's Lament* by M. J. Swanton, "'The Wife's Lament' and 'The Husband's Message': A Reconsideration," *Anglia* 82 (1964): 269–90; W. F. Bolton, "'The Wife's Lament' and 'The Husband's Message': A Reconsideration Revisited," *Archiv* 205 (1969): 337–51; or M. H. Landrum, "A Fourfold Interpretation of 'The Wife's Lament'" (Ph.D. diss., Rutgers University, 1963). This present study, for different reasons from Harris's, also understands the wife to be a living speaker but views the allegorical possibilities of the poem as harmonious with its pagan Germanic themes.

[17] OE *wic* means 'house, hall, village, town, street,' and the Grimms' 'Heerlager' (*Deutsches Wörterbuch*, under *wikinger*). ON *vīk* means 'bay, inlet, harbor,' a shift in semantic reference from the ancient germanic meaning 'Dorf, Wohnstätte.' The generic reference of both *wic* and *vīk* would seem to be '[fortified] shelter.'

[18] Alfred L. Kellogg, "Susannah and the 'Merchant's Tale,'" *Speculum* 35 (1960): 275–79, notes that Susanna and her accusers in the enclosed garden

fines the allegorical Susanna, the Church. The wife as Church, I submit, imagines herself to be abandoned in a dark and allegorical wilderness, to suffer the pain of divorce from her husband for all time.

Time therefore moves and stands still in *The Wife's Lament*. The wife herself, whose thoughts move restlessly in and out of the past and present, also sees her future as still more suffering, endlessly repeated in measurable time. The *uhtceare* 'worry in darkness' which she has already known (line 7) persists *on uhtan* 'in the midnight darkness' of her present exile (line 35). With the accusative of extent of time her life is figuratively compressed to run through a single *sumorlangne dæg* 'long day of summer' (line 37), where the creeping hours hold only the conventional wintry miseries of sitting and weeping (lines 37–38) and pacing alone (line 35). This intolerably long symbolic day comes from an anguished state of mind which recurs, like the habitual sorrow before dawn, without apparent end.

As the wife comes to resemble Susanna in her innocent suffering and the earthly Church in her waiting, the contradictory endless summer-and-winter day begins to look like a riddle on liturgical time. The insistence on *uht* fits some hour or hours of the Benedictine night office, most probably midnight, *media nocte*, the darkest hour of poetic sorrow. The summer-long day of abandonment and lament fits the darkness of Good Friday and Holy Saturday, the end of the Benedictine liturgical winter and the loneliest time of the church year.[19] In this hour the wife as Bride feels an especially keen sense of loss. Her Husband, who

---

were a standard subject of medieval art as early as the ninth century. This essay is reprinted in Alfred A. Kellogg, *Chaucer, Langland, Arthur: Essays in Middle English Literature*, pp. 330–38.

[19] James M. Ure, ed., *The Benedictine Office*, pp. 100–101, shows OE *uht* as the designation for nocturns, the office sung *media nocte*. But the night office varied somewhat according to the seasons—winter (November 1 to Easter) and summer (Easter to November 1)—as established in chap. 8 of the Benedictine Rule. Thus the term *uht* might have been generic for 'night.' In the OE Benedictine office, matins is *dægred*, the next climactic hour after *uht* in *The Descent into Hell* (lines 1, 9, 17).

as in the Old English *Dream of the Rood* has just done battle armed only with his divine will, has left the mortal world in riddlic guise—a Germanic hero who has sailed into exile over the seas. These waters, which flow intermittently in several poems of *The Easter Riddle*, here represent two things: the boundary between the life and death of the mythical hero and the unfathomable gulf between the earthly sojourn and the distant heavenly kingdom of the Spouse. It is this divine *leodfruma londes* 'lord on land' (or, locatively, 'in the land') whom the wife mistakenly seeks in line 8.[20] Having failed to grasp the meaning of the husband's exile *ofer yþa gelac* 'over the welling of waves' into death, she is looking in vain for his kingdom in the "land" of this world.

In the wife's literal and worldly terms the husband's departure from her seems selfish and cruel, and in touches of Old English legalese she implicitly cites the law of mortal men against him. The much-emended b verse of line 15, divided by the end of a manuscript line, is probably a unique poetic instance of a legal phrase [*her*] [*h*]*eard niman*: the wife has been ordered to domicile, 'take up a home here,' i.e., in the lonely wasteland of her banishment.[21] Under earthly law, by which the wife claims a *ful*

---

[20] For instances of the locative genitive *londes* especially in Anglo-Saxon law, see Liebermann, *Gesetze*, 1:178 (*VI Æthelstan* 8.2), 400 (*Antworten auf Klage um Land*), which shows the rhyming phrase *landes ne strandes* 'on land nor strand.' Similar legal usage might have been the origin of Mod Dan *til lands og søs* and Mod Swed *till lands och sjös* 'on land and sea.'

[21] The MS reads *her/heard*, but has been emended to *herheard* (ASPR 3:210); *herh-eard* (*hearg-eard*) (ibid., 3:352, n. on line 15; J. R. Clark Hall, *A Concise Anglo-Saxon Dictionary*; and Wentersdorf, "The Situation of the Narrator," pp. 503–509, who thinks of a reference to a heathen place of sanctuary as the *locus* from which *The Wife's Lament* is spoken). There are other emendations, rejected for various reasons by Emily Doris Grubl, *Studien zu den angelsächsischen Elegien*, pp. 143–44. The spelling *heard* for *eard* in Anglo-Saxon law (Liebermann, *Gesetze*, 2:1, 59, 113) would tend to confirm a reading of line 15b as *her eard niman*, by Rudolf Imelmann, *Forschungen zur altenglischen Poesie*, pp. 17–18; Sieper, *Elegie*, p. 136; Leslie, ed., *Three Old English Elegies*, pp. 47 and n., 53–54. Heinrich Leo, *Angelsächsisches Glossar*, p. 74, line 4 cites *eard niman* twice in the OE *Genesis*; and C. W. M. Grein, *Sprachschatz der angelsächsischen Dichter*, adds a citation from the metrical version of Psalm 64:8.

*gemæcne monnan* 'man fully matched to [her]' (line 18), her lord's command and his leaving imply desertion and the breach of marital promise. She is especially saddened by his state of mind, which seems ruthless and brooding even to the point of murder (lines 19–20). But in her accusations the wife has forgotten that her husband's exile was not a worldly matter at all. His journey over the waves was divinely imposed and just as divinely under-taken, though, as his time drew near, he knew just such human sorrow as the wife describes. The syntactical division of lines 20–21 is much debated in scholarship, but the frequency of OE *oft* in initial position, the unambiguous accusative grammar of *bliþe gebæro* in line 44a, and the emergent allegorical identity of the husband argue for the true paradox of his spirit. More deeply than any mortal spouse, the Christ of Passion Week could be regarded as both *morþor hycgend[n]e* 'dwelling on murder,' i.e., his own, and *bliþe gebæro* 'peaceful in manner,' as in his calm behavior during his capture and trial.[22] It is precisely his identity which is hidden in the seeming paradox of these phrases, for the wife and the reader alike are left to think of a Germanic hus-band whose *fæhðu* 'blood feud' (line 26) makes his spouse bear alone the disastrous legal consequences of her sex.

In riddlic terms the divine Husband has not broken his vows to the wife at all. Indeed, he has strictly kept the provision of lines 22–23a, that no other thing *nemne deað ana* 'except death alone' should ever separate the two of them. In the same breath the wife accuses her husband and speaks of her *felaleofan* 'dearly beloved' (line 26), a word that tacitly acknowledges his fidelity. Thus it is impossible to tell whether in her epilogue the wife be-friends her absent spouse or curses him, for in essence she does

---

[22] Since the full grammar of OE +*bæru* is unknown, the phrase *bliþe gebæro* in line 21a must be speculatively treated. In line 44a, however, the same phrase is acc. dir. obj. of *habban* and suggests (perhaps as a riddlic device) that *bliþe gebæro* of line 21 is acc. as well. If so, it ends in seeming paradox the series of accusative descriptions of the husband's mood. But some modern editors (e.g., ASPR 3 : 210) understand *bliþe gebæro* in line 21 as the instrumental beginning of the passage on broken marriage vows which follows.

both.[23] On the whole she receives the gnomic prescriptions of heroic behavior as true: a young man should indeed be stoic in his composure—*geomormod* 'stern in his mind' and *heard heortan geþoht* 'hardened [in] the thought of his heart—and have *bliþe gebæro* 'cheerful bearing' as well (lines 42–44a). What is more, he should be able to maintain such calmness in the face of *breostceare* 'breast care' and under *sinsorgna gedreag* 'a throng of ceaseless sorrows' (lines 44b–45a). His heroic spirit should prevail 'be all his joy in the world from himself alone, be he banned far away in some distant country' (lines 45b–47a).

But at line 47b the subjunctive mood of gnomic prescription ceases. Beginning with *þæt* (I think perhaps for *Eala, þæt,* or some other unwritten sigh of woe), the wife abruptly turns to indicative verbs and refuses to apply her gnomic wisdom to herself.[24] In her final thoughts she imagines her husband's far-away suffering in language strongly reminiscent both of the Old English Seafarer's wintry misery on shipboard (*Seafarer* 8–9, 14–17, 23, 29–30) and her own banishment on land (*sitta[n]*, line 27, and *siteð*, line 47; *eorðsele*, line 29, and *dreorsele*, line 50; *uhtceare*, line 7, and *breostceare*, line 44, and *modceare*, line 51; *wic wynna leas*, line 32, and *wynlicran wic*, line 52). The indicative verbs and oddly specific scenery of the last six lines show that the

---

[23] Such older scholars as Grein, Moritz Trautmann, and especially Svetislav Stephanovic, "Das angelsächsische Gedicht 'Die Klage der Frau,'" *Anglia* 32 (1909): 399–433, thought of the wife as hating her husband and cursing him in lines 42–53. This view of the poem appears also in Francis P. Magoun, Jr., *The Anglo-Saxon Poems in Bright's Anglo-Saxon Reader*, p. 28, where the final lines are subtitled "Closing Malediction." Stanley B. Greenfield, "*The Wife's Lament* Reconsidered," *PMLA* 68 (1953): 907–12, also subscribed to the "curse theory" about the poem. Bouman, *Patterns*, pp. 58, 80, argues for a grieving wife rather than a hostile one; and Wentersdorf, "The Situation of the Narrator," p. 495, views the last lines as the wife's "philosophical reflection." For a thorough review of major critical positions on the poem, see Douglas D. Short, "The Old English Wife's Lament: An Interpretation," *NM* 71 (1970): 586n.1.

[24] In prominent modern editions (e.g., ASPR 3 and Leslie, ed., *Three Old English Elegies*) the syntax of the wife's epilogue is almost unreadably complex. To unravel it, as well as to emphasize the suddenness of the change in verbal mood, I read a new (expletive) sentence at line 47b.

wife knows some of her absent husband's distress firsthand, and the similarity of her word *dreorsele* with the numerous ship kennings in *-hus*, *-reced*, *-ærn*, etc., in the Old English *Genesis* and *Elene* suggests that *dreorsele* is a riddle word for the husband's ship.[25] But especially if the word element *dreor* also puns on 'blood,' the scenery becomes an allegory of the divine Husband's tomb *under stanhliþe* 'beneath a stone cliff' (line 48), icebound amid the storm of earthly life through which, perhaps, the Seafarer must also steer and engulfed by the symbolical waters of death. Moreover, if by *dreorsele* the poet also means the ship of the Church, a well-known theme of plastic art, then the wife as Church is complaining of suffering too much like her husband to remain apart from him.[26] Hers is the lament of an entombed spirit, shut up in an *eorðsele* in this dark and hopeless life. At the same time her daily course takes her endlessly *geond þas eorðscrafu* (line 36), a plural which suggests that she is regarding the world in her allegorical person as the Church.[27]

From the wife's failure to distinguish between the husband's bodily death and her own spiritual one, her lament concludes in a gnomic outburst of woe. In this cry the impersonal subject *þam*

[25] The images of storm, ice, cliff, and imprisonment on the waves appear, in great lexical similarity to these last lines of *The Wife's Lament*, in *The Seafarer* 8–9, 14–17, 23a, 29b–30. For a rather long list of kennings from *Genesis* and *Elene* that designate a ship as a 'house,' a 'hall,' etc., see Hertha Marquardt, *Die altenglischen Kenningar*, pp. 226, 229. For yet another suggestion that the husband's *dreorsele* is a ship, see Karl P. Wentersdorf, "The Situation of the Narrator's Lord in *The Wife's Lament*," *NM* 71 (1970): 608–10. If *dreor-* in *dreorsele* is a double entendre on 'dreary' and 'bloody,' then perhaps an allegorical allusion to the Holy Sepulcher is also intended. My article "ON *víkingr* and the OE *Wife's Lament*," *MScan*, suggests that *wic* of line 52a is a nonce riddle word for a ship, and therefore also an incidental clue for the obscure and disputed etymology of *Viking*.

[26] For the commonplace image of the Church as ship, with the Cross as mast, see D. Winzen, "Church, Symbols of," *New Catholic Encyclopedia* (1967 ed.), 3: 724b–26b.

[27] Harris, "A Note on . . . Current Interpretations," p. 205, suggests that the plural phrase *geond þas eorðscræfu* perhaps alludes to a deserted settlement of the type well known to archaeologists.

might seem to refer to the husband, but actually it begs pity for the wife. This is her worst moment, the liturgical hours after her Spouse's departure on Good Friday, when the world seems a hostile place, its hills and valleys impassably high and low. Tormented by living *gewidost in woruldrice* 'farthest apart in the world' (line 13) from the leveled hills and valleys of hopeful prophecy, the wife is in mortal jeopardy of mistaking her own despair for wisdom.[28]

Unlike, however, the husband's and wife's identities, the places of their separate exiles, or the liturgical time of the complaint, the wife's error is not confirmed in her lament alone. Indeed, as a riddlic reflection of Susanna and the suffering Church, *The Wife's Lament* once probably told a true story of undeserved misery. It seems possible that *The Husband's Message*, with its strong echoes of the wife's words and themes, was once the immediate answer to her complaint. But in the Exeter Book a number of poems borrowed from various nonelegiac traditions have been copied between *The Wife's Lament* and *The Husband's Message*. These intervening poems are neither as alien nor as intrusive as they seem. *Judgment Day I* and *Resignation*, which follow *The Wife's Lament*, also pursue the suggestion of falseness in the woman's grief. For wrongly accusing her Husband of worldly cruelty and desertion, she is reminded that he is none other than the God of the Last Judgment, which will be both merciful and stern. In *Resignation*, which appears to be two poems fused together by the accidental loss of a folio page from the manuscript, she responds to the warning of *Judgment Day I* in two ways. First, a sinner speaking in the penitential tradition confesses some nameless sins against God and asks his forgiveness. In the second part, after the lost page, a speaker names the specific offense of *tæle* 'calumny' (line 106), which also describes well enough the

[28] Isaiah 40:4, a lesson of the Advent season. In liturgical time these leveled hills and valleys are *gewidost in woruldrice* from the dark hours of Holy Saturday, the time when the wife as forsaken Bride would most appropriately speak of the looming hills and deep valleys of her imprisonment. In other words, Holy Saturday would be the moment when the promise of the Advent season seems farthest away.

wife's imputations against her heavenly Spouse. In a voice that recalls the wife's as strongly as it anticipates the husband's later message, the penitent of *Resignation* describes every exile as *sefa geomor* 'sad in mind' and *morgenseoc* 'downcast at dawn' (lines 95–96) and then reflects on a personal voyage which cannot be made for the want of gold or friends to buy the ship (lines 96–104), i.e., the powerlessness to flee from the exile of worldly life. Moved by such thoughts to understand past sins, the speaker arrives at gnomic acceptance of a lot which cannot be changed. Such resignation implicitly cancels the extravagance of woe at the end of *The Wife's Lament*.

Immediately *The Descent into Hell* opens with the walk of the sorrowful Marys toward the Holy Sepulchre *on uhtan* 'at midnight' (line 1), at *dægred* 'dawn' (line 9). But as their trek begins, still *on uhtan* (line 17), angels will have come to show that the *eorðærn* 'earth vault' (line 19) stands miraculously open. In riddlic terms the spiritual exile (*wræcsið*) of allegorical womankind, the wife's hard journey from despair to obedience, is at its end. In the next poems the scene changes to the Husband's own triumphant exile journey in and out of the stronghold of death and his mystical return to the world in the Easter Eucharist. The hidden connection between the first and last poems of *The Easter Riddle* is then especially strong: the *eald eorðsele*, the weary temple of flesh of the wife's imprisonment, becomes in *The Ruin* the celestial vision of salvation—the glorified temple of resurrected Man.[29]

### Judgment Day I: A Riddlic Rejoinder

Like Wulf's bride in *Riddle 1*, the banished wife seems not to know the falseness of her own sorrow. In implicit disbelief of such joy as there is in Isaiah's Advent promise, she has allowed the hills and valleys of her landscape *on þissum life* to grow im-

---

[29] Thinking of the physical body rather than the possibility of spiritual allegory, William C. Johnson, Jr., "*The Ruin* as Body-City Riddle," *PQ* 59 (1980): 397–411, also argues that *The Ruin* conceals the "riddlic" temple of the flesh.

passable in her mind. Rather than beneath the scriptural fig tree of life, she sits under the Germanic oak tree of death. She closes her lament as though her exile were hopeless, her waiting endless, her husband's promise unkept.

Suddenly, after her bitter final words, the poem known as *Judgment Day I* follows with a vision of the end of time and the destruction of the world. The poet has imagined the Last Judgment essentially in the Petrine fashion (2 Pet. 3), as the rebuttal of all mockers, scorners, and doubters; and the Easter Riddler has placed this message next to the wife, who would accuse her *hlaford* of delaying his promise. But the ancient prophecies of Judgment and the divine and apostolic call to watchfulness mean that "the Lord does not delay in keeping his promise—though some consider it 'delay' (2 Pet. 3:9)." The Petrine certainty of Judgment appears baldly almost at the outset of *Judgment Day I*: *Hafað him geþinged hider þeoden user on þam mæstan dæge* 'Our Prince has pledged himself to come hither on the Last Day' (lines 5–6). Like the mocking and sneering men of the last days (2 Pet. 3:3–6, 16), the *gromhydge guman* 'cruel-minded men' who scorn their Lord now (*nu*, line 13b) will find their eternal place in hell (lines 13–18). The word *nu* gives *Judgment Day I* the familiar apocalyptic urgency of much other Anglo-Saxon writing. In spirit, if not in words, the poet's earnestness about Judgment is akin to the Petrine reminder that the day of the Lord will come like a thief (2 Pet. 3:10).

Similarly persuaded of the nearness of Judgment, the riddler and Pseudo-Peter also share a marked detachment from time. In Petrine thinking, God cannot be accused of delay, since in his might he is free from human time: "In the Lord's eyes, one day is as a thousand years and a thousand years are as a day." *Judgment Day I* states this central paradox of time and timelessness with thematic play on water and fire. Like 2 Pet. 3:5–7, the early lines of the poem enclose all created time in references to three of its greatest events: the creation of the world from the waters, the first destruction of the earth by water, and the promised destruction by fire. Ostensibly *lagu* and *flod* refer to the sea and to floodwaters, the shapeless *wæteres sweg* 'noise of water; the *fisces eþel* 'dominion of fish' (lines 38–39) that fills the world before the Creation, after the ancient Deluge, and again after the flames of the final holocaust have cooled. But the futurity in *sceal*, *floweð*, and *bið* (lines 1–2) and the words *lagu* and *flod* allude also to the conflagration yet to come—the stock poetic image of *weallendan leg* 'welling flame' of *Almsgiving* 5–6.[1] In answer to the wife's complaint, the Easter Riddler has set both the warning and the lesson of *Judgment Day I*: the husband's promise has not been broken or delayed; rather, all created events, from first to last, belong to one and the same divine promise, whose days no man can reckon. Both as an individual doubter and as a figure of the exiled and impatient Church on earth, the wife has erred in seeking to know the days of her misery.

In the arranged poems of the Exeter Book, therefore, *Judgment Day I*, of itself a poem of didactic commonplaces, would become a riddle that employs the Petrine understanding of the Last Judgment to refute *The Wife's Lament*. As in *Riddle 1*, stock words and themes repeated across the texts bridge the allegorical lament of the wife with the instruction on the Last Judgment. In *Judgment Day I* the poet sets the limits of human knowledge with a question: Who has the wisdom to tell the heights of the heavens, or to describe heaven itself in all its prepared goodness (lines 30–33a)? This challenge is a sly but pointed criticism of the wife, who has complained of her numberless days on earth and wrongly described her absent Bridegroom's dwelling as a sepulchral *dreorsele* like her own. In her bitterness she has taken her lord's departure from the world as betrayal, and has missed the joy in heaven (*Judgment Day* 64–67), where exultation reigns ever since salvation was accomplished at the Crucifixion. Whereas the wife expects to grieve forever *on þissum life*, her husband's commitment to a day of judgment assures an end of all mortal life (lines 526–54):

---

[1] *Christ* 1250 has *weallende leg*, and *Genesis* 2544 has *weallende fyr*. Perhaps we may suspect the poet of *Judgment Day I* of wittily trading in a poetic commonplace, for he seems to think of the world as beginning and ending in 'waves' of water and fire respectively.

> Ne bið nænges eorles tir
> leng on þissum life,     siþþan leohtes weard
> ofer ealne foldan fæþm    fyr onsendeð.

> No man's fame will last
> any longer in this life once the Keeper of Light
> sends fire over all the reaches of earth.

On Judgment Day the wife, as the Church on earth, will also be released from the accumulated suffering of her countless members through the ages.

Against her collective human impatience with that suffering the argument of *Judgment Day I* proceeds to warn. The poem describes hell in parallel phrases, as neither a *betlic bold* 'grand dwelling' nor a *hyhtlic ham* 'joyful home' but rather a *sarlic siðfæt* 'sad journey's end' (lines 23–25). The voice of the poem becomes a teacher's, secretly upbraiding the wife with riddlic comparisons to her view of earthly life. Hell is worse than any *wic wynna leas* on earth, a *siðfæt* incomparably more bitter than any worldly (*wræc*)*sið*. Unlike the sweeping valleys and hills of the wife's overwrought imagination, hell is a cramped prison, *ufan . . . enge ond . . . innan hat* 'blocked from above and hot from within' (line 22). It allows no escape, not even the freedom of aimless movement around and around a place. It is a *mircan gesceaft* 'murky creation' (line 26): by implicit comparison the earth, upon which the wife so excessively mourns, is a *beorhte gesceaft* 'fair Creation' indeed (line 58). Hell, not earth, is the place to lament of waiting and longing *butan ende, ece* 'forever, without an end' (line 27).

For the Easter Riddler, the wife's legalisms have conceptual echoes that reverberate in *Judgment Day I*. There are references to (or sometimes wordplays on) a court of assembly (*gemot*, line 36; *gesomnad*, line 103), proclamations (*cyþan, gecyþed, cuþ*, lines 62, 74, 114), verdicts (*spræc, spræce*, lines 6, 101), sentences (*onsægd*, line 28), laws (*ryhta*, line 105), and opinions rendered by both judges and prophets, for the word *cwide* (lines 33, 114) has both applications in Anglo-Saxon law.[2] In *The Wife's Lament* the

---

[2] Felix Liebermann, *Die Gesetze der Angelsachsen*, 2:1, 44.

legal vocabulary wrongly equates the law of the wife's *hlaford* with blind and erring human injustice. But the legal words of *Judgment Day I* help refute the wife's view, for they are used to describe the omniscient—and therefore perfectly just—prosecution of the Divine Law on the day of Judgment. Insofar as it suggests a legal complaint, *The Wife's Lament* is without grounds, since the wife has forgotten God's promise to be a stern but merciful judge at the end of the world.

As the story of Susanna teaches, God's law is the ultimate refuge against human enemies. In answer to the wife's outcry against her husband's evil kinsmen, *Judgment Day I* offers a certain measure of consolation. The worldly power of cruel-hearted men, of the insinuator who *sibbe ful oft tomældeð mid his muþe* 'from habit separates friends with his mouth' (lines 25–26), will end in *brogna hyhst . . . helle grund* 'the direst of dreads . . . depths of hell' (lines 23–24). But these assurances are also riddles laden with double meaning. To the wife they will bring comfort, but also fear, because her own offense resembles the crime of the men she hates. Her lament implicitly blames her *hlaford* for her exile, which, however, is largely self-imposed. Her rebellious mouth has endangered her own *freondscipe* with her husband: their marriage *is nu* * * * *swa hit no wære* not by any fault of her spouse but by reason of her own complaining. On Doomsday, when the *firena . . . þeawas ond geþohtas* 'crimes, . . . habits and thoughts' (lines 35–36) of all men will be revealed, she might be judged as severely for this infidelity to God as her enemies for their *dyrne geþoht*.

The first eighty lines of *Judgment Day I* may therefore be read as a sober riddlic warning. Even the unwatchful feasters of lines 77–80 seem to me to riddle on Christ's description of the revelers before Noah's flood (Matt. 24:37–39). As they frolicked unconcerned until the disaster overtook them, so the wife in her collective unreadiness for the Last Judgment would only repeat their mistake. In her other allegorical guise as the individual sinner, the wife, unlike the foolish revelers, must also reckon seriously with the death and destruction of her body (lines 98–100). Together these passages seem to disclose the wife's full identity, and also her forgetfulness. Since all life (line 2) and all bone and blood (line 40) will have an end, neither the single believer nor the community of the faithful may neglect the fear of judgment. Those who come unprepared before the Cross (*æt þære rode*, line 105) will pass from the newly cooled ashes of earth (line 37) into the sealed furnace of hell.

At line 81 a large, ornamented initial *W* marks the only scribal division of the text. From this point onward, *Judgment Day I* is given over to gentler teaching. As the wife's complaint has weighed her present *wræcsið* against the memories of exile in her past, so the hope of believers for the Judgment is now poised against their dread. By the "generous patience" of God, who "wants none to perish but all to come to repentance" (2 Pet. 3:9), goodness is promised to *þam þe his synna nu sare geþenceð* 'the one who now sorrowfully ponders his sins' (line 83). He will know kindness after death, *þæs þe he swa geomor wearð, sarig fore his synnum* 'because he has thus become mournful, sorry for his sins' (lines 87–88). I take *swa* and *geomor* as riddling words for the salutary *geomormod* overlooked by the complaining wife. This healing *modbysgung* 'distress of mind' (line 84) will lead not to the *unbetlic bold* of hell (line 23) but to the splendor of the mansion (*boldes*, line 90) which the glorious Father himself prepares. Upon this *sele* (line 91) of lasting adornment, and not upon the temporary gloom of the wife's *eorðsele* or even the husband's *dreorsele*, the faithful must learn to wait. Those who know and repent of their sins will not try vainly to *heofona heahþu gereccan* 'reckon the height of the heavens' (line 31) but will want to *heofona heahþu gestigan*—rise to those same heights instead (line 97). Such assurances also have their conceptual affinity with Petrine thought: "What we await are new heavens and a new earth where, according to his promise, the justice of God will reside" (2 Pet. 3:13). Thus *Judgment Day I*, like the rest of Old English Judgment Day poetry, guides the sinner in "heart searching" with reflections on the Lord's sternness and mercy at Judgment. Since such instruction belonged prominently to Anglo-Saxon rites of penance, the Easter Riddler would seem to have placed it after the wife's complaint to suggest the voice of the confessor in his customary teaching role.[3]

As *The Wife's Lament* ultimately argues for despair, so *Judgment Day I* provides in the end a message of hope. Words and themes suggesting terror and destruction before line 80 are sometimes repeated or slightly varied after line 81. When they recur, as in the second mention of the heavenly heights, they advocate not the terrible sternness of God's punishments but rather his faithful devotion to mercy. The bright Creation which trembles (*beofað*) fearfully under the din of high heaven (lines 58–59) also trembles (*beofiað*) in obedient response to God's call (lines 112–13). Phrases meaning 'it shall come to pass' refer in the beginning to the annihilation of the world (*þæt gelimpan sceal*, line 1) but then to the resurrection of the body (*þæt gegongeð*, line 98) and finally to the initiation into glory (*hit . . . gelimpan sceal*, line 116). The heat of the conflagration will be increased (*Hat bið onæled*, line 9), but then, unlike the furnace of hell, cooled once again (*Hat biþ acolod*, line 37); and all men will see fairly judged their deeds *hates ond cealdes, godes oþþe yfles* 'both hot and cold, whether good or evil,' (lines 106–107a). Twice the poet presents a *cwide* '[legal] decree,' apparently to be spoken aloud and the more firmly remembered. First (lines 34b–46a), the final clash of arms and the complete desolation of earth and skies, the passing of men and all their deeds *godes oþþe yfles*, will alarm the sinful mind. Yet the promise of Judgment also means that the wife's *freondscipe* is not yet dissolved *swa hit no wære*, since she will once again encounter the husband himself. The second *cwide* (lines 114b–119) then looks beyond Judgment Day to the fulfilled promise of eternal life. The immutable *wyrd under heofonum* 'fate under the heavens' (line 115), an expedient in God's plan of salvation, must be welcomed as a comfort, not lamented in despair.

---

[3] For the general purpose of Old English Judgment Day poems, see Graham D. Caie, *The Judgment Day Theme in Old English Poetry*, pp. 115–16; L. Whitbread, "Notes on Two Minor Old English Poems," *SN* 29 (1957): 123–29. For the prominent catechetical role of the Judgment Day theme in the Anglo-

This truth specifies what is meant by obedience, the salvific wisdom already urged upon the *deophydigra* '[men] of deep mind' in lines 95b–97.

Only as a riddlic rejoinder to *The Wife's Lament* does *Judgment Day I* show its own true deep-mindedness. It shows the mortal danger of the wife, whose impatience for the husband's coming has slipped into the gravest doubt. At the same time it presents the divine pledge of the Last Judgment to liberate the wife from her deep gloom. An editorial voice, in the whole context of *The Easter Riddle* the voice of the teacher-confessor, urges the praise of God but also implies a corollary sin—the wife's complaint against him (lines 46b–52a):

> Forþon ic a wille
> leode læran    þæt hi lof Godes
> hergan on heahþu    hyhtum to wuldre,
> lifgen on geleafan,    ond lufan dryhtnes
> wyrcan in þisse worulde,    ær þon se wlonca dæg
> bodige þurh byman    brynehatne leg,
> egsan oferþrym.

> [Thus I want always
> to teach the people to lift the praise
> of God to the heights in hope of glory,
> to live in faith, and always to win the Lord's love
> in this world, before that dread day
> herald by trumpet the burning-hot flame,
> the unchecked force of fear.]

Like Caedmon's famous hymn, these lines perhaps take a cue from the ubiquitous formula *we sculon herian* as well as from other thoughts from the meditations of the canonical hours. The lines on the trumpet blast, which God's voice will drown at the final summons (lines 109–12a), have a rough parallel in *The Lord's Prayer II* read at prime: *þu . . . ealra cyninga þrym, clypast*

---

Saxon penitential rite, see Allen J. Frantzen, *The Literature of Penance in Anglo-Saxon England*, pp. 155, 161, 165–66, 181.

*ofer ealle* 'You . . . the majesty of all kings, will call out above all.'[4]
But if the Lord's coming is a thought for the full rise of day,
prayerful readiness for the Judgment is the special business of
the midnight office:

On uhtan we sculon God herian ealswa Dauid cwæð: . . . "To mid-
dre nihte ic aras (and andette drihtenes doma rihtwisnesse)." Crist
sylf bead þæt we georne wacian sceoldan; he cwæð: . . . "Waciað
georne forðam þe ge nyton hwænne eower drihten cymð"; and eft
he cwæð: . . . "Eadige beoð þa men þe se hlaford wacigende gemet
þonne he tocymð" (þæt is ure drihten þonne he to dome cymð
þonne he wile witan hwa wacigende beo on godum dædum).

[At nocturns we must praise God exactly as David said: ". . . At mid-
night I arose (and acknowledged the righteousness of the Lord's
judgments)." Christ himself commanded that we should keep good
watch; he said: ". . . Watch well, because you do not know when
your Lord will come"; and he also said: ". . . Blessed be those whom
the Lord finds awake when he draws near" (that is, our Lord as he
comes for the Judgment, when he will know who would be keeping
a watch of good deeds).][5]

In *Judgment Day I* this same watchfulness is urged against the
darkness of hell and sin, and good deeds have the same vital role
in the watch. Christ is himself the knower of all good deeds (lines
67b–68a) and their requiter in afterlife (lines 85–88a). Thus the
meditations of nocturns only express more succinctly what *Judg-
ment Day I* also teaches with almost belabored repetition: that the
prayerful wait for the husband's coming is a duty and chief good
deed of mortal life. The corollary lesson is that it is in fact rebel-
lious to complain of such a duty. In *The Easter Riddle* the corol-
lary underlies the argument of *Judgment Day I*, a stern yet heart-
ening correction of the sinner in *The Wife's Lament*.

Yet despite its sober and persistent didacticism, *Judgment Day I*
closes with a firm and hopeful promise: *Welan ah in wuldre se nu*

---

[4]See James M. Ure, ed., *The Benedictine Office*, pp. 50–57, 104. Ure concludes
that *The Lord's Prayer II* is either an alternate reading for *The Lord's Prayer III*, in
the long meditation at prime, or else a fragment of a separate office.

[5]Ibid., pp. 100–101 (translation mine).

*wel þenceð* 'He who thinks well now will own rich goods in glory'
(line 119). In the larger arrangement of poems this same thought
counsels the wife to leave her bitter exile and turn toward obe-
dience. Her new journey will require her to look inward to find
at last the resignation of the following poem. Along with her, the
solver *se nu wel þenceð* is guided subtly onward into the pentiten-
tial preparation for Easter.

## *Resignation*: A Change of Heart and Voice

For the poem which follows *Judgment Day I*, modern scholar-
ship has almost settled on the title *Resignation*, though the apt
name *The Penitent's Prayer* is also still used. The text opens with a
large, bold initial *A* and a solitary half line which is also a short
line in the manuscript: *Age mec se ælmihta God* 'May the almighty
God own me.' As at the end of many other riddles, here also,
after the end of *Judgment Day*, the scribe has left no extra space.
He entered the word *helpe*, which properly begins the second
line of *Resignation*, near the vertical center of the large *A*, but the
*ge* of *Age*, the true beginning of the poem, near the top of the
initial. Unlike the world *Wile*, at *Judgment Day* 80 just on the re-
verse side of folio 117, *Age* has no further block letters and no
very discernible emboldening to aid the eye. Thus the words *Age
mec se ælmihta God* are almost concealed by the large initial and
the surrounding long manuscript lines. In his pioneering edi-
tion of the Exeter Book, Thorpe overlooked this opening verse
and understood the large *A* as a verbal prefix in the following
manuscript line, which he mistakenly began as *Ahelpe mec se halga
drihten.*[1] Probably the scribe's spacing in this place was simply
bad, or perhaps Thorpe was fooled by graphic trickery designed
to hide the lexical bridge in the verb *agan*. The word appears as
*ah* 'owns' in the final line of *Judgment Day*, and again as opt. subj.
*Age* just seven words later, where *Resignation* begins. Just to the
left of the capital *A* there is an untidy penciled cross, perhaps by

[1] Benjamin Thorpe, ed. and trans., *Codex exoniensis: A Collection of Anglo-Saxon
Poetry, etc.*, p. 452.

the same unknown reader who marked with a cross the first line of *The Soul's Address*.[2]

In the repeated word *agan* at the beginning of *Resignation*, a first-person speaker offers the self as property to God. It is a distinctly womanly thought, all the more in the veiled eroticism of the next few lines. There the speaker offers soul, body, words, deeds, *ond eal min leopo* 'and all my limbs' (line 8a) to be possessed, in strong reminiscence of the scriptural bride of *Song of Songs*. But a still more sweeping clue to the bond between *Judgment Day* and *Resignation* appears in the gnomic sentiments which close the two poems. *Judgment Day* ends with the advice to 'think well now,' and *Resignation* seems to take this advice with the closing that gives the poem its modern name: an earthly lot which cannot be changed is best borne well. In turn, both of these endings overturn the gnomic bitterness in the final line of *The Wife's Lament*. That is, the wife's last outcry of *Wa biδ*, etc., appears to be canceled by the hopeful wisdom that closes *Judgment Day*: think well 'now,' i.e., during the trials of this life, and own rich goods in the glory of heaven. In a manner akin to riddling the converse wisdom is left unsaid: think bitter thoughts, like the lamenting wife's, and reap all the sternness of the Judgment.

Already the first words of *Resignation* look like the wife's prayerful response to the wisdom in *Judgment Day*, but riddlic confirmations of her identity do not arise until much later. At line 91 the phrase *wineleas wræcca*, the wife's very term for herself in *The Wife's Lament* 10, reappears in the third person; and just as the wife has known *uhtceare* and *hyge geomor* in a *wic wynna leas*, so the exile of *Resignation* 89ff. is described as *morgenseoc, sefa geomor, leodwynna leas*. In lines 96b–104 the penitent abruptly introduces a self-told tale of a sea journey thwarted by friendlessness and poverty, and the words recall both the opening lines of *The Wife's Lament* and a major theme of *The Husband's Message*. But in the end the penitent's own wisdom of accepting the unchangeable closes the debate on the proper attitude toward suffering. By such clues the speaker of *Resignation* gradually appears to be

[2] See the concluding discussion in Part One above.

the banished wife herself, in whom the lessons of *Judgment Day* have created a changed heart. From this large perspective *Judgment Day* and *Resignation* seem to work as an extended dialogue between the voices of a teacher-confessor and his penitent, who at the end of *Resignation* understands the *cwide* of wise obedience assigned to her at the end of the previous poem.

*Resignation* may therefore be said to consist of two inseparable major themes: obedience learned through penance undertaken. The favorite thoughts of penitential books and of the penitential devotions of the Bendictine office appear over and over— prayers for mercy (lines 26ff., 49–52a), healing (63b–64a), and strength against the devil (15b–18, 52b–56, etc.).[3] Necessary steps in penance are discovery and confession of sin, and as in much other penitential literature the wife's sinfulness appears to her to be great (*bitre bealodæde*, line 20a) and manifold (*firendæda fela*, line 26a), more *grimra gylta* 'grievous wrongs' than even a merciful God has allowed (line 28). Amid this rather generalized confessional language, a few oddly vivid hints of more specific crimes also appear. The wife has endangered her soul (lines 65b–66a) because she has *Gode . . . abolgen* 'provoked God' (lines 78b–79a) with her *tæle* 'calumny' (line 106). These offenses go unexplained in *Resignation* alone, but *tæle* seems to name in retrospect the sin of *The Wife's Lament*, wherein the wife has wrongfully charged her husband with her own breach of faith. If, as more than one critic has said, *Resignation* itself is a confused

---

[3] As E. G. Stanley, "Old English Poetic Diction and the Interpretation of *The Wanderer, The Seafarer,* and *The Penitent's Prayer,*" *Anglia* 73 (1956): 451, points out, *Resignation* seems to have no direct sources in other penitential literature. Perhaps this is because the poet was simply trading in commonplaces. Thomas H. Bestul, "The Old English *Resignation* and the Benedictine Reform," *NM* 78 (1977): 18–23, demonstrates the close affinities in content and tone between *Resignation* and the private devotional and penitential literature, including confessional poetry, inspired by the mid–tenth-century English Benedictine reform movement. Bestul thinks tentatively of the reign of King Edgar (959–75) as the time of composition of *Resignation*. This guess matches my own suspicion, based on the literal matter and the language of *The Ruin* and on the probable method of arrangement of *Riddle 1* and *The Easter Riddle* as a whole, that both sequences might have been finished shortly after 973. See the concluding remarks in the Introduction above.

poem, then perhaps the muddle is artistically justifiable as the turbulent thoughts of a guilt-ridden sinner.[4] But even more important, the confusion seems to be deliberate, for in connection with other poems of *The Easter Riddle* it makes a deep-lying sense.

For example, the rather long passage on exile and seafaring at first looks utterly out of place in *Resignation*. But in the larger view it carries both backward and forward to weightier events. As perhaps also in *Wanderer* 1, the *anhoga* of *Resignation* 89b becomes the exile separated by sin from God, but the separation is also lamented in words much like the wife's. At line 97 the penitent, by this conspiracy of words wife and sinner, abruptly confesses not sins but rather a yearning to go to sea. Frustrated, however, by the want of gold or patronage and unable to buy a boat, she seems to give up hope of a voyage. In lines 103b–110a her words sound like bitter complaint if they are read alone. But lines 110b–111a would also reverse the meaning of some crucial words from *The Wife's Lament*. The same wife who once believed that the exile's worldly joy *sy . . . æt him sylfum gelong* '[might] be . . . from himself alone' has now been instructed in more lasting wisdom: *Is seo bot æt þe gelong æfter life* 'The cure comes from you [the Lord] after this life.'

By acquiring her own spiritual remedy in place of the gold she desires, the penitent has moved willy-nilly toward a familiar ideal wifehood in Scripture (1 Pet. 3:3–4):

The affectation of an elaborate hairdress, the wearing of golden jewelry, or the donning of rich robes is not for you. Your adornment is rather the hidden character of the heart, expressed in the unfading beauty of a calm and gentle disposition.

[4] See Stanley, "Old English Poetic Diction," p. 416; and Carl T. Berkhout, "The Speaker in *Resignation*: A Biblical Note," *N&Q* 219 (1974): 122–23, who finds "penitential and exile motives . . . curiously intertwined" in the poem, whose main argument may either favor or disfavor its speaker. Berkhout suggests the Vulgate Job 14:7–10, and perhaps also Gregory the Great's *Moralia in Job* 12.6 as possible sources for the figure of the wood bursting from the death of winter into spring (lines 105–106a). For Berkhout, *wyrd* (lines 107–18) seems to be a double force that perpetuates nature even as it punishes the "unregenerate decay" of the sinner.

Thus *Resignation* follows the wife as she learns to put on the adornments of humility and patience, and the instrusion about seafaring may possibly have been fitted in as a riddle on her spiritual journey. Her words *ic me sylf ne mæg . . . willan adreogan* 'I cannot myself . . . fulfill my desire' (lines 103b–104) are not the complaint they seem to be, but a proper acknowledgment of and submission to the power of God. By such meekness the wife stands to inherit, if not the earth, then the far greater riches promised at the end of *Judgment Day*. Later the husband will send from exile his message that the wife's ship and gold await her. First, however, her riddlic journey will also lead over the baptismal waters of *The Descent into Hell*, *Pharaoh*, and *Alms-giving*.

Quite aside from these numerous suggestions of links with adjacent poems, however, *Resignation* is in a sense a divided text itself. The evidence of a missing folio leaf at lines 69–70, between the folios now numbered 118 and 119, seems too weighty and varied to doubt.[5] First, a gathering of the codex appears to have been rearranged to accommodate such a loss. Although they were once probably folded and sewn in the same way, the two gatherings bridged by the text of *Resignation* are now conspicuously different. Folio 112, the first page of the gathering in which *Resignation* also begins, is pasted to the sewing strip of folio 118, which was originally a singleton. This patchwork sug-

[5] The following paleographical arguments summarize the full and detailed argument of Alan J. Bliss and Allen J. Frantzen, "The Integrity of *Resignation*," *RES*, n.s. 27 (1976): 385–402. Marie Nelson, "On Resignation," in Martin Green, ed., *The Old English Elegies: New Essays in Criticism and Research*, pp. 133–47, argues by analysis of themes and speech acts that *Resignation* is a unified "testament of courage" and a preparation of the soul for death. I agree with Nelson that the poem can be read to show the speaker "making progress toward self-understanding and toward true comprehension of God's grace" (p. 138), but I cannot dismiss, as Nelson would, Bliss and Frantzen's cogent argument for the loss of a MS leaf at the present lines 69–70. In the larger context of *The Easter Riddle* the lines now known as *Resignation*, probably originally two adjacent texts sharing confessional penitential themes, can reasonably be perceived as a textual rather than a conceptual muddle.

gests that folio 112, like the first page of the next gathering, is the surviving half of a double sheet. A second half, like the corresponding last page of the next gathering, seems to be missing.[6]

A number of linguistic discontinuities at this same point also imply some lost text. *Resignation* 69, which seems to round out folio 118b, is given in modern editions as *no þæs earnunga ænige wæron mid*. But whereas the word *mid* could perhaps be read adverbially, as in *Dream of the Rood* 106, it is not needed to complete the sense of *Resignation* 69, whose versification it also disrupts. On the other hand, *mid* cannot possibly belong to the *hwæþre* clause which begins folio 119a. This last word on folio 118 therefore appears to be disconnected, as though it once began a sentence which continued onto a page that is now lost.

Certain lexical and thematic shifts converge on *Resignation* 69–70 as well. The words *sawol* and *gæst* of earlier lines yield after line 70 to the synonymous *ferð* and *mod*. The occasional Anglian words in *Resignation* stop at *meorda* 'goodness' of line 68. God is repeatedly invoked in the second person until line 67b but is spoken of only in the third person from line 76b onward. Traces of the versified OE *Paternoster* and *Gloria* and of the metrical Psalms, probably influences from penitential literature, color the first 69 lines but do not appear after 70. Indeed, after line 70 the riddlic mood of penitential prayer could have been adapted from a lament almost without changing a word.[7] To-

---

[6] For the discovery of the other missing leaf in the gathering, between the present fols. 125 and 126, see John C. Pope, "An Unsuspected Lacuna in the Exeter Book: Divorce Proceedings for an Ill-matched Couple in the Old English Riddles," *Speculum* 49 (1974): 615–22.

[7] Bestul, "The Old English *Resignation*," who was unaware of the work of Bliss and Frantzen, "The Integrity of *Resignation*," thinks of the break between the elegiac and penitential portions of *Resignation* as occurring at line 75 and of the whole poem as an innovative attempt to combine native elegy with the tradition of Latin penitential poetry based on the seven penitential Psalms. Bliss and Frantzen believe that the two contradictory moods of *Resignation* can be explained by the loss from the MS of parts of two separate poems. Perhaps, since we cannot hope to recover that loss, it is best to take the closing advice of *Resignation* itself and make of the surviving confessional-penitential text the best conceptual unity we can.

gether these dichotomies build a sound case for a missing leaf, perhaps with an initial which once began a separate poem, between folios 118 and 119. Apart from the manuscript, however, only careful inspection of the word *mid* will show the disappearance of some sixty lines of poetry after *Resignation* 69b. In the present edition *mid* is followed by an ellipsis and enclosed in brackets to represent the gap.

The careless Anglo-Saxon reader might not have detected the break in *Resignation* much more easily than latter-day readers have done. In spite of their halting meter, the words *no þæs earnunga ænige wæron mid* make a kind of sense when *mid* is read as a prepositional adverb. At the top of folio 119a the lines beginning with *hwæþre* have acceptable meter and syntax and show no obvious interruption in sense from folio 118. With their riddlic double perspective the later lines of *Resignation* might be either venting spite and rebelliousness or showing humble submission to the will of God. It is thus possible to read both halves of *Resignation* as mainly penitential in their somewhat different ways.

The narrative of *The Easter Riddle* moves through human time, in an order of ecclesiastical events beginning with the bitter exile of Good Friday and looking toward the reunion of Husband and Wife at Easter, a conceptual order of events that has a likely analogy in another poetic manuscript.[8] But in the faith and doc-

---

[8] Allen J. Frantzen, *the Literature of Penance in Anglo-Saxon England*, p. 181, observes a tandem order of penitential poems also in MS 201 of Corpus Christi College, Cambridge. In Frantzen's view *Exhortation to Christian Living*, *A Summons to Prayer*, *The Lord's Prayer*, and *Gloria* would have been read in their MS order as a series, "a movement from contrition and confession to absolution and prayer." Since in that MS the poem just preceding *Exhortation* is the 306-line *Judgment Day II*, and since *Exhortation* itself urges in homiletic fashion "especially the abundant bestowal of alms [to] safeguard against the perils of the approaching Judgment" (ASPR 6, p. lxxii) quite probably the middle poems of *The Easter Riddle*, from *Judgment Day I* through *Almsgiving*, *The Lord's Prayer I*, and *Homiletic Fragment II*, show a tandem arrangement largely similar to the penitential grouping that Frantzen sees in Corpus Christi MS 201. This latter grouping, however, would seem to begin with the conventional penitential instruction in *Judgment Day II* rather than with *Exhortation* as Frantzen suggests. There is no doubt of the

trine of the Church the movement from exile to reunion is already accomplished in eternity, whose promise men share through the Resurrection. Toward the end of *Resignation* these human and eternal events merge into symbolic time, wherein the great deeds of salvation history may occur simultaneously, or even out of their narrative order. I have thus moved the word *nu*, usually placed at the end of line 116, to start a new sentence at line 117a. With the usual editorial addition of *selast* to fill out line 117a, the relocated word *Nu* changes line 116b from a questionable to a regular b verse, and line 117a from a regular *a* verse to a regular *b* verse. Thematically the words *Nu giet* betoken the next event, the opening scene of *The Descent into Hell*, where the *dægred* 'dawn' of Easter can be glimpsed even before the conquest of hell is told. *Nu giet* 'even now,' as the wife achieves her peace of heart and mind, the drama of her salvation is gathering force. The riddler's point seems to be that God comes to the sinner at the very moment when the sinner elects to return to him. With the final turn to spiritual obedience in *Resignation* and the analogous turning from sorrow to amazement and joy in the quem quaeritis theme which begins *The Descent into Hell*, the Easter Riddler has arranged a major dividing point in his scheme. In the first seventeen lines of *The Descent into Hell*, lines which (to borrow again the words from *Wulf and Eadwacer*) perhaps "never were joined" in this place before, the troubled journey of allegorical Womanhood comes to a happy end. The answering journey, the Husband's exile into death and hell and his mighty return to glory, can now begin.

---

eighth-century inspiration of *Judgment Day II*, since it is a "rather close translation" (ASPR 6 : lxxi) of Bede's (or perhaps Alcuin's) *De die iudicii*; but the laxity of alliteration in the Old English version suggests authorship of the late tenth or early eleventh century. Corpus Christi MS 201, which dates from the late-eleventh century, therefore contains some likely support for my view of *Riddle 1* and *The Easter Riddle* as older poetry, at least in part, reworked into new schemes that originated in the Benedictine Reform. On some scholars' attribution of *De die iudicii* to Alcuin, see Stanley B. Greenfield, *A Critical History of Old English Literature*, pp. 133–34 and nn. 9–10.

## *The Descent into Hell*: Out of Exile

*The Descent into Hell* tells of Christ's mighty invasion of the fortress-prison of souls but does not overtly deal with his triumphant march out again. Instead, the figure of John the Baptist, riddlic chief petitioner among the hell dwellers, serves to introduce the theme of baptism, a typological journey into and out of the water of spiritual purgation and rebirth.[1] But the poem opens with a distinct liturgical echo, an antiphonal paraphrase, embedded at lines 1–5 and again at lines 9–11a, of the quem quaeritis trope that sprang from the Benedictine Reform.[2] *The Descent into Hell*, then, not only closes the private spiritual journey of Womanhood but also begins the public journey of liturgical celebration.

In one sense the lamenting wife, who is also the dramatic speaker in *Resignation*, has a hidden identity as Susanna, and therefore typological connections with the Church. But in her intensely personal complaint and confession she also represents the individual doubter who must regain her strength through the riddlic *folgað* she seeks, the collective mystical body of Christ. In the early poems of *The Easter Riddle* the wife's oneness with the Church is a true identity from which, as she confesses in *Resignation*, she has wrongly separated herself. From *The Descent into Hell* through *The Husband's Message* the absent Husband answers the repentant wife through his own invisible identity with the Church. In the main his response takes the appropriate form of riddling on the Easter liturgy. Thus the poet of *The Descent into Hell* did not need to show the literal march back from hell itself,

---

[1] See Thomas D. Hill, "Cosmic Stasis and the Birth of Christ: The Old English *Descent into Hell*, Lines 99–106," *JEGP* 71 (1972): 387–88; and R. E. Kaske, "The Conclusion of the Old English 'Descent into Hell,'" in Harry George Fletcher III and Mary Beatrice Schulte, eds., *Paradosis: Studies in Memory of Edwin A. Quain*, p. 48 and n. 3.

[2] For a detailed explanation of the embedded antiphons of the early lines and some proposed sources, see Patrick W. Conner, "The Liturgy and the Old English 'Descent into Hell,'" *JEGP* 79 (1980) 180–83.

for the rites of the Easter liturgy also trace the progress of that victorious return trip.

The first lines of the poem present and then deliberately suspend the human discovery of the Resurrection. The grieving Marys begin their trek toward the Holy Sepulchre *on uhtan* (line 1), the hour given as *media nocte* in the Divine Office. With heavy but resigned hearts, as the end of *Resignation* also implies, they reach the tomb at *dægred* 'dawn' (line 9), the liturgical hour of matins.[3] But, as the poet tells, an *engla þræt* 'crowd of angels' has already arrived there *on uhtan* (line 17), at the very moment when the women first set out. This timing implies that the resurrected Christ could have passed the two Marys in the dark hours of the morning, when, like the wife, they were engrossed in their own sorrow, unaware of the parallel between their own trek and the hell journey which Christ has just completed.[4] Perhaps this is the dramatic possibility which yielded the incipient English *quem quaeritis* of the Winchester *Regularis concordia*, an almost exact contemporary of the Exeter Book.[5]

The introductory lines of *The Descent into Hell* follow the women to the brink of their discovery at dawn by the empty tomb. In line 19a, speaking for them in his own voice, the poet exclaims in wonder, *Open wæs þæt eorðærn* 'Open was the earth vault!' This revelation to men, however, lags behind the divine

[3] In the OE Benedictine office *uht* means 'nocturns', and *dægred* means 'matins.' Conner, "The Liturgy and the Old English 'Descent into Hell,'" p. 183 and n. 8, also remarks that the liturgical words *uhtan* and *dægred* seem to have borrowed native Germanic terms for the dark and dawning hours of the morning. In the context of *Descent into Hell*, however, *uht* and *dægred* make the best sense as clues of the liturgical hours. See the discussion of the word *uht* in *The Wife's Lament*, text and n. 19 above. Contrary to most translators, I take *uht* even in that first poem of *The Easter Riddle* as an early liturgical clue of a specific hour of the wife's grief, the dark midnight hour of Good Friday–Holy Saturday.

[4] The dramatic parallel of the earthly and divine journeys is also pointed out by Richard M. Trask, "*The Descent into Hell* of the Exeter Book," *NM* 72 (1971): 426.

[5] Conner, "The Liturgy," p. 182, notes that the quem quaeritis of the *Regularis Concordia* confirms the reading of *uht* and *dægred* in *The Descent into Hell* as two different times of the day during which the Marys travel. The OE Benedictine

truth. Beginning at line 20b, therefore, the poem flashes back to an earlier moment in the process of triumph over death—the instant (by inference from the Benedictine office, on *dægred* of Holy Saturday) when the earth shook, and the hell dwellers below it also shook with exultant laughter at sensing Christ's approach.[6] Thereupon the poem describes the great Holy Saturday prelude to the Resurrection: Christ's deliverance, through baptism, of human nature from necessary confinement in hell.

The rescue of the patriarchs and solemn baptism, the two great events of Holy Saturday, occur simultaneously in hell and on earth. Thus *The Descent into Hell* seems to be divided between these two achievements. But the division is hardly a radical one, for the harrowing and baptism signify in common the liberation of men from the exile of Adam. As has been pointed out, the baptismal suggestion in the apocryphal tradition of Adam's penance, forty days up to his neck in the Jordan, may also have influenced the poet.[7] The Easter riddler, too, might have been think-

---

Office, whose basic text predates the mid–tenth-century reform movement, does not mention the Marys or their visit to the tomb. The quem quaeritis material at the beginning of *The Descent into Hell* thus suggests that the arranged *Easter Riddle* was a fresh product of the Benedictine Reform when it was copied into the Exeter Book between about 950 and 990. However, Thomas H. Bestul, "The Old English *Resignation* and the Benedictine Reform," *NM* 78 (1977): 20 & n. 13, cites the opinion of Kenneth Sisam, *Studies in the History of Old English Literature*, p. 108, that the Exeter Book anthology might very well have been compiled much earlier, during the reigns of Alfred, Edgar, or Æthelstan (871–939). One might perhaps suspect that the anthology in the Exeter book as we have it is an expanded version of an earlier, pre-Reform collection.

[6] The meditation for matins of the Benedicine Office ( James M. Ure, ed., *The Benedictine Office: An Old English Text*, p. 82) associates that liturgical hour with the moment when Christ *of deaþe aras and of helle gelædde ealle þa ðe he wolde*, etc. Hill, "Cosmic Stasis," p. 338, sees in *The Descent into Hell* an order of events "in a pattern which bears on the present moment," and Conner, "The Liturgy," p. 187, agrees. Inasmuch as the liturgy commemorates the events of salvation history over and over until the end of the world, it may be said to make these events timeless, or, in Hill's terms, to freeze them in a "cosmic stasis" of meaning independent from time.

[7] Trask, "*The Descent into Hell*," pp. 421–22, discusses the simultaneous penitential and baptismal significance in the apocryphal *Vita Adae et Evae*.

ing of this penitential connection as he chose this spot in the Exeter Book for *The Descent into Hell*. Nevertheless, the theology of baptism now displaces penance as the riddler's controlling idea. In line 23 the appearance of John the Baptist among the waiting prisoners of hell unites the harrowing and baptism as the major accomplishments of a single chosen witness. *The Descent into Hell* depicts John, arguably the central figure of the poem, as a kind of personal typology—the man who twice prepared the way. His second preparation gives *The Descent into Hell* its major dramatic focus.

There is a twofold propriety, both corporeal and spiritual, in twice calling John the *mæg* 'kinsman' of Christ (lines 25, 57). However much it might conjure associations with Adam or someone among the famous patriarchs and prophets of lines 44–46, the crucial phrase *burgwarena [o]rd* 'foremost of fortress dwellers [in hell]' (line 56) accompanies the second instance of the word *mæg* and can hardly designate anyone other than John.[8] The riddle word *ord* also confirms John as the 'front man

---

[8]Ferdinand Holthausen, "Zur altenglischen Literatur, V., 21, 'Christi Höllenfahrt,'" *Anglia Beiblatt* 19 (1908): 49–53, and ASPR 3, pp. lxi–lxii, argue that the *burgwarena ord* of line 56 is Adam. C. L. Wrenn, *A Study of Old English Literature*, p. 156, assumes that the *burgwarena ord* is Adam. Stanley B. Greenfield, *A Critical History of Old English Literature*, p. 141, thinks of either Adam or John. Among newer studies, Kaske, "The Conclusion," assumes from the outset that the speaker of lines 56ff. (and therefore also necessarily the *burgwarena ord*) is John; and Conner, "The Liturgy," pp. 183–84, argues for John on thematic grounds. Trask, "*The Descent into Hell*," pp. 422ff., assumes without direct argument that John is the speaker who addresses Christ in the poem but thinks of John's voice as gradually merging with the poet's, which then addresses Christ and John together with the problematical dual *git* at line 135. Trask's solution seems to be a reasonable way out of the difficulty when one is reading the poem by itself. My proposal of a concealed second voice, distinct from both Christ and John, is, of course, based on my sequential reading of *The Easter Riddle*. For the tradition of John as *ord* in the sense of '[military] chieftain,' see J. E. Cross, "*Blickling Homily XIV* and the *Old English Martyrology* on John the Baptist," *Anglia* 93 (1975): 148. The list of patriarchs in lines 44–46 occurs in the Sarum rite of baptism (see E. C. Whitaker, *The Baptismal Liturgy: An Introduction to Baptism in the Western Church*, pp. 76, 78–79). The names in the poem might therefore have been taken wholesale from an early baptismal rite.

of a [military] formation' which will follow Christ, pictured in line 40 as a warrior-king on horseback, on the ensuing march to freedom. Born before Christ, and therefore for riddling purposes the last Old Testament figure to enter hell, John is also the *ord* 'first' to turn and meet his divine cousin, the mounted Warrior who will reappear in another context and form in *The Husband's Message*. Having now been assigned to prepare the Lord's way for the second time, John announces the royal horseman's approach even before the locks and bars fall from hell's gate (lines 39–40) or the unprecedented light gleams on the doors of ancient darkness (lines 50–55). Indeed, as the small capital *F* for a new rhetorical division at line 33 seems to show, Christ advances on hell only after John's special mission, the announcement in lines 26–32, has been performed.

In part of its riddlic meaning the word *ord* suggests a liberated army which will march without needing to fight. The Lord's power, alone and unaided, has burst the gates and penetrated the hostile realm (lines 37–42a). By making Christ the only rider (*Cyning in oprad*, line 40b), the poet contrasts the lordly might of the Son of God with the manly strength of his marchers. In lines 70b–73, then, where John gratefully remembers the armor once given to him by his Lord, he is not speaking of battle armor, for which he has no need. Instead he riddles on the armor that, as he says, he received when Christ *end to me insipadest* 'the other time came inside me' (line 71). John's defenses, *sweord ond byrnan*, *helm ond heoroscearp* (lines 72b–73a) are spiritual weaponry borrowed from Eph. 6:10–17: the sword of the spirit, breastplate of jutsice, helmet of salvation, armor of God.[9] This armor of the spirit John received *end* 'the other time' at the Visitation, the moment when he was designated to prepare the way in the desert with his baptism. Now, therefore, in his third meeting with God at the broken gates of hell, John has the understanding and the riddlic authority to continue speaking beyond line 76, where the focus of the poem shifts from the harrowing to baptism itself.

---

[9] "Trask, "*The Descent into Hell*," p. 421, also identifies Eph. 6:11ff. as the source of the "armor" of which John speaks.

Yet, as the dual second-person reference *git Johannis* shows, John has yielded to another speaker somewhere before line 135. The dramatic voices of *The Descent into Hell* thus appear to be a cardinal riddlic matter.[10]

In the addresses to Gabriel, Mary, Jerusalem, and the Jordan of lines 76–106 the poet seems to have applied to John some of the same thoughts which refer to Christ in the Creed of the Benedictine office.[11] Ultimately, as has long been assumed for the Advent lyrics of *Christ I*, these apostrophes beginning with *Eala* probably derive from "Great O" antiphons (from the Latin 'O' of

[10] The widely different editorial boundaries for John's second speech and the different views of the number and identity of the voices in the poem are hints that the speeches and voices there are intentional theological riddles. Hill, "Cosmic Stasis," would mark John's second speech from lines 56–76; Conner, "The Liturgy," from lines 56–132; ASPR 3 and Kaske, "The Conclusion," from lines 56–137 (the end of the poem); and the present edition, from lines 56–117. Conner, "The Liturgy," p. 183, sees two voices in the poem—that of John and a "primary voice" of a liturgical celebrant, who would "traditionally have one or more secondary voices." Less specifically, Hill, "Cosmic Stasis," p. 382n.2, thinks that after line 76 the poet speaks as "a Christian for the community of the faithful." Some scholars, such as Kaske, "The Conclusion," make elaborate but ultimately unconvincing efforts to explain *git Iohannis* of line 135 as possibly spoken by John to eliminate the need for a second speaker in the final lines. Some editors have tried to avoid the (apparently illogical and undesirable) shift in point of view in line 135 by emendation: of *git* to *gio* (Genevieve Crotty, "The Exeter *Harrowing of Hell*: A Reinterpretation," *PMLA* 54 [1939]: 357–58) or to *wit* (a verbal suggestion by J. E. Cross, noted in Kaske, "The Conclusion," p. 50 & n.10). But the clear and unaltered MS reading *git Iohannis* seems to need not emendation as much as a good explanation. The present argument, based on riddlic themes, which agrees with Conner that the second speaker is a liturgical celebrant, also takes note of the paleographical division at line 118 in the MS.

[11] The names of Gabriel, Mary, and Bethlehem appear together in the meditation on the first clause concerning the Second Person (Ure, ed., *The Benedictine Office*, p. 87, lines 30–31; p. 88, line 9). The phrase *in Iudeum* in the poem (lines 99, 103, 128, 131) might have been inspired by a thought like this one from the meditation at Terce: . . . *on undern-timan Crist wæs ðurh þara Iudea dom to deaðe fordemed* 'at Terce Christ was condemned to death by the judgment of the Jews,' etc. (ibid., p. 95, lines 27–28). Whether or not under the influence of the Divine Office, the poet aligned the public careers of Christ and John closely enough to make the word *mæg* a central witticism of the text.

reverential address of the Godhead) for the appropriate liturgical season.[12] John's career, of course, belongs to both the Advent and the Easter seasons. While still in Elizabeth's womb, he greeted the newly conceived Word and acknowledged his own destiny as its herald. As annunciator of the swordlike Word, with its *gleaw ond scearp* 'shrewd and sharp' (line 76) penetration of the Virgin's womb, Gabriel is wittily compared with John, whose own spiritual armor has a *sweord* as well (lines 72b, 76b). The apostrophe to Mary of the Visitation (lines 84–98), another reminder of that miraculous beginning of John's career, is badly damaged at its midpoint for several lines.[13] In line 91, whose first word is perhaps irrestorably lost, the words *mægburg usse* 'our kindred' are almost surely addressed to Mary by John, since he has twice before been called the *mæg* of Christ. John covertly likens Mary to his own *byrnan* in two ways—as fleshly protector of Christ in her womb (lines 84–88a) and, perhaps through her *murnende* 'mourning' (line 91), as intercessor for men, who except for the armor of her prayers would disarm themselves and fall into the devil's hands (lines 95b–98).

The next two apostrophes, to Jerusalem and to the Jordan, associate John with the central places and events of Easter as well as with the lessons of the Epiphany, his traditional place in the liturgical year. As watchman, soldier, and statesman next to Christ in hell, John continues also in these later lines of the poem to be the *mæg* 'kinsman' of Jesus during the three days of divine victory over death. Thus *The Descent into Hell* becomes a non-

---

[12] Conner, "The Liturgy," p. 185. Trask, "*The Descent into Hell*," p. 431, thinks of the apostrophe to Mary as especially antiphonal: "a lament concerning the evil spirit's power yields to a celebration of the deliverance through God." This little movement, from lament to celebration, parallels the grand scheme of *The Easter Riddle* as a whole.

[13] A passage in *Blickling Homily XIV* connects John's first leap in the womb with his grasping of the weapons with which he will later fight to prepare his kinsman's way. The homilist says that John *wæpn gegrap mid to campienne, ærþon he to his lichoman become* 'grasped weapons to fight with before he would enter into his body.' This idea, pointed out by Crotty, "The Exeter *Harrowing*," pp. 354–56, helps show how the prominent themes of John's weapons and armor and his joyful prenatal leap could have been associated in our poet's mind as well.

heroic poem with a distinctly heroic flavor, and John attains a composite Germanic and scriptural identity something like the lamenting wife's. With these common bonds of thought the Easter riddler was able to merge two poetic traditions, native Germanic and Roman Christian, into a single riddling scheme.

The Easter riddling of the Jerusalem and Jordan apostrophes also deals in theological witticism of a high order. Jerusalem, the locus of Christ's sacrifice, where the helmet of salvation of 1 Thess. 5:8–10 was given to all, is fixed immovably (*stille*, line 100) in an earthly place as well as in the suspended time of the Easter triduum.[14] Since John, who died in the fortress of Machaerus, in Galilee, was himself one of the many who did not reach the earthly Jerusalem, these lines perhaps allude to his death. Next comes the apostrophe to the Jordan (lines 103–106), an equally fixed place in which John's preparation of the Lord's way on earth was visibly and audibly sanctioned from heaven (Matt. 3:16–17; Mark 1:11; Luke 3:21–22; John 1:32–34). The riddling on the Jordan, so intimately connected with John's life, extends the power of the baptismal waters far beyond their place *in Iudeum* 'among the Jews' (lines 99, 103). Baptism provides a spiritual armor to all pilgrims on earth (line 106), including those many who cannot ever hope to wade in the geographical Jordan. If line 105a, grammatically unintelligible in the manuscript, is emended for exact parallelism with line 101a, a plausible riddlic contrast between the two places *in Iudeum* of lines 99–106 results: the Jordan, by the power of baptism, flows everywhere, but no one can *geondferan* 'walk through' (line 101) the Jerusalem of salvation before the universal waters of the Jordan, i.e., of baptism, have been joyfully used (line 106).[15] These waters are in part the legacy of John.

[14] The word *stille* in lines 100 and 104 can mean 'quietly,' as Conner renders it ("The Liturgy," p. 188). But the meaning 'fixed, stable' is also possible there and fits especially well the idea of "cosmic stasis' proposed by Hill. Perhaps both of these meanings are intended.

[15] In the apostrophe to the Jordan, line 105 is insolubly ungrammatical as it stands in the MS: *Nales þu geondflowan foldbuende*. The difficulty has been variously handled in scholarship, usually by emending the line. For example, T. A.

With the credential of his life and the lasting inheritance of his baptism thus subtly established, John can now turn without riddling to his true purpose and the event at hand. At line 107, with a bold capital *N* perhaps intentionally distinguished from the four capitals of the apostrophes, John addresses his Lord in plain speech. *Nu* 'now' his business is a petition. He begs for deliverance for *us* (line 109), i.e., himself and his companions in hell. He appeals first by the divine mercy (lines 109–14) and then to the divine power, for which he also has skillful praise (lines 115–17). Cleverly he insinuates that the Lord, who attends to all nations on land and each grain of sand in the sea, will surely also rescue his faithful servants under the Old Law. John therefore appears to speak twice in the poem—once to announce Christ's approach toward hell (lines 26–32) and again, starting at line 59, to plead with elaborate diplomacy for release from bondage there. But as with the Marys, whose quem quaeritis drama stops just short of its miraculous resolution at the tomb, John's petition ends without the literal march of the patriarchs to freedom.

A script capital *S* and the riddle word *Swylce* begin line 118. 'Likewise,' i.e., like John, a second *ic* takes up the plea for deliverance, this time of all the world, through baptism. This second

---

Shippey, *Poems of Wisdom and Learning in Old English*, pp. 116–17, eliminates the puzzling negative sense from the line, which he emends to *Mostes þu geondflowan foldbuende* and translates 'You could flow over all the people on earth.' Conner, "The Liturgy," pp. 186–88, leaves the line unemended and, with thematic help from the *Vidi aquam* antiphon, translates 'You do not rush upon the dwellers of the earth,' which cannot entirely explain the grammar of the MS reading. My own guess, which assumes the scribal error of an omitted word and a mistaken *þu* for *þe* (perhaps because the scribe inattentively took *Nales* for a verb), restores full grammatical parallelism with line 101: *Nales [mostan] þ[e] geondflowan foldbuende* 'Earth's citizens [could] not at all stream through [you],' a witty reverse image in which not the Jordan but rather the pilgrims who seek the waters are visualized as a stream. Fortunately, line 106 makes the general sense of the passage clear: a conscious tension between the literal Jordan, fixed in one place, and the theological Jordan, the water of baptism, which is everywhere and can be joyfully used throughout the earth.

petitioner, whose presence should perhaps be understood all along, now emerges as a dramatic voice uttering supplications probably based on litanic prayer.[16] He is a baptized man: *Wit unc in þære burnan baþodan ætgædre* 'We two [i.e., I and you, Christ, in your spiritual presence] bathed in that spring [of the figurative Jordan] together,' line 132. This new pleader's litanies—by Christ's childhood, wounds, and Resurrection; by the name of Mary and by the angels (in damaged but intelligible lines); and finally by Jerusalem and the Jordan—are close parallels with the verse antiphons spoken by John. Somewhat like messengers in the heroic tradition both speakers offer their knowledge of famous persons, deeds, and places as their credentials to address the Lord. But unlike John, with much more of the spirit of the baptismal liturgy, the second speaker invokes Christ's deeds and Mary's name without claiming any blood kinship with them. Nevertheless, he shares John's confidence. His last lines—*Oferwurpe þu mid þy wætre* 'May you splash with that water,' etc.—both ask and command Christ's presence in all baptisms, which descend from the baptism of *git Iohannis* 'you [Christ] and John' in the Jordan of Judea (line 135).[17] By all these clues the supplicant

---

[16] Conner, "The Liturgy," pp. 190–91, identifies this "second petition" of the poem with the very similar second part of the litany as recited on Holy Saturday. While Conner recognizes the thematic and structural integrity of lines 118–32 of the poem (p. 190 n.24), he nevertheless assigns this "second petition" to John. But the fact that it is a second petition, and demonstrably litanic besides, suggests all the more the (riddlic) introduction of a second voice, the liturgical celebrant, at line 118.

[17] Unless the last lines of the poem are given to a second voice who can logically pronounce the words *git Iohannis* 'You [Christ] and John,' the reader must use considerable ingenuity to explain why John would refer to himself in the second person. Otherwise, several lines must be reinterpreted with even more ingenuity still, as Kaske does in "The Conclusion." Taking the apostrophe to the Jordan in lines 103–106 and two Anglo-Saxon illustrations of the personified Jordan (in imitation of Roman illustrations of river gods) as evidence that the Jordan can be personally addressed, Kaske suggests that *git* means 'You [Christ] and the water,' that *Iohannis* is gen. sing., and that lines 135–37a can be read 'just as you two [you and the water], by the baptism of John in the Jordan, graciously inspired all this world' (p. 59). But as Kaske admits (pp. 55, 59), such a reading requires con-

of the last twenty lines is the liturgical celebrant, already encountered as the implicit confessor-catechist in *Judgment Day I* and *Resignation*. His voice will be heard again in the riddling of *Pharaoh* and *The Husband's Message*.[18] The priest's closing words will advance us, newly resigned to patience and assured of the success of John's able advocacy, to the riddlic preparations for Holy Saturday baptism itself.[19] Like the Marys with whom *The Descent into Hell* began, we are now well along the way to discovering the mystery of Easter.

### *Almsgiving*: To Prepare the Heart

To judge from its nearest neighbors alone, the poem called *Almsgiving* seems to occupy a chosen rather than an accidental place in the Exeter Book. A possible thematic connection between the *reþehygdig wer* 'upright man' of *Almsgiving* 2 and the *reþust ealra cyninga* 'sternest of kings' of *The Descent into Hell* 36 has already

---

siderable lexical, syntactical, and thematic maneuvering and therefore hardly compares with the simplicity of taking *git Iohannis* as an elliptical dual 'you two [Christ and] John.'

[18]Conner, "The Liturgy," p. 183, thinks of a "narrating celebrant of the liturgy" as the primary voice of the poem, i.e., as the persona for the poet himself. Trask, "*The Descent into Hell*," pp. 434–35, also perceives liturgical, especially litanic, influence in this final passage of the poem, which he assigns to two voices at once, John and "Everyman," the poet speaking for all men. But the two distinct voices of *Pharaoh*, a dialogue riddle, and of *The Husband's Message*, apparently based on a convention of ancient Germanic statecraft, will help show how lines 118–37 of *The Descent into Hell* could be spoken by a separate and concealed voice as well. See the discussions of *Pharaoh* and *The Husband's Message* below.

[19]Kaske, "The Conclusion," pp. 47–48, gives a very probable rendering of *oferwurpe* (line 133) as opt. subj. 'may you sprinkle,' etc. Conner, "The Liturgy," p. 188 n. 20, cites the connecton made by Edmond Martène, *De antiquis ecclesiae ritibus libri*, vol. 3, col. 440, between the antiphon *Urbs beata Jerusalem* and the service for the blessing of the font before baptism. It is attractive, if also uncertain, to think of the blessing of the font as the liturgical moment being paraphrased in lines 118ff. of the poem.

been duly noted in scholarship.[1] The righteous man, who *sawla lacnað* 'heals souls' (line 9) by increasing the yield of Christian virtue through almsgiving, is the proper image of the just God who rescues men through baptism from the death sentence of their sinful human nature.[2]

As the principal charity of a redeemed man, almsgiving also had close ties with baptism in the thought of Cyprian and other church fathers.[3] Indeed, in the very early Church almsgiving seems to have been a practice of the adult catechumenate and an important test of worthiness for baptism. According to Saint Justin Martyr (100?–165?), the moral lives of advanced catechumens of early days were scrutinized to see "whether they lived devoutly, whether they honored widows, visited the sick, and practiced every good work."[4] Justin's reference to "every good work" and specific mention of widows suggest that, besides their regular prayers and fasts, candidates approaching baptism were to perform some charity of alms. Such almsdeeds would have helped cleanse the heart for baptism as baptism in turn prepared the soul for Easter. Moreover, the importance of alms was

[1] Carl T. Berkhout, "Some Notes on the Old English 'Almsgiving,'" *ELN* 10 (1972): 85.

[2] Berkhout, ibid, p. 82, says the usual emendation of MS *sawla* to sing. *sawle* misses the poet's theological subtlety. I agree, and I would add that *sawla* must be plural here because of the riddlic connection of the word to Christ's rescue of the souls of the Patriarchs from hell.

[3] Ibid, pp. 83–84; Berkhout quotes Cyprian on this point. Although its own themes are explicitly baptismal, the little poem *Almsgiving* seems to fit *The Easter Riddle* in several ways at once. The Anglo-Saxon connection between alms and penance, and in turn between penance and the Lenten season, discussed by Allen J. Frantzen, *The Literature of Penance in Anglo-Saxon England*, pp. 161–64, 180, 183, has already been noted, as has the urging of almsgiving in preparation for the Judgment in the poem *An Exhortation to Christian Living*, found in Corpus Christi College, Cambridge, MS 201. The poet of *Almsgiving* and the Easter riddler (if they were not one and the same) appear to have been thinking of alms in their most ancient (baptismal) connections rather than their penitential ones.

[4] J. A. Jungmann, "Catechumenate," *New Catholic Encyclopedia* (1967 ed.), 3:238b.

still a lively subject even in late Anglo-Saxon times, as, for example, the Blickling homily for the third Sunday of Lent shows.[5] It would probably have been a matter of course for the compiler of the Exeter Book to place *Almsgiving* with *The Descent into Hell* and *Pharaoh*, both poems with explicit baptismal themes.[6]

*Almsgiving* 5–7 also explains the saving virtue of almsdeeds in terms of wisdom paraphrased from Scripture: the almsgiver cures the wounds of sins as water douses fire and rescues a burning city. The source of the poet's thought is Sirach 3:9: "Water quenches a flaming fire, and alms atone for sins." The analogy means that the charity of alms has the virtue, as the waters of baptism also have the power, to deliver the righteous man from hell, the place of unquenchable fire (Matt. 3:12, 18:8, 25:41; Mark 9:43; Luke 3:17; Jude 7). More directly, Old Testament wisdom teaches that "almsgiving frees one from death, and keeps one from going into the dark abode" (Tobit 4:10), and also (Tobit 12:8–10) that "prayer and fasting are good, but better than either is almsgiving accompanied by righteousness. . . . It is better to give alms than store up gold; for almsgiving saves one from death and expiates every sin." From such scriptural authority the poem of *Almsgiving* takes as its real subject not the gesture of alms itself, which by divine command (Matt. 6:2–4) is too private for liturgical expression, but rather the theological significance of the gesture: its power to atone for sin and deliver from hell. In riddlic fashion, *Almsgiving* figures the untold drama of the previous poem, the escape of the righteous out of hell. The righteous, however, are now redefined. They are no longer just the patriarchs rescued by Christ but also the *repehygdig wer*, who in imitation of Christ *sawla lacnað* 'heals souls' by deeds of alms. From *Almsgiving* 5–7, therefore, the reader is challenged to look figuratively backward at the fiery

[5] See Marcia A. Dalbey, "Themes and Techniques in the Blickling Lenten Homilies," in Paul E. Szarmach and Bernard F. Huppé, eds., *The Old English Homily and Its Backgrounds*, pp. 222, 226, 227.

[6] Berkhout, "Notes," p. 85, makes this observation.

*burg* of hell in *Judgment Day I* 22ff. and *The Descent into Hell* 35, 38, and 56.[7]

Finally, *Almsgiving*, in a different way from *Resignation*, prepares the heart for the coming events of *The Easter Riddle*. As in many medieval saints' legends (e.g., Martin of Tours) Jesus is the disguised recipient of alms, so the almsgiving Christian who opens a *rume heortan* 'an ample heart' (line 2) also prepares for the return of Christ, in liturgical "disguise," in *Homiletic Fragment II*, *Riddle 30b*, and *The Husband's Message*. In *The Ruin* the *repehydig wer* will be shown the celestial reward of Jesus, who has urged his hearers to "sell what you have and give alms. Get purses for yourselves which do not wear out, a never-failing treasure with the Lord" (Luke 12:33).

## *Pharaoh*: Typological Destruction

The little poem *Pharaoh*, only eight lines long, is ostensibly about a familiar biblical subject, the destruction told in Exodus 14 of Pharaoh and his army as they attempt to pursue the Israelites across the Red Sea. The text belongs to a ubiquitous and complex genre known as the question-and-answer dialogue, used in ancient and medieval schools for such diverse purposes as instruction in literacy, philosophical disputation, dramatized or fictionalized argument modeled largely on the Socratic dialogues of Plato, catechisms in rhetoric and rudimentary theology, and (to judge from the number of riddlic questions and answers in medieval dialogue collections) entertainment.[1]

---

[7] Ibid., p. 82, does not connect the (ostensibly) earthly *burgum* of *Almsgiving* 7b directly with a riddle on the fires of hell, as I do, but he does observe that the word *burg* occurs frequently as a metaphor for hell in Old English poetry. As examples he cites *Christ II* 561, *Juliana* 545, and the several instances in *The Descent into Hell*.

[1] On the vast and diverse tradition of the question-and-answer dialogue, see the immensely learned English-language introduction by Lloyd William Daly to Daley and Walter Suchier, eds., *Altercatio Hadriani Augusti et Epicteti Philosophi*,

In Old English the question-and-answer dialogue is preserved in the prose and poetic *Solomon and Saturn* and the prose *Adrian and Ritheus*, though these examples are only distantly related to *Pharaoh*.[2] More specifically, *Pharaoh* represents the *dic mihi* (OE *saga me*) dialogues popularized by, among others, Isidore of Seville.[3] Very often miscellaneous in their themes, the medieval dialogues nevertheless spent much wit on Old Testament exegesis, especially of Genesis and Exodus, as well as on the time-honored exercise of philosophical or catechetical instruction.[4] Most probably, therefore, *Pharaoh* is neither an isolated fragment from a longer dialogue nor, as has also been proposed, the abandoned start of a new collection.[5] It appears instead to be a specimen of question-and-answer exegesis, perhaps even catechism, borrowed to suspend the reader momentarily between Holy Saturday baptism and the liturgical reappearances of Christ at Easter.

Like *Almsgiving*, *Pharaoh* looks backward to the preceding

---

esp. pp. 15–44. See also H. Musurillo, "Dialogue (Literary Genre)," *New Catholic Encyclopedia* (1967 ed.), 4:849a. The complex tradition of the dialogue is also mentioned in passing by L. Whitbread, "The Old English Poem 'Pharaoh,'" *N&Q* 190 (1946): 53b and n. 2.

[2] The other famous Old English examples of the question-and-answer dialogue are cited by Whitbread, "Pharaoh," p. 54a, and Joseph B. Trahern, Jr., "The *Ioca Monachorum* and the Old English *Pharaoh*," *ELN* 7 (1970): 165–68. Daly's study of the numerous subgenres of the dialogue, however, suggests that the other extant OE dialogues resemble *Pharaoh* mainly in form.

[3] Daly, Introduction, Daly and Suchier, eds., *Altercatio*, p. 31.

[4] Ibid., pp. 26–29. Besides the well-known Socratic question-and-answer dialogues, Archer Taylor, *The Literary Riddle Before 1600*, pp. 14–16, discusses and shows examples of ancient Vedic (Sanskrit) question-and-answer dialogues which riddle on matters of catechesis as well as other kinds of wisdom. Some of Taylor's examples are given and discussed in the Introduction to this book.

[5] Whitbread, "Pharaoh," pp. 53–54b, weighs Dobbie's view of the poem as an isolated fragment against his own suggestion of an abandoned experiment. He concludes (p. 54b) that "[t]here is nothing in the linguistics of the lines to militate against so late a date of composition as this theory would entail." *The Easter Riddle*, however, like *Riddle 1*, appears to be composed in some indeterminate (but probably large) part of borrowed and "joined" poetry added to some original composition.

baptismal themes. The drowning of Pharaoh's army is cherished as a figure of the drowning during baptism of the sinful nature which all men inherit through the fall of Adam. Thus the closest known analogue of *Pharaoh*, in the eighth-century *Joca monachorum* ('Simple Games of the Monks') from Saint Gall, also poses the question of the Egyptians' numerical losses: *Quod milli Egyptii persecuti sunt filiis Israel?* The cryptic answer *Xdccc* '1,800,' by treating the problem as something of a riddle, accounts for the javelinist or archer, shield bearer, and driver in each of the "six hundred first-class chariots" destroyed in Exodus 14:6–7. But in a strange way atypical of its genre, the literary Pharaoh riddle of the Exeter Book seems wittier still.[6] First the questioner demands in lines 1–3 to know *weorudes ealles . . . on Farones fyrde* 'in full the troop strength in Pharaoh's army,' a query which actually excludes numerical precision, for Exodus 14 implies only that Pharaoh's whole army was vast, or even innumerable. To be sure, the respondent of *Pharaoh* dutifully mentions, in the damaged but readable words of lines 6–7, the 'six hundred cars' of the Egyptians, the only armed force of *gescyred rime* 'measured count' in the story.

For a poem of such modest size *Pharoah* has an endearing liveliness that makes its textual damage especially regrettable. Besides the words *gescyred rime*, which compromise tactfully on the real question, there is also the solver's deferential protest that he does not know the answer *be wihte*, loosely 'right on the nose' (line 4).[7] There are several proposed restorations of the missing

[6] Trahern, "The *Ioca Monachorum*," points out the analogous relationship of the Pharaoh question in the Saint Gall *Ioca monachorum* to the Old English *Pharaoh* and observes (p. 166) that the answer in the Old English poem, which dodges the precise information sought by the questioner, is "not at all typical of the genre." Trahern thinks (p. 167) that "the Old English poet sought . . . to provide the reader with enough information for him to solve the puzzle without stating the answer outright." But I think the answer is hidden in line 4: *Nat ic hit be wihte* 'I don't know it right on the nose'; i.e., there is no numerical answer to the question as it is posed.

[7] In generic terms *be wihte* has the sense 'precisely,' as Whitbread, "Pharaoh," p. 52b, demonstrates. But I also suspect a witty pun on *wiht* 'man, creature' and

word after 'six hundred' in line 6, including a rather improbable suggestion for confirming the answer "1,800" in the *Joca monachorum* and a much likelier word *gecorena*, which would identify the *screod[a]* of line 5 as the *currus electos* 'chosen chariots' of the biblical narrative.[8] Assuming that the letters at the front edge of the hole in line 7 are *yþ-* rather than *sl-*, one plausible guess at the missing words supplies *yþ[a fǽrgripe]* 'the sudden grip of the waves,' an attested poetic image which would fit the damaged space, the grammar of the lines, and the notion of a *wraþe wyrde* 'cruel fortune' which overwhelmed the Egyptians without warning.[9] Such hypothetical recovery of the lost text seems less important, however, than the solver's polite refusal to attempt the unanswerable question in the first place. Among riddlic dialogues *Pharaoh* seems remarkable mainly for failing its own riddlic challenge.

---

*wiht* 'whit, thing,' etc. If this guess is right, then the unique phrase *be wihte*, in the context of the Pharaoh riddle, means '[according] to the [last] man' or '[according] to the [last] detail.' To render both the generic meaning 'precisely' and the possible pun, I have translated *be wihte* as 'right on the nose.'

[8] Whitbread, ibid., p. 53a, reviews previous restorations of the gap in line 6 as follows: (1) Grein and early editors: *siex hun[dred]a*, too few letters to fill the gap; (2) Holthausen (1894): *siex hun[dred godr]a*, which fits the hole but gives an unlikely form of 'hundred' in the series 200 to 900; (3) Mackie: *siex hun[d þusend]a*, a literal attempt to count Pharaoh's whole army, as the question asks, but at the expense of the clear scriptural basis for *siex hund . . . screoda*; (4) Holthausen (later): *siex hun[d ealr]a*, which, as Dobbie objects, is too short for the gap; and, as Whitbread himself observes, would be redundant in view of *eal* in line 7. Trahern, "The *Ioca Monachorum*," p. 167, thinks of *siex hun[d þrifeþen]a* on the analogy of the answer "1,800" in the Saint Gall *Joca monachorum* and on the phrases *þreo feðan (foeðan)*, glosses for *ternos stantes* and *ternos statores* in the Canterbury and Vespasian psalters. There is no known evidence, however, of the compound word that Trahern supplies. Trahern's alternative *gecorena*, a thematic match for the special mention of *electos* 'chosen' chariots in the biblical account, seems more probable. But if the hole in the MS would accommodate the extra letter, I would suggest *gecorenra*, an indef. gen. pl. adjective to describe *screoda*.

[9] Again, Whitbread supplies a valuable review of previous restorations of line 7: Grein and earlier editors: *yþ[a geblond w]raþe*, etc., probably based on *Beowulf* 1373; Holthausen (1894): *yþ[a flodes w]raþe*, etc.; Dobbie (ASPR 3): *yþ[a streamas w]raþe*, etc. On the models of *Beowulf* 464 and 848, Whitbread also thinks of *yþ[a gewealc w]raþe* or *yþ[a geswing w]raþe*, but finally argues seriously (p. 53b) for *yþ[a*

Besides avoiding a count of the total Egyptian force, *Pharaoh* also omits the constructive themes of baptism. The narrative of Exodus 14 tells the Egyptian disaster only to focus on the miraculous preservation of the Israelites. Their joyous emergence from the Red Sea prefigures not only the liberation of the patriarchs from hell, as the typology of Pharaoh for matins of the Benedictine office explains, but also symbolizes the rising of the New Man from the waters of baptism.[10] Moreover, in *The Descent into Hell* 53–55 the victorious Light opens the gates of hell, as later he also opens the Tomb on earth. Therefore, in the Easter Vigil, that poised moment between Holy Saturday and Easter, the final rescue of the Israelites from Pharaoh, typifying the deliverance both of the Patriarchs and of Man, is a prescribed Old Testament reading since the earliest days of the liturgy.

It thus seems likely that the little poem *Pharaoh*, perhaps borrowed from an analogue of the Pharaoh question in the *Joca monachorum*, is intended to riddle on that suspended moment before the vigil service begins. It is the time when the entire vast communion of the faithful, numberless as Pharaoh's army or the saved throng of Israelites, anticipates the Easter joy. Their old natures drowned in the spiritual Jordan encountered near the end of *The Descent into Hell*, the expectant believers, collected into one voice, are examined with a riddle, once again by the dramatic voice who has spoken as catechist, confessor, and liturgist, about the true meaning of the death of Pharaoh. By seeming to falter on the superficial answer, this collective solver finds a truer one, a "numberless number" representing herself. In *The*

---

*færgripe w]rape* 'the sudden grip of the waves,' which would make especially good thematic sense with *wrape wyrde* 'grim fate' and the singular verb *fornam* in line 7. (Whitbread translates *fornam* as 'seized,' but I read it more literally as 'took away.') Moreover, Whitbread can offer the close parallel *færgripe flodes* in *Beowulf* 1516, and in closing gives a discussion and full translation of *Pharaoh* on pp. 53a–b. Trahern, "The *Ioca Monachorum*," 167 and n. 10, cautions that the usual reading *yþ-* in line 7 is disputed in, among other places, the British Museum transcript, which reads *sl-*. However, as Trahern also notes, the requirements of alliteration argue strongly for *yþ-* and against *sl-*.

[10] James M. Ure, ed., *The Benedictine Office: An Old English Text*, p. 82.

*Easter Riddle* she may be imagined as the Wife, the Church who waits with the 'ample heart' of *Almsgiving* to kindle the New Fire and the Easter Light of the coming poems. Her death and re-birth in baptism have prepared for the Resurrection of Easter. The Resurrection, in turn, will prepare the Church for her de-struction in this world and her glorious delivery into the next. That destruction and rescue will be the concealed subjects of *The Ruin*.

### The Lord's Prayer I: Eternal Bread

The eleven-line metrical Paternoster on folio 122a of the Exeter Book is numbered to distinguish it from two longer versions, *The Lord's Prayer II* and *The Lord's Prayer III*, both connected with the Old English Benedictine office.[1] In the office the Latin Pater-noster is anatomized phrase by phrase, and each phrase is ex-panded into an instructional meditation in Old English verse. While *The Lord's Prayer I* has no Latin headings, it shares with the other two metrical Paternosters an expanded paraphrasing. Like them, too, it addresses both God the Father and Christ, the "hal-lowed Name," who is called *nergend* 'Savior' and *helpend* 'Helper, Benefactor' in all three poems. Like *The Lord's Prayer II* the Exe-ter Book poem calls God *soðfæst* 'true-sworn,' and *The Lord's Prayer III* also describes God as *soð* 'true' and *hyge-cræftum fæst* 'firm in powers of thought.' These and other less marked resem-blances suggest that *The Lord's Prayer I* once also belonged to the Benedictine office. But no matter what his direct source may have been, the Easter riddler probably also had in mind the tra-ditional English association of the Lord's Prayer with Lenten penitential rites.[2]

---

[1] See James M. Ure, ed., *The Benedictine Office: An Old English Text*, pp. 85–87, 103–106.

[2] See Allen J. Frantzen, *The Literature of Penance in Anglo-Saxon England*, pp. 161, 163–164, 175, and the discussion in the Introduction to Part Two and n. 8 above.

Unlike the metrical Paternosters of the office, *The Lord's Prayer I* is an incomplete text. It is also quite brief—only eleven lines compared to 38 Old English lines plus Latin headings for *The Lord's Prayer III* and 122 Old English lines plus headings for *The Lord's Prayer II*. *The Lord's Prayer I* gets its brevity from simply paraphrasing the Paternoster in several places, and from expanding no phrase by more than three half lines. Moreover, the conspicuous absence of certain elements of the Paternoster, when weighed against the extended parts, makes the abridgment of *The Lord's Prayer I* look like careful, even riddlic, selection, a shaping of the poem to its hidden task. There is no mention of the balanced forgiveness of debts, presumably because the penance done in *Resignation* and the themes of purification in the baptismal texts already stand for canceled sin. On the other hand, the most elaborated petition of *The Lord's Prayer I* is the request for food. In a notable departure from the scriptural words of the prayer, the food of *The Lord's Prayer I* is called not 'daily bread' but *hlaf userne . . . þone singalan* 'our loaf . . . the eternal one' (lines 7a, 8a), perhaps in reference to the eternal Bread of Life in John 6. Yet the poet also follows the Paternoster in asking for this eternal bread *to dæge* 'today' (line 6a). The resulting lexical play on time and eternity seems to set the dramatic moment when *The Easter Riddle* has passed the liturgy of solemn baptism and now anticipates the returning Eucharist. The light of the Easter Vigil can shortly be expected, and then, still *to dæge*, the Church's prayer for its eternal bread will once again be answered. In calling the loaf of the Eucharist *domfæstne blæd* 'a lawful blessing,' *The Lord's Prayer I* looks ahead to the legal words and theme of *The Husband's Message*.

There is also an accidental break in the text. An extensive hole in the middle of folio 122 has swallowed up all of the opening half line except for the serifed upper tip of an initial with a left-hand vertical stroke, the final *g* of an adjective in *-ig*, and the letters *-der* of the next word. What remains of the capital looks like neither the *U* of *Ure* nor the *A* or *Æ* of *Ælmihtig*, for which the damaged space also seems a bit too long. But the initial might have been *H*, or more probably *L*, as a comparison of the upper tip of the large block initial *L* of *Wulf and Eadwacer* (folio 100b) shows. If the first letter of *The Lord's Prayer I* could have been an *L*, then the opening word might have been the expletive *La* rather than an adjective or pronoun. A detailed argument in the Textual Notes shows how *The Lord's Prayer I* may have opened on a note of deliberate intensity: *[La, eallhali]g [fæ]der*.

### *Homiletic Fragment II*: Toward the Light

*Homiletic Fragment II*, so distinguished in the Anglo-Saxon Poetic Records from *Homiletic Fragment I* of the Vercelli Book, appears in the Exeter Book on folios 122a–b, as the dramatic climax of Easter draws very near. As its tone and title suggest, this poem would deserve little notice for itself, but to *The Easter Riddle* it gives a quiet moment of doctrinal preparation for the events at hand.

Like *The Lord's Prayer I*, *Homiletic Fragment II* develops no specifically liturgical ideas. It gives instead a riddlic measure of the passing of liturgical time. The narrative present of the poem (*nu*, line 1) offers both joy and consolation in God. The opening verses, *Gefeoh nu on ferðe . . . ond þinne dom arær* 'Rejoice now in spirit . . . and lift up your honor' (lines 1–2), only vaguely resemble the exhortation Sursum Corda. This invitation to rejoice, well known as the preface to the canon of the mass, is also spoken before the Paschal proclamation of the Easter Vigil. A very loose paraphrase of the Sursum Corda would imply that *Homiletic Fragment II*, like *The Lord's Prayer I* just before it, occupies the unliturgical moment between *fulwiht* 'baptism' of Holy Saturday (line 9) and the beginning of the Easter Vigil. With no demonstrable liturgical connections *Homiletic Fragment II* appears instead to be the final instructional preparation for Easter. The poem is a rather careful assortment of ideas which advance the salvific movement of Creation and Time while liturgical time briefly stands still.

An especially noticeable break at lines 8–9 suggests that the riddler was constructing his poetry from more than one source.

At line 8 the argument shifts abruptly, by implied rather than expressed contrast, from the impermanence of the world and the wavering promises (*wordbeot*, line 6) of human oath swearers (*treowgeþofta*, line 5) to the eternal oneness of the God of Faith. These proclamations of divine oneness come almost wholesale from the famous scriptural parallelisms of Eph. 4:5–6: "There is one Lord, one faith, one baptism, one God and Father of all," etc. Lines 8–9 are also marked by small capitals and raised punctuation, perhaps the same scribal tactic by which certain other Exeter Book riddles appear to have been deliberately spliced.[1] It appears, therefore, that the Easter Riddler has noticed how handily the poet's Pauline echoes also serve his own dual purpose: to refer both to the liturgical moment of baptism just past and to introduce God the Father, the beginning of a concealed Trinitarian argument that extends throughout the rest of the poem.

Starting at line 8, *Homiletic Fragment II* argues in its own order the central tenets of the Creed, the fundamental pronouncement of faith in which Anglo-Saxon penitents were widely instructed.[2] Like the penitent's submission to God at the end of *Resignation*, this confession of faith is the vital human assent without which the divine plan cannot move forward. After the Father has been adored for the glories and joys of his Creation (lines 10–11), a certain shadow, not to be confused with the primeval darkness, extends over the world until the time of Mary (lines 12–14). Before her deep-minded obedience (lines 15–16) the accomplishment of Creation, glorious though it was, stood darkened, shrouded by trees (lines 13–14). With this somewhat extraneous (and perhaps "joined") thought the riddler binds his profane and sacred themes. The covering trees are the same Germanic groves of this life in which the lamenting Bride has

<hr />

[1] See James E. Anderson, "Two Spliced Riddles of the Exeter Book," *In Geardagum* 5 (June, 1983): 57–75, which reinterprets *Riddlers 42/43* and *47/48* as texts "joined" by the same graphic signals, the small capital and the raised point, which are also found at lines 8–9 of *Homiletic Fragment II*.

[2] Allen J. Frantzen, *The Literature of Penance in Anglo-Saxon England*, pp. 161, 163–64, 175. See Introduction to Part Two and n. 8 above.

endured her long exile (*The Wife's Lament* 27–41) and from which the Husband will soon command her to flee (*The Husband's Message* 37b–40). But in the person of Mary the hope of a new light has been realized. The Holy Spirit, the third Presence of the Creed, has been pleased to settle brightly in a riddlic place, barely legible around the damage to line 19a as *on breos[tum]*, a reading confirmed by *The Descent into Hell* 110–11a and by the phrase *beorhtan bosme* of *The Ruin* 40. That riddlic place is the inviolate womb of Mary, and the riddlic masculine pronoun *se* of line 20 therefore designates the ultimate theme of *Homiletic Fragment II*, the Incarnate Second Person of the Trinity.

It is he whose light now appears, as before to John at the doors of hell. Now he, who is *beorht on breos[tum]*, approaches to relieve the *breostceare* of the lamenting Wife. She, as the Church, has already been instructed to rejoice in her heart (line 1). He comes to amend the feeble *wordbeot* of men with the divine promises (*wordbeotunga*) of *The Husband's Message* 32. *Homiletic Fragment II* moves men from the last darkness of Easter exile to the *ordfruma ealles leohtes* 'primordial point of all light' (line 20). This is the light of the risen Christ. In a return to liturgical thinking, however, it is momentarily still just a 'point,' the first glowing spark of the Easter Fire.

### Riddle 30b: The Journey of Light

The nine lines of *Riddle 30* stand twice in the Exeter Book, as *Riddle 30a* on folio 108a and again on folio 122b–123a as *Riddle 30b*. Although only *Riddle 30b* strictly belongs to *The Easter Riddle*, both poems together tell a great deal about the riddler's method of composition. In this case he has done almost wholesale borrowing, making deceptively few and minor changes in the text. Thus the two poems are enough alike to restore the slight damage to *Riddle 30b* (folios 122b–123a) by comparing it with *Riddle 30a* (folio 108a; variants italicized for convenient reference):

## Riddle 30a

Ic eom leg bysig,       lace mid winde,
bewunden mid wuldre,      wedre gesomnad,
fus forðweges,      fyre gebysgad,
bearu blowende,      byrnende gled.
5  Ful oft mec gesiþas      sendað æfter hondum,
þæt mec weras ond wif      wlonce cyssað.
Þonne ic mec onhæbbe,      *ond* hi onhnigað to me,
monige mid miltse,      þær ic monnum sceal
ycan upcyme eadignesse.

## Riddle 30b

Ic eom *lig* bysig,      lace mid winde,
*w[uldre bewunden*,      we]dre gesomnad
fus forðweges,      fyre *gemylted*,
bear[u] blowende,      byrnende gled.
5  Ful oft mec gesiþas      sendað æfter hondum,
*þær* mec weras ond wif      wlonce *gecyssað*.
Þonne ic mec onhæbbe,      hi onhnigað to me,
*modge miltsum*,      *swa* ic *mongum* sceal
ycan upcyme      eadignesse.

But from these small textual variants arise vastly different answers and meaning. The connection between the two riddles is itself a riddlic matter: as alike as they seem, the two texts must ultimately be read and answered apart.

As long ago as 1901, however, F. A. Blackburn solved both texts together as one, introducing the view that still prevails in scholarship. Over the years Blackburn's solution has provoked an ambivalent response. His proposal of multiple wooden objects—"tree," "beam," "trumpet," "cross," etc.—under a single general theme of *beam* 'wood' seems to defy most good riddling, wherein an interlocked system of clues normally produces a single answer. Yet even though Blackburn's answer has not been widely accepted, his generic supposition "wood" continues to inspire most

of the well-received interpretations of *Riddle 30*.[1] Unfortunately
the theme of "wood" is based partly on misreadings: a once com-
mon but happily abandoned emendation of *leg/lig* to *lic* in line 1
and misunderstanding of the riddlic language in line 4. The
words *bearu blowende*, *byrnende gled* in fact do not specify wood
but describe instead a kind of wood fire. All the clues of lines
1–4 reveal the type of *lig*, a heaped fire of flame and gleed,
fanned by the wind and blowing sparks from wood as it mixes
with the *wedre* (line 2b), a word still used in Germanic languages
to mean 'open air.'[2] The correct theme of "fire" then shows the
major riddlic tension between lines 1–4 and the rest: the solver
must discover a speech-bearing "flame" which can also be passed
from hand to hand, kissed, and knelt down to. To 'men and
women' (line 6) the handling of such a fire must bring not harm
but an 'elevation in bliss' (line 9).

[1] Blackburn's interpretation of *Riddle 30b*, which considers *Riddles 30a* and *30b*
as variants, is in "The 'Husband's Message' and the Accompanying Riddles of the
Exeter Book," *JEGP* 3 (1901): 1–13. W. S. Mackie, ed., *The Exeter Book, Part II,
Poems IX–XXXII*, p. 190, called *Riddle 30b* "Riddle 30 (Second Version)." ASPR
3:337–38 (n. on *Riddle 30a*) assumes that "[t]here are two texts of Riddle 30 in
the Exeter Book," etc. Frederick Tupper, *The Riddles of the Exeter Book*, p. 142,
speaks of "both versions" of *Riddle 31* (his numbering) and argues for Black-
burn's solution. Craig Williamson, ed., *The Old English Riddles of the Exeter Book*,
p. 229, says of *Riddle 28* (his numbering), "This is the only riddle in the Exeter
Book for which there are two texts." Unlike Tupper, Williamson prints both texts
and calls them *Riddle 28a* and *Riddle 28b*. He solves them together as "tree
[wood]." Kevin Crossley-Holland, trans., *The Exeter Book Riddles*, p. 116, says, "For
some reason there are two widely separated, virtually identical texts of Riddle 30
in the Exeter Book." He prints both texts, designating them as *Riddle 30a* and
*Riddle 30b*, following ASPR, and considering it "agreed" that they are a pun on
OE *beam* 'wood.' Michael Alexander, trans., *Old English Riddles from the Exeter
Book*, gives only one very free translation based on his supposition that "the final
guise of the wood is a cross" (p. 69).

[2] See *OED*, *weather* n., 1j; 2d; Jacob Grimm, Wilhelm Grimm, et al., *Deutsches
Wörterbuch*, in Wetter (Etymology), which cites the word as a frequent gloss for
*aura*. Joseph Wright, ed., *Old English Vocabularies*, ed. Richard Wülcker, 1, col.
698, line 27, has *Hec aries*, weder. Cf. Mod Dan *gaa i vejret* 'to rise into the air.'
The poet's figure on rising smoke perhaps comes from an ancient folk riddler's
theme. Archer Taylor, *The Literary Riddle Before 1600*, p. 43, cites Greek and Ital-
ian riddles on smoke as a creature which flies upward to the clouds.

In *Riddle 30b*, among the texts of the Easter sequence, this challenge is solvable first as a liturgical reference. Coming just after the 'primordial point of all light' at the end of *Homiletic Fragment II, Riddle 30b* describes the Easter Fire in its several identities, both literal and symbolic. The early lines, with their dancing flame and their blowing sparks rising to mingle with the air, play on the New Fire of the Easter Vigil. Struck on heaped wood from a flint spark, the New Fire stands in the open air outside the church door.[3] In line 2a this fire is 'surrounded with splendor,' i.e., by the priest and celebrants in Easter vestment, by the white-robed newly baptized whose unexpressed presence has nevertheless been felt in the previous poems, and by the congregation of the faithful.[4] All of these participants, *weras ond wif*, are *wlonce* 'proud, splendid in majesty' (line 6b), either in their festive clothes or in their manner of reverence, since *wlonce* can be either a plural adjective or an adverb. In line 3b the riddlic

[3] W. J. O'Shea, "Easter Vigil," *New Catholic Encyclopedia* (1967 ed.), 5:10a, says that the New Fire, of Gallic origin and traceable to eighth-century Germany, was originally performed outside the church because it involved the "cumbersome" striking of fire from flint. The blessing of the New Fire (as opposed to the mere kindling of the fire itself) has been traced to tenth-century Germany. According to O'Shea the New Fire gained its present symbolic meaning (as coming from stone just as "light comes from the risen Christ, the cornerstone") only gradually, "with the passing of time." However, the final lines of *Homiletic Fragment II* and *Riddle 30b* together show that the lighting of the New Fire, perhaps the blessing of it, and certainly its christological symbolism were also known in tenth-century England with its many and intimate Gallic connections. It seems probable that the eighth-century Anglo-Saxon missionaries in Germany would also have made the rite of the New Fire known to their correspondents in England.

[4] According to J. A. Jungmann, "Baptism (Liturgy of)," *New Catholic Encyclopedia*, 2:60b, "[f]rom the fourth century [Ambrose, *De mysteriis* 7] there is evidence of the white clothing received by the newly baptised to symbolize the innocence of his new life." The name *Dominica in albis depositis* given to the Sunday after Easter reminds us that the newly baptized once wore their white garments through the Easter Octave. E. C. Whitaker, *The Baptismal Liturgy: An Introduction to Baptism in the Western Church*, pp. 50–51, says that at some time during the Middle Ages the white vesture was reduced to "no more than a white band around the head." Possibly the words *wlonce weras ond wif* of *Riddle 30b* refer to whatever white baptismal garments were being worn in tenth-century England.

'flame' is also *fyre gemylted* 'melted by fire,' yet in line 5 it moves *þær* to some unspecified new location. In this new place the flame is handed about, kissed, and, as it raises itself (line 7a), adored by kneeling men and women (line 7b). These clues identify the Easter Fire in other shapes, first as the Paschal candle, a 'flame' also 'melted by fire' as it burns, and elevated and knelt before as the vigil procession moves from the place of the New Fire into the church. With line 5b, *sendað æfter hondum*, this 'busy' flame spreads to the tapers lighted from the Paschal candle and carried in the hands of everyone present. The flame of *Riddle 30b* rightly calls itself 'busy' at the outset, for it then assumes all the liturgical forms of the Easter Light: New Fire, Paschal candle, and tapers 'sent along' to drive the evening darkness from the church as the vigil begins.

But none of these flames can literally be 'kissed' (line 6), and no evidence exists for a devotional kiss of the Paschal candle itself. To add to the challenge, *gecyssað* appears to be a deliberate variant of *cyssað* in *Riddle 30a*. With the added perfective prefix, the altered word seems to riddle on the spiritual preparedness shared by *weras ond wif* in the Pax Domini, or kiss of peace, widely given just before communion.[5] In that case the men and women of the riddle would be "kissing" not a physical flame but an inward one. Begun as the point of light shining *beorht on breos[tum]* (*Homiletic Fragment II* 19a), this "kissed" flame would now leap not only in Mary's bosom but also in all mutually greeted hearts. In this spiritual flame is found the *upcyme eadignesse* 'elevation in bliss' which closes *Riddle 30b*. In the absence of scriptural connections between fire and the kiss the riddler was perhaps thinking of the liturgical rubrics which explain the pax as purifier of the heart, and of the "purifier" also as flame.[6]

If, as it seems, the riddlic kiss is the Pax Domini, it is also of

[5] On the place of the Pax Domini, usually before the Offertory in early centuries, but moved to the end of the canon before 417 and later attached to Communion, see B. I. Mullahy, "Kiss, Liturgical," *New Catholic Encyclopedia*, 8:207a.

[6] Archdale A. King, *Liturgies of the Past*, p. 456 and n. 4, gives an eighth-century Nestorian explanation of the Pax Domini along these specific lines. On the kiss as removal of the "defilement of enmity" from pre-Nicene times, see Dom Gregory Dix, *The Shape of the Liturgy*, 2d ed., pp. 105–106.

great thematic moment. It would mean that the very brief *Riddle 30b* must move swiftly from the New Fire almost to communion of the Mass of Easter. Such narrative haste would follow the symbolic movement of the Easter liturgy itself: the Easter Vigil leads without pause into the Easter Mass, just as in *The Descent into Hell* the light of Christ rises on hell's gates only an instant before John addresses Christ in person. Indeed, the liturgical gestures of the vigil announce the imminent Resurrection partly by duplicating the eucharistic rite in symbolic ways. The obeisances done to the flame of *Riddle 30b* are a little later done to the risen Presence in the Eucharist as well. The words *sendað æfter hondum*, by which the light spreads into the hands of all the people, also anticipate the delivery of the Host into the outstretched hands of the 'many' (*mongum*, line 8).[7] The elevation and genuflection associated with the Paschal candle (lines 7–8) also suggest the Host, which is both adored at the consecration and shown at the Little Elevation of the doxology. The phrase *modge miltsum* 'sincere [though also 'bold'] in their meekness' (line 8a), another change from *Riddle 30a*, perhaps alludes to a special prayer of "both humility and confidence," such as the ancient words *Domine non sum dignus* spoken by all partakers just before communion.[8] The very notion of a riddlic kiss applies well enough to eucharistic bread about to be eaten, and even better to the sacramental wine, for the drinking cup is the most frequently "kissed" object of Anglo-Saxon poetry.[9] In sum, the *forðweg* of *Riddle 30b* appears to be the swift 'departure' of the rising *lumen Christi* until it reenters the world in the Eucharist, to whom all kneel, as the speaker says, *þonne ic mec onhæbbe* 'when I lift myself up' (line 7a). This theme of a shifting flame, with one riddle told in several voices, returns us strangely to Blackburn. If he had only thought of several kinds of fire rather than multiple objects of wood, he might long ago have answered *Riddle 30b*.

In *Riddle 30a*, however, the speaker describes itself somewhat

[7] J. A. Jungmann, *The Mass of the Roman Rite: Its Origins and Development (Missarum Sollemnia)*, trans. Francis A. Brunner, 2:378–82.

[8] Ibid., p. 355.

[9] Williamson, ed. *Old English Riddles*, p. 232, n. on *Riddle 28* 5–6.

ominously as *fyre gebysgad* 'busied' or even 'worried' by fire. Because *forðweg* is so often a poetic word for the journey of death (notably in *Beowulf* 2625), the phrase *fus forðweges* (line 3a) has been tentatively read as 'eager to pass away.'[10] But the flame of *Riddle 30* does not clearly speak of or allude to death. There are no hints that it is the fire of cremation, nor do our two fullest accounts of Germanic cremation, by the *Beowulf* poet and a tenth-century Arab traveler among the Volga Rus, mention any gestures of handling, kissing, or kneeling as in the riddle.[11] The Easter riddler therefore does not seem to have turned pagan death fires into his liturgical riddle on the Fire of Life. But *Riddle 30a* no longer conveys its own answer, which emerges only after close study of the next poem in *The Easter Riddle*. In incorporating *Riddle 30* into his text of *The Husband's Message*, Blackburn was once again both right and wrong.

### The Husband's Message: Runes and *Geryne*

Blackburn's proposal to begin the text of *The Husband's Message* with *Riddle 30b* appeared in 1901. But his solution for *Riddle 30b* itself—multiple answers based on the general theme *beam* 'wood'—seemed to violate riddlic unity for the sake of doubtful allegory. One of Blackburn's answers was "cross," hardly a welcome suggestion among his contemporaries, who generally admired the supposed paganism of the Old English elegies. Largely ignoring Blackburn, the scholarship and major editions of the following years began *The Husband's Message* with the manuscript's capital *N* and the words *Nu ic onsundran þe secgan wille*, etc., after the first colophon on folio 123a. Thus separated from *Riddle 30b* and "Riddle 60" (folios 122b–123a, lines 1–17

[10] Ibid., n. on line 3.

[11] See Beowulf's cremation, lines 3137–55; and H. M. Smyser, "Ibn Fadlan's Account of the Rus with Some Commentary and Some Allusions to *Beowulf*," in Jess B. Bessinger and Robert P. Creed, eds., *Franciplegius*, pp. 92–119. This is a complete English translation of the Ibn Fadlan's famous account of the Rus.

in the present book) *The Husband's Message* was read and interpreted as a poem of about 53 lines.[1]

In 1967, however, Robert E. Kaske, returning to some of Blackburn's ideas through patristic writings and certain themes of the Old English *Dream of the Rood*, published a text which incorporated "Riddle 60" into *The Husband's Message*, and made them one poem.[2] Guided by older solutions of "Riddle 60" as "reed," Margaret Goldsmith next interpreted the longer text of *The Husband's Message* as *obscura dicta* about a reed pen made to write in familiar exegetical ways of the scriptural mystery of Christ the Victor.[3] Kaske's and Goldsmith's different views strongly imply that not only "Riddle 60" but in fact all of *The Husband's Message* belongs where it is found, squarely among the riddles of the Exeter Book. More recently, in an ingenious paleographical reconstruction of the damaged lines of *The Husband's Message*, John C. Pope considers "Riddle 60" and *The Husband's*

[1] Modern editions which begin *The Husband's Message* at *Nu ic onsundran þe secgan wille* are still in the majority. They include the manuscript photofacsimile (R. W. Chambers, Max Förster and Robin Flower, eds., *The Exeter Book of Old English Poetry*); W. S. Mackie, ed., *The Exeter Book, Part II: Poems IX–XXXII*, pp. 192–97 (who counts 55 lines); ASPR 3:225–27 (53 lines); Roy F. Leslie, ed., *Three Old English Elegies: The Wife's Lament, The Husband's Message, The Ruin*, pp. 49–50 (54 lines). John C. Pope, "Palaeography and Poetry: Some Solved and Unsolved Problems in the Exeter Book," in M. B. Parkes and Andrew G. Watson, eds., *Medieval Scribes, Manuscripts, and Libraries: Essays Presented to N. R. Ker*, pp. 57–59, gives a 54-line text but urges readers (p. 55) to consider "Riddle 60" (also given) and *The Husband's Message* as one poem.

[2] Robert E. Kaske, "A Poem of the Cross in the Exeter Book: 'Riddle 60' and 'The Husband's Message,'" *Traditio* 23 (1967): 41–71. For an elaborate view of the runic passage in *The Husband's Message* as symbolic of the Crucifixion (in line with Kaske's view of the poem), see Kjell Meling, "Cruciform Runes in the Manuscripts of Some Old English Poems" (Ph.D. diss., SUNY/Binghamton, 1972), pp. 183–206.

[3] Margaret Goldsmith, "The Enigma of *The Husband's Message*," in Lewis E. Nicholson and Dolores Warwick Frese, eds., *Anglo-Saxon Poetry: Essays in Appreciation for John C. McGalliard*, pp. 242–63. A medieval reed riddle by the Spanish Jew Jehuda Halevi (early twelfth century), cited in Archer Taylor, *The Literary Riddle Before 1600*, p. 36, uses the (folk-riddling) clues "hollow," "little staff," and employs the theme of pen, "small destroyer of reputations, bringer of pain and

*Message* as separate texts while admitting the possibility that they are one poem, whose speaker he reaffirms as a Germanic rune-stave rather than a reed or cross.[4] Despite their ostensible separation in the manuscript, therefore, "Riddle 60" and *The Husband's Message* more and more appear to be united in theme, recounting together the making and message bearing of a runic artifact with magical speech and a hidden identity.[5] The rune-stave's secret ultimately becomes the great central mystery of the riddler's faith.

In fact, *Dream of the Rood* and "Riddle 60" resemble one another mainly in their shared narrative device of the speaking wood which reflects upon its transformed life. Possibly both poems somehow grew from the same riddlic convention of the reshaped tree, which also appears at least twice more in the Exeter Book riddles, in *Riddle 53* ("battering ram") and *Riddle 73* ("spear"). The similarities between *Dream of the Rood* and "Riddle 60" are therefore real, but they are also somewhat beguiling. As the Rood tells the dreamer of its origins in the forest, so in the first lines of "Riddle 60" a wooden object speaks of its firm-rooted home by the shore, where at dawn it once knew the caress of the breaker. Just as the Rood recalls being hewn down and shaped into the Cross, so after a few lines the waterside tree is speaking in some new nature or shape, wondering at the miracle of its own mouthless speech. At lines 15–17 it talks of announcing secretly an *ærendspræce* 'message in speech,' apparently a unique member of a family of legal compound words beginning

---

singer of songs." Neither such clues nor the writing theme appears in *The Husband's Message*, which therefore does not appear to be built on a reed riddle. Goldsmith's reading depends in part on some older scholarly solutions of "Riddle 60" as "reed" (see ASPR 3:361), but that answer does not satisfactorily explain all the clues of the text.

[4] Pope, "Palaeography and Poetry," esp. p. 53 and n. 71, p. 54 and n. 73.

[5] This view of the relationship between "Riddle 60" and *The Husband's Message* is presented in full textual detail in James E. Anderson, "Strange, Sad Voices: The Portraits of Germanic Women in the Old English Exeter Book" (Ph.D. diss., University of Kansas, 1978), pp. 159–223.

in *ærend-*.[6] But whereas the talking Rood inhabits a dream, the talking wood of "Riddle 60" is not a dream figure at all. It is instead the pseudoparadoxical silent voice known from several other Exeter Book riddles, the noiseless speech of written language. From lines 12–13 we know the source of this alleged miracle: not the pen, but most particularly the knife point, the right hand, an earl's inmost thoughts and the knife point together. These words introduce the themes of runes and rune carving, vehicles of magic and wonder from early Germanic times. In its wonderment the runic object, quite unlike the Rood, does not speak of itself as wounded or victimized; on the contrary, it seems to participate too willingly in its own transformation to be identified exclusively with the Cross.

A second reference to the rune carving 'earl,' the man *se þisne beam agrof* 'who engraved this wood,' comes at line 30b, just after the next modest initial in the manuscript. Amid the extensive damage to the manuscript between the capitals at lines 18 and 30 appears the relatively unscathed word *treocyn[ne]* 'kind of tree' and also the phrase *ic tudre aweox* '[? from what] kinship I grew.' As Pope's reconstructed text helps confirm, these defective lines appear to tell the 'kind' of wood being inscribed.[7] In the words *treocyn[ne]* and *tudre* resides a play on species and worthy ancestry, the conventional messenger's recitation of pedigree and authority. Between the two capitals at lines 18 and 30, then, the earlier themes of runes and rune cutting take a riddlic turn. The capitals themselves, which prompted Thorpe in 1842 to divide "Riddle 60" and *The Husband's Message* into two "riddles" and *A Fragment*, mark a rhetorical deception—a change of audience at line 18 and a change of speakers at line 30.[8] One of Thorpe's old

---

[6] Felix Liebermann, *Die Gesetze der Angelsachsen*, 2 : 1, 7 gives *ærendgewrit* 'Sendschreiben' and *ærendwreca* 'Bote.' *ASD* cites nonlegal meanings for these same compounds, however. On *spræce* as a simplex, see Liebermann, ibid., 1 : 200 under *sprecan*.

[7] Pope, "Palaeography and Poetry," pp. 44–53 and plates 7 and 8.

[8] Benjamin Thorpe, ed. and trans., *Codex exoniensis: A Collection of Anglo-Saxon Poetry, etc.*, pp. 471–75. Thorpe entitled *Nu ic onsundran þe* and succeeding lines

divisions, at line 18, began the mistaken amputation and independent naming of "Riddle 60," which is in fact the true start of *The Husband's Message*.

Since a poem which opens with riddling becomes at least to some degree a riddle itself, the other interpretative cruxes of *The Husband's Message* emerge as deliberate puzzles to be solved. In line 30b the wood has suddenly stopped talking, to become, in third person, *þisne beam*. Many modern editors have followed Thorpe, who believed that this abrupt change in point of view introduced a separate speaker and therefore an independent text. Pope, recalling that the Rood speaks of itself in both first and third person, suggests that no change of speakers need be imagined at line 30.[9] The thematic riddle, however, partly upholds both views.

The dual voice of the poem hides the custom in medieval law and statecraft of sending a truthful message or petition by two envoys, such as Egil and Arinbjorn before Erik Bloodaxe at York, two messengers before Harold of England's captor in a scene on the Bayeux Tapestry, or Rosencrantz and Guildenstern unwittingly bearing to England first Hamlet's death sentence

---

"III" (of three "Riddles," including *Riddle 30b* and "Riddle 60") and began "A Fragment" with *Hwæt, þec þonne biddan het*, etc., line 30 of *The Husband's Message*.

[9] Pope, "Palaeography and Poetry," p. 52. More recently Peter Orton, "The Speaker in 'The Husband's Message,'" *LeedsSE* 12 (1981): 43–56, argues that the scribal divisions tell nothing conclusive about the so-called division of voices in the poem and observes that other speakers in poetry, notably the Cross in *Dream of the Rood*, refer to themselves in third person. Earl R. Anderson, "Voices in *The Husband's Message*," *NM* 74 (1973): 238–46, notes the scribal divisions especially at lines 13 and 26 (lines 30 and 43 in the present edition) and suggests two voices as in *Dream of the Rood*, a human prologue followed by extended prosopopoeia uttered by a runestave, an order of speakers opposite to that suggested in this book. In *The Husband's Message*: Persuasion and the Problem of *Genyre*," *ES* 56 (1975): 289–94, Anderson reconsiders his earlier position to suggest that the human messenger can be strongly argued to speak the entire poem. Thus the number and identities of the voices in *The Husband's Message* and the boundaries of the speeches continue to generate controversy. Orton, "The Speaker in 'The Husband's Message,'" p. 52, thinks of a deliberately enigmatic speaker without trying to identify or solve the enigma.

and then their own. Conversely, the lone go-betweens of medieval literature, from Hild of the Heodening Saga and Ganelon to Iago, often shuttle the false testimony which leads to war and tragedy. In *The Husband's Message*, whose early lines 'dare to pledge an honor-bound promise' (lines 28–29), an alert Anglo-Saxon reader might well have looked for a second messenger to guarantee this proffered truth. The suspicion of two messengers is rewarded by clues in at least two places: the shifting viewpoint of line 30, which implies a second speaker of the message, and the runestave's change from the dual pronouns *unc* and *uncre* (lines 15, 17) to the singular *þe* (line 18), which implies two listeners, a fellow envoy and the wife. *Widdor* 'more widely' of line 17 also slyly invites us to read 'farther.' If we do so, *onsundran* of line 18 seems to imply a new text but really acknowledges a new audience. The argument now turns to *þe onsundran* 'aside to you,' i.e., not the silent messenger addressed as *þe* in line 14 but rather the equally silent wife. Thus on either side of the traditional break at line 18 lurk riddling words and themes which squint at each other as independent texts probably would not do. This duality of speakers has already occurred twice in *The Easter Riddle*: toward the end of *The Descent into Hell*, where the phrase *git Iohannis* betrays the second voice, and in *Pharaoh*, whose obvious dialogue hides a cunning lapse of riddlic form.

After line 30 a human messenger, who has no need to riddle on his own speech, invests his argument with the hidden force of law. First he recalls the spoken promises (*wordbeotunga*, line 32) by which the husband and wife once ruled together the mead towns of their homeland. Since these promises were also spoken *oft . . . on ærdagum* 'often . . . in former days' (line 71), riddlic play on notable Old Testament promises—Psalm 44, known to medieval exegesists as the epithalamion of Christ and Ecclesia, or the tree from Jesse's *treocyn[ne]*, i.e., his lineage (Isa. 11 : 1), or the inscribed rod of Ezekiel 37—was almost surely on the poet's mind. Likewise, to a monastic riddler whose daily spiritual exercises were filled with psalm singing, the oath taking at the end of *The Husband's Message* would have echoed the sworn promise of

Psalm 88:4.[10] But in *The Husband's Message* 36, as also in *The Wife's Lament* 25, the old contract of husband and wife is known as *freondscipe*, the Germanic legal word for the mutual protectorship of the clan and comitatus as well as for the analogous protectorship of marriage.[11] In *The Wife's Lament* and *The Husband's Message* alike the original allegorist has concealed his ultimate secret in coincidental scriptural and Germanic themes.

Once again, too, a principle of Germanic law is applied to the familiar Germanic predicament of exile. In lines 36b–42 the wife is urged to honor her old contract by rejoining her exiled husband across the sea. The messenger cannot guarantee an easy voyage: it is to begin with the mournful death cry of the cuckoo, and it is threatened by possible resistance from 'living' men. But against these troubling thoughts the message offers legal encouragement in the form of an exile's success story.

The titles *þeoden* 'king, lord, prince' (line 46) and *þeodnes dohtor* (line 65) suggest that the royal marriage contract of husband and wife has outlasted their separation. Lines 61–64 declare not only that the husband has 'won out over [the] woes' (*wean oferwunnen*) of his hasty boat journey into exile but also that he has once more acquired a princely abundance of noble treasures, horses, and jewels in his new home. The damaged passage beginning with *he genoh hafað fedan go[ldes]* (line 52) and including the words *eþel healde* (line 54) appears to have reported the husband's accession to great rank and power in a new land.[12] Since the twelfth-century *Norðleoda laga* stipulates that to

[10] Goldsmith, "The Enigma of *The Husband's Message*," p. 254. Anderson, "*The Husband's Message*," p. 292, also notes the hint in *ærdagum* that the promises were sworn long ago but does not propose a reference to Old Testament times because (Anderson, "Voices in *The Husband's Message*") he is among those readers who do not wish to read the poem allegorically.

[11] Leslie's observation of the analogy between legal protectorship and marriage appears in his commentary on *The Wife's Lament* (*Three Old English Elegies*, pp. 4–5). But his remarks also apply to *The Husband's Message*, which treats marriage explicitly as a legal theme.

[12] Anderson, "Voices in *The Husband's Message*," pp. 240–41, concludes that if the husband is to be identified as Christ then the *elþeode* (of line 55) must be the

be ranked above a *ceorl* a man had to own a helmet, a byrnie, a *golde fæted sweord*, and five hides of land, perhaps the words *fedan go[ldes]* and *epel healde* allude to such particular emblems of distinguished rank.[13] More certainly these damaged lines once testified to the husband's regained wealth, and Pope's paleographic suggestion *feohgestreona* for line 52b is all the more attractive for the lexical parallel in *eorlgestreona* (line 64b).[14]

These promises of riches are made not to woo the wife but to remind her of a point of law. The same legal force and intent that shows at the end of the runestave's long exordium also underlies the gentle persuasion of the second envoy. The runestave's assurance, *Ic gehatan dear pæt pu pær tirfæste treowe findest* 'I dare to pledge that there [in the husband's mind] you will find an honor-bound promise' (lines 28–29), is rife with words (*gehatan, dear, treowe*) borrowed either from codified law or from the law of custom. The second messenger, with professional humility and due respect for the woman he addresses as *peodnes dohtor*, nevertheless finishes his account of the husband's triumph with a condition: the husband's success will be complete only *gif he pin beneah* [from *benugan*] 'if he may have enough of you' (line 65b). The argument spanning the lost text on folio 123b thus begins and ends in the telling lexical parallel *genoh/beneah*: the man who has enough poured gold must still have 'enough' of his wife in order to crown his victory. 'Enough,' one might suspect, is litotes for 'all.' Though they take pains to convey the husband's abiding

---

angels and saints in heaven, a reading which Anderson then rejects but which appears to me to be exactly the poet's meaning. As Anderson himself notices (pp. 239–40), the poet's word *sigepeode* (line 37) suggests a powerful and victorious people. Both *sigepeode* and *elpeode* appear to make the best sense as riddle words in allegory, *elpeode* implying foreignness with respect not to the husband but to the earthbound wife, the 'far folkland' in which she has imagined the husband to be sitting in *The Wife's Lament* 47. It is true, as Anderson says (p. 240) that the phrase *ofer eorpan* (line 64) refers to worldly joys. But the messenger is saying that the husband's new joys will far outshine any joys on earth once he and the wife are reunited.

[13] See Liebermann, *Gesetze*, 1:460–61 (*Norðleoda Laga* 9–10). This provision apparently defines a man's rank for the purpose of determining his *wergild*.

[14] Pope, "Palaeography and Poetry," p. 59 and plate 10.

marital faith and love, the two messengers have also been sent to reclaim the wife as her husband's property before the law. The claim answers the desperate prayer at the beginning of *Resignation*: *Age mec se ælmihta God*, etc. But the second messenger makes his legal duty especially clear with the phrase *aþe benemnan* 'declare with an oath' in the last lines of *The Husband's Message*. These words remove all doubt of the major Germanic theme of the poem: the medieval *Treugelöbnis*, or formal promise, sealed with a solemn oath.[15]

The final lines of *The Husband's Message* also show the runes which, by giving magical speech to the transformed wood, have begun the riddlic embassy. Closely bound as they are to the legal formula *aþe benemnan*, the runic letters somehow help consummate an implied drama of contractual love. If Pope's very plausible reading of *ofer* as 'above and beyond' is accepted, *The Husband's Message* closes with formal supercession of an old promise (*gebeot*, line 66a) of faithfulness (*winetreowe*, line 69b) and marital covenant (*wære*, line 69a).[16] *Wyrd*, that old shoulder companion of Anglo-Saxon scholars, has badly obscured a crucial single letter of this final passage: the stem consonant of its one and only main verb. The remaining shadow of the damaged letter looks too angular for the *c* which some editors supply.[17] With much strain the naked eye can discern the feet of an *h* or an *n*, but even ultraviolet light does not show through the dark smudges at the top of the letter. Thus the reading *genyre*, which

---

[15] The words and themes of *The Husband's Message* can be precisely accounted for by matching them against the language of the *Treugelöbnis*. See Paul Puntschart, *Schuldvertrag und Treugelöbnis des sächsischen Rechts im Mittelalter: Ein Beitrag zur grundauffassung der altdeutschen obligation*. Ada Broch, *Die Stellung der Frau in der angelsächsischen Poesie*, p. 70, makes the only published statement I have found which specifically links *The Husband's Message* to the *Treugelöbnis*. In speaking of the runes near the end of the poem, Broch says, "Whatever the runes may signify, the conclusion is apparently only a reiteration of the frequently pledged faith." Translation mine.

[16] Pope, "Palaeography and Poetry," p. 59 (in the prose translation under the OE text).

[17] Ibid., p. 63 n. on line 50a, also rejects *gecyre* as "totally erroneous" and "misread."

requires some philological and thematic ingenuity, is also physically uncertain.[18] But the frequently suggested reading *ge[h]yre* makes sound riddling sense. Returning to the pseudoparadox of runic speech which opens the poem, the human messenger would close simply by claiming to 'hear' the five runes witness the husband's sworn promise.[19]

In accord with the theme of the *Treugelöbnis* in *The Husband's Message*, the runes themselves should also be giving testimony of some kind. Separated by bold raised points around and between them but also ambiguously joined by the riddle words *ætsomne* and *geador* (line 66), the runes have been interpreted both individually and as letters in various scrambled words. All the anagrammatic solutions require the last of the runes to be a *D*, but the letter looks nearly the same as the unquestioned *m* rune of *The Ruin* 23, only about half a folio page ahead.[20] In favor of the

[18] Kaske first suggested *genyre* on the authority of an ultraviolet-light reading, which, however, establishes in his published photograph nothing beyond what the naked eye already sees. His argument, with photograph, is found in "The Reading *genyre* in *The Husband's Message* Line 49," *MÆ* 33 (1964): 204–206 and facing p. 169. Later, in "A Poem of the Cross," pp. 45–46 and n. 35 and pp. 69–71, Kaske cites the philological concurrence of Kemp Malone with the reading *genyre* and argues that the poet means to "constrain" the runes into a message that speaks allegorically of the Cross. Anderson, "*The Husband's Message*," p. 290, takes Kaske's *genyre* as beyond doubt and offers two examples from *ASD* of *genyrwan + ofer*. But he reads lines 66–67 as 'I superimpose . . . ofer eald gebeot' and thus gives to *ge[n]yre* a meaning quite different from Kaske's. Orton, "The Speaker in 'The Husband's Message,'" p. 49, argues against *genyre*.

[19] The reading *gehyre* has been proposed by Moritz Trautmann, "Zur Botschaft des Gemahls," *Anglia* 16 (1894): 207–25; Mackie, *The Exeter Book, Part II*, pp. 196 and n. on line 51, 197; Leslie, *Three Old English Elegies*, p. 50 and p. 66n.; Goldsmith, "The Enigma of *The Husband's Message*," pp. 251–52; Pope, "Palaeography and Poetry," pp. 59, 63 n. on line 50a; and Orton, "The Speaker in 'The Husband's Message,'" p. 50.

[20] Leslie, *Three Old English Elegies*, p. 15, inclines toward reading the last rune of *The Husband's Message* as M because it resembles the *m* rune in *The Ruin* 23. On p. 51 of his edition of *The Ruin*, Leslie enters the word *mon* in the place of the *m* rune itself and reads line 23b as *mondreama full*. Meling, "Cruciform Runes," pp. 230–31, argues on the same grounds as Leslie's for reading the last rune in *The Husband's Message* as M. Pope, "Palaeography and Poetry," p. 63n. on lines 50b–51a, believes that the doubtful rune in *The Husband's Message* is M and "al-

*D*, and against published views of these runes as cult symbols based on the English Runic Poem, or alternately as the initials of five persons (conjurors of the oath?), W. J. Sedgefield's old idea of an anagram for *sweard* (*sweord*) 'sword' is partly supported by a runic artifact from across the English Channel.[21]

From Arum, in Frisia, comes a small wooden effigy of a sword or knife, carefully worked and fire-polished along the blade by a sixth- or seventh-century craftsman. The Arum Sword Effigy is housed in the Fries Museum, in Leeuwarden.[22] On one side of the blade, framed by occult marks, is an inscription in runes of characteristic English form: *edæ* : *boda*. The two *d* runes look like the disputed final rune of *The Husband's Message*.[23] The second word, *boda* (or *bodæ*; there is some doubt about the slant strokes of the last rune), is generally identified as OE *boda* 'messenger.' The word *edæ* has been variously read, either as the proper name *Ede* or as OE *ad* 'fire,' the latter suggesting the ancient Germanic custom of sending around a spearpoint as a levy for war.[24]

----

most certainly not *D*," a judgment he does not explain. But the arguments for *M* in *The Husband's Message* must be uncertain because of the riddling nature of the poem: perhaps the scribe failed, deliberately or otherwise, to distinguish the form of the last rune in *The Husband's Message* from the *m* rune in *The Ruin*. The fact remains that all the other groups of runes in the Exeter Book riddles, as well as Cynewulf's signature in *Christ II*, spell out words. In *The Husband's Message*, reading the last rune as *M* does not produce an anagrammatic word, but *D* gives a very plausible one.

[21] A convenient review of solutions for the runic lines appears in Kaske, "A Poem of the Cross," p. 44 n. 2. The fruitful (though not entirely correct) anagrammatic solution *sweard* 'sword' is in W. J. Sedgefield, *An Anglo-Saxon Verse Book*. A representative solution based on rune names and (supposed) runic magic is R. M. W. Elliott, "The Runes in the Husband's Message," *JEGP* 54 (1955): 1–8. Goldsmith, "The Enigma of *The Husband's Message*," pp. 251–54, 259–60, gives a partial solution involving rune names and exegetical symbolism rather than pagan magic.

[22] Klaus Düwel, *Runenkunde*, p. 119.

[23] The Arum Sword effigy is pictured in R. M. W. Elliott, *Runes: An Introduction*, plate IV, fig. 9. The *a* and *o* runes of the inscription look distinctively English.

[24] R. I. Page, *An Introduction to English Runes*, p. 100, reads *edæ* : *boda*, taking the last rune as *A* with a stray mark rather than *Æ*. Konstantin Reichardt, *Runen-*

Nonetheless, *The Husband's Message*, with its persistent legality, more plausibly suggests the OFris word *ed, eth,* OE *að* 'oath.'[25] The words and runes on the Arum Sword would then recall the strong Anglo-Frisian connections of the sixth and seventh centuries: and the inscription *edæ : boda* (or *bodæ*) would mean either OE *aða boda* 'bringer of oaths' or, more probably, *aðe boda* 'messenger with (i.e., accompanied by) an oath' to be delivered across the sea.[26] The Arum Sword Effigy would perhaps represent the real sword upon which an oath was sworn, or the reiterated knife (lines 12–13) which gave the oath its runic voice.

While the shape of the artifact from Arum would seem to confirm Sedgefield's anagram *sweard* (*sweord*) for the runes of *The Husband's Message*, the legal spirit of the poem itself hints that *sweard* (in any case an otherwise unrecorded spelling for *sweord*) is either a coincidental resemblance or a pun. The runic word in *The Husband's Message* is more probably *sweard,* or *swearð,* 'swearing,' clearly given once elsewhere as *aðswyrd,* with a final *d.*[27] The

---

*kunde,* pp. 61–62, reads *edæ : bodæ* and pictures the inscription in Fig. 6. Helmut Arntz, *Handbuch der Runenkunde,* 2d ed., p. 124, discusses the runes in the Arum inscription. For the interpretation of *edæ* as an inflected form of OE *ad* 'fire' (or an OFris cognate) see Page, *An Introduction,* p. 100; Reichardt, *Runenkunde,* p. 62; Arntz, *Handbuch,* p. 287. Düwel, *Runenkunde,* p. 62, cites W. J. Buma's reading 'Für Ede, (den) Boten,' which does not seem to fit the grammar of the inscription. Düwel himself reads the inscription as *edæ : boda* and says that it is customarily understood to mean *renuntius* 'rückkehrender Bote.' Although I do not agree with this reading, the idea of a 'returning messenger' might help meet the objections of Pope ("Palaeography and Poetry," pp. 52–53) and Anderson ("Voices in *The Husband's Message,*" p. 242) to the idea of a runestave making voyages *ful oft* (line 23) across the sea. To me the poet seems to be thinking both literally of a runestave and figuratively of its function as messenger in the complex arrangements and counterarrangements of the Germanic marriage promise, a duty which might easily cause several trips. See n. 31 below.

[25] *ASD,* under *að,* gives OFris *eth, ed.* Jacob Grimm, Wilhelm Grimm, et al., *Deutsches Wörterbuch,* under *Eid,* gives OSax *ed. Woordenboek der nederlandsche Taal,* under *eed,* gives OFris *eth.* The *OED,* for *oath,* gives OFris *eth, ed.*

[26] On the close Anglo-Frisian relations especially of the sixth and seventh centuries, see F. M. Stenton, *Anglo-Saxon England,* 3d ed., pp. 56–57, 221, 240.

[27] MS *aðsweorð* in *Beowulf* 2064a was emended by Thorkelin in his transcription to *aðsweord,* and this reading has been followed in some editions. C. L.

word *sweard* would thus carry the same basic message as the Arum Sword, long-distance testimony of a sworn oath to an absent person across the sea.[28] In the first damaged lines of *The Husband's Message* the runestave seems to talk of its shuttling back and forth *ofer heah hofu* 'across the open seas,' and the Arum Sword, too, appears by the form of some of its runes to have been made in England and taken to Frisia, where it was found.

The Arum Sword is made of yew wood, whose natural and magical properties are recorded piecemeal. Another Frisian runestave, also made of yew and called Westeremden B, twice mentions the ability of yew to calm stormy seas.[29] Besides explaining the meaning of the words *ofer heah hofu*, then, these Frisian runestaves also seem to elucidate the talk of a shoreline origin and of peaceful coexistence with the wave in *The Husband's Message* 1–7.[30] All of the runestave's claims of intimacy with the sea sound like thematic riddling on yew wood as the wife's magical protector on the difficult voyage she will undertake when the cuckoo calls. The English Runic poem describes the yew as 'hard and fast in the earth,' an idea echoed in the phrase *frumstapole fæst* 'firm in [my] first home' in *The Husband's Message* 3. The

---

Wrenn, *Beowulf With the Finnesburg Fragment*, rev. W. F. Bolton, p. 174 n. on line 2064, rightly objects to Thorkelin's emendation but notes the occurrence of *aðswyrd* 'iuramentum' in the *Vespasian Psalter Gloss.*

[28] Although two much-disputed runic inscriptions, the Arum Sword and the runes in *The Husband's Message*, are here compared in a necessarily circular fashion, the oath swearing of the poem and the acknowledged word *boda(e)* 'messenger' on the artifact hint of one and the same Germanic custom, otherwise unknown: the practice of long-distance runic oath sending by halidomes of symbolic sword shapes and generic rather than specific messages, presumably so that they could be used more than once.

[29] See Arntz, *Handbuch*, p. 208 and n. 2.

[30] Leslie, *Three Old English Elegies*, pp. 49 and 60 n., emends MS *hofu* to *h[a]fu* on the grounds that *hofu* would mean 'buildings' and be "out of context." I agree with Leslie that *ofer heah hofu* means 'over the high seas,' but not that MS *hofu* requires emendation if the vowel was sounded as /ɔ/, for which spellings in *o* are more common in the Exeter Book than spellings in *a*: e.g., MS *gopes* 'of the gaping one,' from ON *gapa* 'to gape,' *Riddle 48* 3.

The Arum Sword Effigy, in the Fries Museum, Leeuwarden. Provenance: Arum, Frisia (Netherlands), A.D. 550–650. The sword, of fire-polished yew wood, is 24 centimeters (ca. 9½ inches) long. The blade contains inscribed runes of probable incidental relation to *The Husband's Message*. The meaning of a single tree rune near the tip of the blade (not clearly visible in this photograph) is unknown. Photograph courtesy of the Fries Museum.

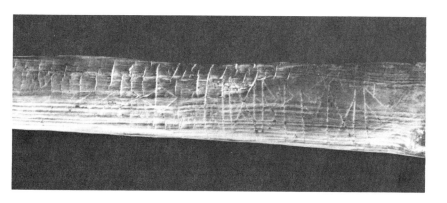

Detail of the runes on the Arum Sword Effigy. The seven grouped runes read *edæ : boda [bodæ?]*, perhaps 'bringer of oaths' or 'messenger with an oath.' Photograph courtesy of the Fries Museum.

same Runic Poem also calls the yew a 'guardian of flame,' a skald-like obscurity which seems to mean that yew keeps a fire alive for a long time, i.e., is slow-burning. This property of yew wood might well account for the fire-working of the blade on the Arum Sword.

With so much riddlic information about the yew among the early lines of *The Husband's Message*, Pope's restored words *iw mec ælde hataŏ* 'men call me yew' for line 19 suit the context as well as they fit the damaged space.[31] In the first damaged lines of *The Husband's Message*, therefore, the wooden "messenger" once divulged its species and elaborately defined its transoceanic mission.[32] By this network of clues the Anglo-Saxon reader was to guess the hidden drama in the runic climax of the poem, as the modern reader can also do with the added help of the Arum Sword. At the very end of the message the human ambassador who began speaking at line 30 is still addressing the silent but attentive wife. He hands her a small yew-wood artifact which "speaks" its own purpose. To satisfy the alliteration and further challenge the solver, the word *sweard*, runic testimony of the husband's oath-sealed promise, has been slightly scrambled: S · R · EA · W · D. Probably the wife is to be imagined as solving

[31] Pope, "Palaeography and Poetry," pp. 48–52 and plate 8. The yew wood of the Arum Sword effigy places Pope's restored word *iw* "beyond reasonable doubt" for archaeological reasons which confirm his very sound paleographical ones. Thematically such riddling on the yew (the species of life, i.e., fertility, afterlife, etc.) would have provided a clue to the larger theme of the marriage oath as well and also a balance against the oak tree (of death) in *The Wife's Lament*. Conceivably such artifacts as the Arum Sword would have aided especially in the making of royal-marriage contracts, which often bound not just different clans but also different nations together and therefore sometimes involved overseas negotiations. In that case the runes of *The Husband's Message* would have been to Anglo-Saxon readers a further clue of the allegorical kingliness of the Husband and Wife.

[32] Pope, "Palaeography and Poetry," pp. 48–52, plates 7 and 8, and p. 57 (text and translation) reconstructs lines 20b–22 to talk of *siþas* 'journeys' (though he translates 'courses') *ellor londes* 'in foreign parts.' See the Textual Notes for full discussion of Pope's complete restoration of *The Husband's Message*.

the runes *ofer meodu* [*-bence*] 'over the mead bench,' as the judicious standard emendation of line 9a reads.[33]

Since in *Beowulf* the sword becomes a *beaduleoma* and *hildeleoma* 'battle flame' (lines 1143, 1523, 2583) and in *The Fight at Finnsburg* 35b–36 the flashing of swords in battle is compared to fire, the Arum Sword also gives a credible answer for *Riddle 30a*: an ancient Germanic oath-swearing ritual. The poem and historical artifact together suggest that a wooden sword effigy with a runic "voice" was laid on a glowing fire, then perhaps held or brandished aloft with its blade aflame. Such a gesture might explain how the blade of the Arum Sword was actually 'worried by fire' [*Riddle 30a* 3) and also how the speaker of the riddle seems to be both wood and flame at once. The *weras ond wif* of the text would then represent the oath swearer and his conjurers or witnesses, all perhaps splendidly dressed for the solemnity of the moment. The Germanic halidome of the riddle, as the embodiment of the oath taker's solemn intentions, appears to be held high, reverenced, and passed around and kissed ceremonially by the sharers in the oath. The joy brought to *monnum* 'men' (lines 8–9) and the 'splendor' of the participants mark such an oath as a happy occasion. Probably, as *The Husband's Message* suggests, *Riddle 30a* describes the Germanic ritual for sealing a wedding promise. Such halidomes as the Arum Sword might have inspired the later Christian custom of the *osculatorium*, or peace board, sometimes of wood and inscribed with a cross, which the faithful passed and kissed at the Pax Domini.[34] If *Riddle 30a* preserved the making of a heathen marriage oath, it would have

---

[33] MS *ofer meodu* is unmetrical. Pope, "Palaeography and Poetry," p. 60 n. on *Riddle 60* 9; and p. 56 (text and translation) sees no reason against the emendation *meodu*[*-bence*], first suggested by Grein and adopted in Frederick Tupper, *The Riddles of the Exeter Book*, p. 43; Mackie, *The Exeter Book, Part II*, pp. 190–91; ASPR 3:225; and Williamson, *Old English Riddles*, p. 103. ASPR 3:362, n. on *Riddle 60* 9, lists alternative (but less successful) emendations in earlier scholarship.

[34] Though peace boards are known from "the latter part of the Middle Ages" (B. I. Mullahy, "Kiss, Liturgical," *New Catholic Encyclopedia* [1967 ed.], 8:207b), it is possible that a peace board is the riddler's connection between *Riddle 30a* and

been a most appropriate text to borrow, and slightly rework, as a signal for the great marriage oath renewed at Easter.

In *The Husband's Message* the runestave's mouthless utterance is, like all other oaths, a holy one. Its sanctity the messenger witnesses *be him lifgendum* (line 70), a riddling variation of *be Gode lifgendum* 'by the living God,' who is the chief witness of men's oaths in Anglo-Saxon law.[35] The husband who would swear by himself, against Christ's prohibition of intemperate swearing (Matt. 5 : 33 – 37), would also invalidate his oath by such blasphemy, unless, of course, he and the living God were one and the same.[36] It is precisely this double meaning with which the pronoun *him* is charged.

---

*Riddle 30b.* On the kissing of holy objects as a very ancient (pre-Christian) practice, see J. A. Jungmann, *The Early Liturgy, to the Time of Gregory the Great*, trans. Francis A. Brunner, p. 128. F. Cabrol, "Baiser. VII: L'osculatorium," *Dictionnaire d'archéologie chrétienne et de liturgie*, 2 : 1, 127b, traces peace boards to the time of Pope Innocent III (1198 – 1216) but also notes that bronze objects thought to be used for the same purpose and dating from the fifth century have been authenticated.

[35] See Liebermann, *Gesetze*, 1 : 396 – 97 (*Swerian* 1, 2), which has *lifiendes Godes*. In poetry the adjective *lifiend* refers to God more frequently than to any mortal person: see *God lifiende, Crist lifiend, se lifigende* (Christ), *lifiendum Gode*, and the like at *Guthlac* 1072; *Azarius* 78; *Christ* 273, 755; *Andreas* 459, 1411; *The Soul's Address* (Exeter Book) 69; *Soul and Body* (Vercelli Book) 69; *Solomon and Saturn* 574; and occasionally in the metrical Psalms. The laws have one instance of a phrase *be libbendum wife* (Liebermann, *Gesetze*, 2 : 1, 134) which means 'in the case of a surviving widow.' C. M. W. Grein, *Sprachschatz der angelsächsischen Dichter*, I, under *libban*, attributes similar human reference to the words *be him lifgendum* in *The Husband's Message*: 'bei seinem [i.e., an earthly husband's] Lebzeiten.' In the present edition the word *Him* in the poetic phrase is capitalized, though it clearly makes better riddling if it is left uncapitalized as in the MS.

[36] Pope, "Palaeography and Poetry," p. 63 n. on lines 50b – 51a, recalls Ernst A. Kock, "Interpretations and Emendations of Early English Texts. VIII," *Anglia* 45 (1921): 122 – 23, who thinks of the last rune as *M* (*monn*) and believes the husband is swearing in runes to conceal his oath on himself, a violation of Christ's command in Matt. 5. Kock's observation comes very close to discovering the riddlic intention of the husband's oath as well as his identity, for only God can swear by himself, as he does in the story of the sacrifice of Isaac (Gen. 22:16: OE *ic swerige þurh me selfne*, etc.).

For the hour of vespers the Old English Benedictine office instructs the brethren to praise God because

. . . on æfen-timan ure drihten offrode æt his æfen-gereorde and dælde his discipulum þurh [h]alig geryne hlaf and win for his sylfes lichaman and for his agen blod.

[. . . at eventide our Lord made offering at his evening meal and by holy runing (i.e., mystery making) gave his disciples bread and wine for his own body and his own blood.][37]

With this same central proposition of his faith in mind, a witty poet-apologist has turned the runes of Germanic oath swearing into the *geryne* 'mysterium' of the Eucharist. Together the two messengers bear witness of the New Covenant, which stands *ofer eald gebeot* 'over and above the Old Promise' because it stands once for all (Heb. 10:9–10). *The Husband's Message* as we have it transcends its Germanic themes just as this new promise, fulfilled in the Resurrection, is understood to replace the law of Moses and the oft-repeated promises of the Old Testament. In riddlic allegory the mouthless runestave which marvels at its own transformation becomes the sacred bread itself, cut with the mere point of a knife but endowed with *eorles ingeþonc* 'an earl's inner thought' (lines 12–13). The emended word *meodu[-bence]* makes a very probable riddle on the divine Husband's altar. At line 30 the concealed second voice, as in *The Descent into Hell* and *Pharaoh*, emerges once again as the priest, the Husband's messenger to the Wife, who is both the individual anima and the collective Church on earth. After recalling the days of this earthly marriage (lines 30–36a), the human speaker counsels the wife to await her Lord's call and then follow him into his former exile of death, of which she has once wrongly complained in *The Wife's Lament*. At the end of her hard voyage the wife may expect to rejoin her Spouse in triumph and abundant riches in a new home to the south [*suð heonan*, line 44), in Bede's exegetical thinking the direction of the fire of love and of Christ's new spiri-

[37] James M. Ure, ed., *The Benedictine Office: An Old English Text*, p. 98.

tual kingdom.[38] In the last lines the human messenger hands the wife the wondrously articulate memorial of the New Promise. This is the moment of the Eucharist, liturgical accomplishment of the Resurrection and sign in heaven of the bond of Husband and Wife *on ærdagum* 'in former days' on earth.

For this long explanation of the Husband's returning an eleventh- or early-twelfth-century artist appears to have devised a single picture.[39] His drawing of a horse and rider is incised in drypoint, upside down, in the bottom margin of folio 123a. The horse's legs disappear into the field of the last line on the page. The horseman is robed and riding sidesaddle, as in the standard Palm Sunday image of Christ entering Jerusalem. But in the drypoint picture the rider seems to have a helmet on the uncertainly drawn crown of his head, for his long hair flows abruptly straight backward from his neck. He appears also to have a shield hanging behind him from the saddle.[40] From this unlikely combination of robe and armor he may be guessed as that same victorious horseman who has already ridden past the burst gates of hell (*The Descent into Hell* 40) and who appears again in Rev. 19:11: "And I saw heaven opened, and behold, a white horse; and he that sat upon him was called Faithful and True, and in righteousness he doth judge and make war." With his own silent and nearly invisible "voice" the anonymous draftsman seems to have answered the central riddle of *The Husband's Message*—the sacred *geryne* present in the runes, who is the faithful and true Bridegroom himself.

Indeed, in the secret of *The Husband's Message* is concentrated

[38] Goldsmith, "The Enigma of *The Husband's Message*," p. 253.

[39] See the description of the seven "rare if not unique" drypoint incisions of the Exeter Book and their date, estimated by Meyer Schapiro as the second half of the eleventh century or the twelfth century, in Max Förster, "General Description of the Manuscript: 4. Ornamentation," in Chambers, Förster, and Flower, eds., *The Exeter Book of Old English Poetry* (photofacsimile ed.), p. 60.

[40] In ibid. these incised drawings have been entered, presumably individually by hand. The drawing of the horse and rider on fol. 123 of the facsimile is admirably faithful to the original. Nevertheless, the reduced line drawing given in this edition makes one or two very slight corrections based on the MS. I am grateful to Mrs. Audrey Erskine, of the Exeter Cathedral Library, for the opportunity to examine the Exeter Book against the facsimile on this very important matter.

the whole meaning of the celebration of Easter. The speech-bearing artifact, a piece of the Germanic yew tree of life, represents the mystery of the Eucharist, which manifests the Passion and Resurrection, the fulfillment of Scripture and the living Word all in One. The deepest *geryne* of the poem is that the Husband and his message are the same accomplished promise of salvation, the only persuasive rebuttal of the agonizing doubt of *The Wife's Lament*.[41] The apocalyptic drawing in the margin not only answers the riddle of *The Husband's Message* with a riddle of its own but also leads to the magnificent visionary finale of *The Easter Riddle*. This is the damaged poem called, with ironic aptness, *The Ruin*.

### *The Ruin*: Wondrous Destruction

The wife has made it clear in her lament that an ocean separates her from her exiled husband. Not only has he departed over the waves, but at the end of the poem he also hugs some far shore in his "dreary hall," by riddlic implication his ship. Alone on land and falsely accused like the apocryphal heroine Susanna, the wife hardly seems to be telling a purely Germanic story. In fact she is imprisoned in this life, while her husband has traveled the greatest possible distance from her, across the symbolic waters of death. In *The Husband's Message* he returns in mysterious form together with a human messenger. They urge the wife to follow across the sea when the cuckoo, bird of both joy and death, gives the sign. As the rich and powerful lord of his far-off kingdom, the husband makes a new promise that supersedes the Old Law and assures the couple's joy forever. In Germanic terms the wife is to leave her oak tree of mortality and sail to the magical voice that speaks to her from out of the yew, the wood of life. Words and images of double reference, such as *uht* 'midnight, nocturns,' *gebeot* 'promise, covenant,' or the oak tree of both Woden

---

[41] Anderson, "*The Husband's Message*," pp. 291–92, thinks of the poem as governed by a "rhetoric of persuasion" to deliver a message mainly of "assurance or reassurance."

and Susanna, infuse Germanic themes with secret allegorical
intent.

From their matching themes of law, the sea and voyages, and
even species of trees, *The Wife's Lament* and *The Husband's Message*
would seem to have been paired allegories when they were first
composed, probably in the eighth century. It is fairly easy to
guess how they were both paired and separated in the tenth-
century Exeter Book. While the great codex was being copied,
or at least not very long before, a Benedictine liturgist and re-
former appears to have conceived of the two poems as the begin-
ning and end of an ambitious Easter poem in riddlic form. In
the considerable space between the wife's false complaint and the
husband's comforting answer, perhaps originally parts of the
same dialogue poem, the didactic, devotional, and liturgical
middle of the Easter triduum was inserted. Various riddlic de-
vices throughout these middle poems contribute to the Easter
argument. A notable riddlic touch occurs in *Resignation* 97b–
104, where exile formulas of a ship and seafaring seem to in-
trude upon a devotional narrative, perhaps to "join" it to the ele-
giac framework of the entire Easter sequence. Repeated words
and phrases in adjacent poems, the ostensible legacy of oral
composition, also advance such bookish Easter themes as water
and light. Thus through texts of diverse genres the solver comes
to the Husband's timeless reinstatement on earth of his briefly
suspended promise to the Wife. An early graphic solver has also
riddled on the eternal faithfulness of the Husband in heaven. As
*The Ruin* opens, therefore, heaven and earth have once again
been joined by means of the accomplished Resurrection.

The text begins on the very bottom of folio 123b of the Exeter
Book and runs to just over the middle of folio 124b—a span of
forty-nine lines in modern editions. The rather poorly made ini-
tial wynn hardly does graphic justice to the meaning of the first
word: *Wrætlic* 'beautiful, wondrous.' A punctuated *m* rune be-
gins the seventeenth manuscript line of folio 124a, and addi-
tional raised points also mark off that entire line:

.  M . dreama full,      oþþæt þæt onwende      wyrd seo swiþe.[1]

[1] Besides the raised points on either side of the *M* rune (at the beginning of a

Perhaps by accident, perhaps to make a riddlic obstacle, the scribe did not clearly distinguish his runic *M* from the *d* rune of *The Husband's Message*. But of the *m* rune in *The Ruin* there can be no doubt: it forms the alliterating arsis of line 23b and is therefore generally given the value of its rune name, *monn* 'man.'[2] The text of *The Ruin* is otherwise unremarkable, without any immediate signs of riddlic purpose.

Nevertheless, *The Ruin* offers a singular physical challenge, for it is something of a ruin itself. By folio 124 the cruel accident to the last pages of the Exeter Book is severely felt. A gaping hole in the page interrupts *The Ruin* twice, once at lines 12–18 and again, even more unluckily, from line 42 to the end. Like the rest of the poem, the shreds of text around the hole include some rare and unique words—largely architectural details more or less enigmatically named. Among several other notable features of the poem, this unusual interest in architecture has caused some recent scholars to challenge the long-accepted view of *The Ruin* as an elegy.[3] The strange and often beautiful language of the poem also defies extensive restoration of its damaged parts.[4]

In addition to its lost lines the text presents one considerable

---

manuscript line), there is also a point, not shown here, at the end of the previous manuscript line.

[2] The ninth-century law code *Judicium Dei* 4.2.1. (in Liebermann, *Gesetze*, 1:409) glosses L *homo* with the *m* rune. See also Liebermann, *Gesetze*, 2:1, 141, under *Mann*.

[3] B. J. Timmer, "The Elegiac Mood in Old English Poetry," *ES* 24 (1942): 33, observes the unelegiac tone of *The Ruin*. An implicit redefinition of the genre of the poem is by Anne Thompson Lee, "*The Ruin*: Bath or Babylon?" *NM* 74 (1973): 443–55. The view of D. R. Howlett, "Two Old English Encomia," *ES* 57 (1976): 289–93, agrees explicitly with Lee's view. William C. Johnson, Jr., "*The Ruin* as Body-City Riddle," *PQ* 59 (1980): 397–411, thinks of the poem as a riddle on the "temple" of the human body but rejects the idea of the poem as allegory (p. 406).

[4] John C. Pope, "Palaeography and Poetry: Some Solved and Unsolved Problems in the Exeter Book," in M. B. Parkes and Andrew C. Watson, eds., *Medieval Scribes, Manuscripts, and Libraries: Essays Presented to N. R. Ker*, p. 42, also thinks of *The Ruin* as impossible to reconstruct. While I do not agree with Pope's remark that the scenery of the poem is full of "unpredictable particulars," I believe that its unusual language would prevent restoration.

editorial difficulty in the form of a doubtful manuscript reading at lines 3–4:

> Hrofas sind gehrorene,    hreorge torras,
> hrim geat torras berofen,    hrim on lime,

The repetitions on the same line of *torras* and *hrim*, probably scribal errors of some kind, are variously handled in scholarship. In line 4a the word *torras* can be fairly safely eliminated to regularize the meter; nevertheless, some early editors chose to read a noun *geat-torras* there.[5] Line 4b gives a regular verse of Sievers's type A, *hrim on lime* 'rime on mortar,' a puzzling detail unless it means that a great deal of mortar is exposed to the weather because the stones are thoroughly broken apart and scattered. But the word *hrim* in line 4a makes no sense, and some attempt, however uncertain, must be made to emend it. For paleographical reasons the best emendations are *hrun*, leading to *hrungeat* (for *hrunggeat*) '?rung gate,' '?barred gate,' or *hrin*, which suggests *hringeat* (*hringgeat*) '?ring gate.'[6] Both in the riddles specifically and in Old English poetry generally, *hring* is somewhat better established than *hrung*.[7] In this place, too, *hring* seems the more

---

[5] C. W. M. Grein, "Zur Textkritik der angelsächsischen Dichter," *Germania* 10 (1865): 422, proposed *hrungeat-torras* for MS *hrim geat torras*. His reading was later accepted by Wülcker. Even earlier, in *Bibliothek der angelsächsischen Poesie*, 1:296, Grein had emended to *hrimge edoras*. But vol. 2, p. 414, corrects to *hrungeat torras*.

[6] Grein first proposed *hrungeat* (i.e., *hrung-geat*; see n. 5 above). Friedrich Kluge, *Angelsächsisches Lesebuch*, 2d ed. (1897) and 3d ed. (1902), proposed *hringgeat*, and was followed by Levin L. Schücking, *Kleines angelsächsisches Dichterbuch*. For fuller details of older emendations of line 4a, see ASPR 3:364 n. on *Ruin* 4. Gary I. Rubin, "MS Integrity, Lines 3a–4b of *The Ruin*," *Neophil* 63 (1979): 297–99, also thoroughly reviews the various emendations of these lines but argues unconvincingly for retaining the MS reading by taking *geat* as pret. sing. of *geotan* 'to overwhelm' and reading all of line 4a as a hypermetric verse (however, of unlikely syntax and grammar).

[7] Old English *hrung* appears certainly only once in poetry, as dat. sing. *hrunge* in *Riddle 22* 10. On the other hand, *hring* appears several times, notably in a phrase *wopes hring*, of disputed meaning, in Cynewulfian texts. In the riddles, especially *Riddle 47* and *Riddle 58* (ASPR numbering 48 and 59), it is a favorite device for wordplay on 'ring' (circle) and 'ringing' (sound), and also a witty testi-

probable choice with the likelier meanings. It would make the first of several obscure references to circularity: the bow of an arched gate or (if riddlic logic as well as deceptive imagery is at work) the 'gate of a ring,' i.e., the entrance to a round courtyard or chamber, or 'gate (decorated) with rings,' an ornamented entrance to a city or building. The reason for these garbled lines cannot be known. The scribe might have been either careless or perplexed, vainly trying to turn the poet's obscurity into sense. *The Ruin* is, after all, an abstruse poem on the whole, full of arcane words and mystifying details.

With walls of stone and roofs of tile (*tigelum*, line 30), with the gnawing of time (*ældo undereotene*, line 6) and the presence of *baþu* 'baths' (lines 40b, 46b) and *stream hate/hate streamas* 'hot stream[s]' (lines 38b, 43b), the crumbled city of the poem is often thought to be Bath or some other fallen glory of Roman Britain.[8] Indeed, many images from the text—the red and gray stains of line 10, the bound or clamped stonework of lines 19–20, the many bath chambers of line 21, the red roof tiles of line 30, and above all the thermal streams and baths of the last lines—have been persuasively matched with the archaeological remains of Bath.[9] Yet, while the repeated word *baþu* perhaps even riddles on the Anglo-Saxon designations *Hat Baþu*, *æt Baþum*, and *Baðan*, the poem also seems to describe a more general, even ideological landscape.

More than one recent scholar has convincingly linked the im-

---

mony of "circular" riddlic argument. A fuller note on *hring* as a riddle word appears in my article "Two Spliced Riddles of the Exeter Book," pp. 59–60 and n. 13.

[8] Gareth W. Dunleavy, "A 'De Excidio' Tradition in the Old English Ruin?" *PQ* 38 (1959): 112–18, thinks of Chester. But Charles W. Kennedy, *Old English Elegies*, argues that the poem seems to refer to natural hot springs and therefore excludes all other places in Britain except Bath.

[9] A strong case for identifying *The Ruin* with Bath is made by Cecelia A. Hotchner, *Wessex and Old English Poetry, with Special Consideration of* The Ruin. See also the good review of scholarly identifications of *The Ruin* with Bath in Roy F. Leslie, ed., *Three Old English Elegies*, pp. 22–28. Karl P. Wentersdorf, "Observations on *The Ruin*," *MÆ* 66 (1977): 171–80, implicitly accepts Bath as well.

personal (and therefore unelegiac) voice of the poet, his tendency to shift from past to present, from dead city to living city and back again, and his special concern with architectural details and hot springs to the rigorous and well-known Classical genre *encomium urbis* 'praise of a city.'[10] Even those scholars who are inclined to view *The Ruin* as an expression of such native ideas as the Anglo-Saxon love for the hall do not entirely dismiss the striking parallels found in the sixth-century *De excidio Thoringiae* of Venantius Fortunatus.[11] But if it were not for the fact that the Anglo-Saxon poet's ruin has stone walls and decidedly un-English architecture, it might have been built by almost anyone. In line 2b the walls are simply called the work of *enta* 'giants,' a poetic hyperbole for 'heroes,' with no suggestion that they were either British or English or Roman. From the badly damaged end of

[10]The Anglo-Saxon names for Bath are given in Leslie, *Three Old English Elegies*, pp. 22–23 and nn. The best work connecting *The Ruin* with the tradition of *encomium urbis* is by Lee, "*The Ruin*: Bath or Babylon?" This study gives a detailed history of the *encomium urbis* from its Classical origins. *The Ruin* is also convincingly related to the *encomium urbis* by Howlett, "Two Old English Encomia," and Wentersdorf, "Observations on *The Ruin*," p. 173 and n. 10.

[11]Kathryn Hume, "The 'Ruin Motif' in Old English Poetry," *Anglia* 94 (1976): 339–60, thinks of a body of Anglo-Saxon ruin poetry generated from "the image-cluster proceeding from the value- and idea-complex of the hall" (p. 341). While an Anglo-Saxon poet's love for the hall might well have given the Latin *encomium urbis* poetry a special appeal, Hume's attempt to trace *The Ruin* mainly to ideas in northern vernacular literatures is not very convincing, since (*a*) *The Ruin* is not only about a single building but also about a *burg* 'city' (line 49) of 'many a mead hall' (line 23); (*b*) the poem is considered together with other Old English "ruin poetry" which it broadly resembles in theme, but in tone hardly at all; (*c*) the architectural details in the poem do not match what is known of the hall: the Ruin is of stone, and Johnson, "*The Ruin* as Body-City Riddle," pp. 404–405, finds no resemblance, for example, between the Anglo-Saxon hall and the references to rings and wires in lines 19–20. The likeness of *The Ruin* to Fortunatus's *De excidio* is first noted by Alois Brandl, "Venantius Fortunatus und die ags. Elegien 'Wanderer' and 'Ruine,'" *Archiv* 139 (1919): 84. Wentersdorf, "Observations on *The Ruin*," p. 173 n. 10, cites J. D. A. Ogilvy, *Books Known to the English, 597–1066*, p. 140, as proof that Fortunatus's works were familiar to the Anglo-Saxons. Dunleavy, "A 'De Excidio' Tradition in the Old English *Ruin*?" gives Fortunatus a prominent place in a *de excidio* genre which might have influenced the Anglo-Saxon poet.

the poem we know only that the ruin, or something associated with it, is a *cynelic þing* 'kingly thing.' The identity of the royal builder, if it was once given in the damaged lines, in any case does not appear in the text as we have it. Throughout the middle lines the fallen city, its dead inhabitants, their departed splendor, and the time of their departure are relentlessly generalized, never particularly described.[12] The poet's subject seems to be not only a literal ruin exposed to physical time and elements but also a riddlic ruin to be exposed to the mind's eye.

As mysterious as the generality of *The Ruin* is the ambiguity of its mood. On the one hand, the theme is the importance of men and the destruction of their mightiest works, and these ideas are suitably dressed in words and images broadly like those of ubi sunt poetry. On the other hand, *The Ruin* yields not the pure sadness of elegy but a melancholy tempered by the apprehension of beauty and wonder.[13] The opening verse, *Wrætlic is þes wealstan*, has exclamatory syntax like the marveling about the Holy Sepulcher in line 19 of *The Descent into Hell*: *Open wæs þæt eorðærn* 'Open was the earth vault!' The similarity will help confirm the truest identity of the ruin.

[12] Daniel G. Calder, "Perspective and Movement in *The Ruin*," *NM* 72 (1971): 445; Stanley B. Greenfield, *A Critical History of Old English Literature*, p. 215; and Alain Renoir, "The Old English *Ruin*: Contrastive Structure and Affective Impact," in Martin Green, ed., *The Old English Elegies*, pp. 148–73, observe in somewhat different terms that time in *The Ruin* is in effect abstracted by means of constant narrative shifts from remote past to dramatic present. For reasons which will become obvious, I cannot agree with Renoir that geography, poetic voice, action, and story are also abstracted away. Instead, I read all of these elements (with the possible exception of voice) as elements of the fundamental riddlic allegory of the poem.

[13] Lee, "*The Ruin*: Bath or Babylon?" pp. 452–54, observes that (unlike elegy) *The Ruin* seems to end "on an appreciative note." Edward B. Irving, Jr., "Image and Meaning in the Elegies," in Robert P. Creed, ed., *Old English Poetry: Fifteen Essays*, p. 154, thinks of *Wrætlic* 'wonderful, marvelous' as "inviting our admiration with the very first word." Howlett, "Two Old English Encomia," pp. 291–92, notes that, whereas all the other Old English elegies "advertise themselves as such" with conventional words for sadness, *The Ruin* expresses what Leslie (*Three Old English Elegies*, pp. 28–29) calls "awe and approval" all the way through, not just after line 21 as Leslie himself contends.

The wall stone of *The Ruin* is *wrætlic* 'wondrous, marvelous' in yet another way. It is also 'curious, to be wondered at,' for it has had both its builders and its *betend* 'restorers' (line 28b), men who, like the walls they once built, have long since fallen to the ground in the repeated word *crungon* (lines 25, 28).[14] The mention of restorers implies that the walls have toppled more than once, an unusual observaton for a poet thinking merely of a literal ruin. But the scriptural (and therefore allegorical) ruins of Babel, Babylon, and Babylon Magna (Rev. 16–18), already proposed in scholarship, do not have restorers.[15] This odd detail matches instead the composite history of the preeminent ruin of Scripture, the Temple of Jerusalem, destroyed and rebuilt in the Old Testament and mourned in the Gospels by Christ himself, who expects a second razing that will not leave one stone upon another (Mark 13:1–2; Luke 19:44, 21:5–6). The frequent reading of *wigsteal* in line 27 as a variant of *weohsteal* 'temples, sanctuaries' thus seems to make especially good riddling sense, not only as a literal reference to the temple of Sulis Minerva at Bath but also as a sly echo of the prophecy of destruction in Amos 7:9: "The high places of the idol [*idoli*: Vulgate] shall be laid waste, and the sanctuaries of Israel made desolate."[16]

[11] Renoir, "Contrastive Structure," p. 159, notes that in lines 25 and 28 both men and their walls *crungon* 'have fallen' without entertaining riddlic possibilities in the echoed word. This study concludes that the ruin is ultimately both the men and their walls, which are one and the same.

[15] Hugh Keenan, "The Ruin as Babylon," *TSL* 11 (1966): 109–17, argues that earthly Babylon is the subject of the poem, whose last lines tell of God's destruction of that city by flood because of its wickedness. I agree with Calder, "Perspective and Movement," p. 442, that such a reading is doubtful. Hume, "The 'Ruin Motif' in Old English Poetry," pp. 341, 343, suggests Babel (Gen. 11:1–9) and Babylon (Isa. 13:19–22; Jer. 50–51), which stands for the world, the "Babylon Magna of the Apocalypse (Rev. 16–18)." But unless the material lost from its damaged passages would radically change its tone, *The Ruin* appears to express wonder, not vengeance or lamentation, at the destruction it describes.

[16] Wentersdorf, "Observations on *The Ruin*," p. 174, suggests this double reference to Bath and Scripture and reads MS *wigsteal* of line 27 as *weohsteal* 'temples,' Lee, "*The Ruin*: Bath or Babylon?" p. 450, also translates *wigsteal* as 'temples.' Lee's authority, and perhaps also Wentersdorf's, is Leslie, *Three Old English Ele-*

With the ruin thus identified, the many obscurities of the poem emerge as riddling devices inspired by Scripture. The riddler's words *hund cnea* (line 8), usually taken to lament the passing of a hundred generations, look back instead to the time of the old rebuilding of the Temple as the prophet Ezra describes it. Beginning with the name of Sheshbazzar Prince of Judah (Ezra 1:8) and continuing through a list of ninety-nine more names (Ezra 2), the prophet remembers the "legitimate houses of Israel," the implied rebuilders of the Temple. Whether or not *hund cnea* marks the envisioned passing of a hundred generations of time, the same words, with *cnea* as a riddle word meaning 'houses, clans' as *cneomaga* means 'kinsman,' precisely count Ezra's list of tribes. Thus the departed *hund cnea* of lines 8–9 secretly become the same people as the fallen *betend* 'restorers' of line 28, whose passing probably confirms the vision of Amos as the source of line 27. As this network of clues for the Temple begins to spread, the surviving words of line 19 seem to hint of a riddler's boast like the closing of *Wulf and Eadwacer*: like the ruin, the poem also shows the subtlety of a *mod* 'mind' which *myne swiftne gebrægd* 'wove a swift design,' an account of several ruins of the same great scriptural monument with one set of words.[17]

All the most puzzling words and ideas of *The Ruin* thus speak

---

*gies*, p. 73 n. on line 27, which, however, does not clearly argue for *weoh* 'idol' in the compound as opposed to the more general reading of *wig* 'war.' The matter is not resolvable from Scripture, since the passage in Amos seems to support one reading, the warfare of the Apocalypse (Rev. 19) the other. The drypoint horse and rider in the margin of *The Husband's Message*, if also taken from Rev. 19, might indicate that the medieval graphic riddler understood this disputed word as *wigsteal* 'places of battle,' and this reading would fit the allegory of the beleaguered mortal body (like the lamenting wife's) here proposed. Leslie's glossary gives 'bastions.' All these readings seem to fit the literal and allegorical themes of *The Ruin* almost equally well. I have decided on the reading 'temples' because of its very attractive pun on the central riddlic theme.

[17] This mind is perhaps to be read as the *wyrd* 'Fate' of line 1, which Renoir, "Contrastive Structure," p. 156, calls a "deliberate force" in the poem. Here, as sometimes elsewhere in Old English poetry (including perhaps even *Beowulf*), *wyrd* seems ultimately to mean the plan or design of God.

literally of Bath but allegorically of the Temple in its various scriptural ages and meanings. The language of the opening lines fits the total second destruction as Jesus foreknows it: there is a *wealstan* without walls (line 1), and much *lim* 'mortar' to be envisioned on the exposed joints of the completely scattered stones. The enclosing wall of the later lines (*weal eall befeng*, line 39) refers not only to the defenses of a city, which are leveled to their foundations, but also to the enemy breastworks to be thrown up around Jerusalem, as Jesus foretells in Luke 19:43: "Days will come upon you [Jerusalem] when your enemies encircle you with a rampart." Similarly, the *stanhofu* 'stone courts' of line 38, the height and width (*stea[þ]*, *geap*) of line 11, the many rooms and bathhouses and high gables of lines 21–22 are riddlic devices, seen in the literal Roman ruin but also imagined from the plans and measurements of the original Temple (1 Kings 6–7) and from the prophet Ezekiel's vision of the restored one (Ezek. 40–46).

The unique word *weallwalan* (line 20), perhaps the riddler's own coinage on the analogy of such a word as *wyrtwala* 'root stem,' matches an architectural detail in the Roman ruins of Bath. The *weallwalan* of the poem are in some way circular, 'bound . . . together with wires, wondrously shaped . . . into rings' (lines 19–20), possibly like the iron-clamped columns which once stood in the baths themselves.[18] If, therefore, the word *weallwalan* means 'wall stems,' i.e., columns or pillars, it corresponds variously also to the many pilasters in Ezekiel's visionary Temple, to the 'hooks and bars of the columns' (Vulgate: *capita cum coelaturis*) around the ancient Ark of the Covenant (Exod. 27:10–11, 38:10), and perhaps also to the "gold chains' and 'bands' of Solomon's Temple (1 Kings 6:21, 34).[19] These bib-

---

[18] Leslie, *Three Old English Elegies*, pp. 25–26.

[19] Ibid., p. 72 n. on line 20, credits Grein *Sprachschatz der angelsächsischen Dichter*, with first suggesting the parallel of *wyrtwalan*. However, Leslie thinks Grein's gloss of *wyrtwalan* as 'radices' "suggests the meaning 'foundations of walls.'" But Alistair Campbell, *Addenda and Corrigenda to An Anglo-Saxon Dictionary*, under *wal*, cites *Beowulf* 1030–31, where *wala* (MS *walan*) seems to mean 'ridge or comb inlaid with wires running on top of the helmet from front to

lical details answer better to the idea of 'wondrously' bound pillars than anything yet discovered at Bath. Moreover, like such wires and columns, the *baþu* (lines 40, 46) and the *hringmere* 'circular sea' (line 45) have multiple scriptural reference to both the bronze laver (*labrum æneum*) of the Dwelling of the Ark (Exod. 38 : 8) and the great bronze circular sea (*mare*) of the first Temple (1 Kings 7 : 23–26).

By far the hardest of these architectural riddles is the destroyed roof of lines 30–31. Of the many attempts to match these lines with the ruins at Bath, the best, perhaps, reads *hrostbeages [h]rof* of line 31a as an allusion to the semicircular barrel vaulting from a second- or third-century reconstruction. This guess would establish a literal reason for the word *betend* 'restorers' in line 28.[20] The fallen tiles, a commodity in the rubble at Bath, do not appear in the biblical accounts of the Temple. However, a shifted reference, to another part of the Temple's "roof," seems to lurk in the hapax legomenon *teaforgeaþa* of line 30. From the analogous *horngeap* of *Beowulf* 82 and *Andreas* 668, *teaforgeaþa* may be read as a participial adjective of the weak declension though without an article, a fairly common feature of po-

back.' Campbell refers to Herbert Dean Meritt, *Old English Glosses (A Collection)*, p. 46 (42, 2), who gives *wala* as 'strip, band, ornament consisting of strips.' Such meanings suggest that *wyrtwala* meant not just 'radix' but 'root stem' and that *weallwala* is a riddle word, perhaps even a nonce word, meaning 'wall stem,' i.e., 'pillar.' The prominence of pillars and pilasters in biblical descriptions of the Temple lends some thematic weight to this guess.

[20] The suggested reference to the barrel vaulting of the reconstruction at Bath is by Wentersdorf, "Observations on *The Ruin*," pp. 176–77, who, however, does not argue the possible application of the word *betend*. Leslie, *Three Old English Elegies*, p. 74 n. on line 31, reads *hrostbeag* and *[h]rof*, and I follow the latter reading to show that I do not take MS *rof* to mean 'bold.' Otherwise the word *rof* could stand unemended as a late spelling of *hrof*. ASPR 3 reads *hrostbeages hrof*. W. S. Mackie, ed., *The Exeter Book, Part II, Poems IX–XXXII*, like many earlier editors, follows the MS reading *hrost beages hrof*. For Bath, the literal ruin in the poem, the usual understanding of *hrostbeag* as some detail of the roof structure, such as the vaulting, is perhaps correct. But the allegorical identity of the ruin has suggested to me that *hringmere* and *hrostbeag* could also be riddlic references to the same object, not the roof but rather something sheltered under it.

etry.[21] The elements of the compound are *teafor*, dialect *tiver* 'tile red,' and *geap*, related to ON *gapa* 'to gape' and to the unique OE *gopes* in *Riddle 48* 3.[22] If *teaforgeapa* means 'tiver-gaped,' i.e., 'red-spanned,' a probable matchup for the word emerges from a detail of Solomon's Temple (1 King's 6:9): "When the temple was built to its full height, it was roofed in with rafters and boards of cedar." Tiver, a familiar hue among the ruins at Bath, would

[21] Wentersdorf, "Observations on *The Ruin*," pp. 175–76, gives a good review of the various grammatical solutions for lines 30–31a but himself reads *teaforgeapa* as a nom. sing. subject of *sceadeð*, which then would not need to be emended to *sceadað*, as has frequently been done. My reading takes [h]rof, the widely accepted emendation of MS *rof*, as the sing. subject of *sceadeð*, also without emendation, and *teaforgeapa* as the participial adj. modifying *hrof*: 'from its tiles the tiver-spanned roof of the roost ring parts.' On the suggested meaning and reference of *hrostbeages* (MS *hrost beages*) see the discussion below.

[22] The *OED* cites *tiver* as sb. dial. 'a red colouring matter,' and vb. dial. trans. 'to mark or colour with tiver.' Henry Sweet, *A Student's Dictionary of Anglo-Saxon*, gives *teafor* as 'red pigment, vermilion.' Joseph Wright, ed., *The English Dialect Dictionary*, gives *tiver* sb. 'red ochre used for marking sheep,' and this authority is cited in *ASD*. Thomas Wright, *Old English Vocabularies*, ed. Richard Wülcker, 1:46, 74, 1:75, 20 glosses *read teafor* and *teafor* as 'minium.' Campbell, *Addenda and Corrigenda*, reads *teaforgeapa* as a noun 'arch of red stone' but notes that "others regard [this word] as [an] adj. *red and curving*." *Riddle 48* 3 has the words *þurh gopes hond*, where *gopa* designates the aider and abettor of a silent and normally earthbound destroyer. The solutions for this riddle are so various that they are ultimately "uncertain" (Craig Williamson, ed., *The Old English Riddles of the Exeter Book*, pp. 289–91). I think the riddle is about "torchlight" taken from its place on the wall or floor and misused to loot and burn, possibly by a Viking who is wittily named (by borrowing his own ON word *gapa* 'to gape, stare stupidly,' etc.) as a 'gaper,' i.e., a staring lout or fool. The adjective *geap* 'wide,' from the same root and found in line 11 of *The Ruin*, would then mean 'spread apart, spanned' in adjectives of architectural reference such as *horngeap* and (as I believe, in disagreement with Campbell) *teaforgeap*. Whatever detail of the ruins at Bath might have been 'red-spanned,' *teaforgeapa . . . [h]rof*, if applied to the Temple, best fits the (red-hued) cedar spars and beams of the ceiling ('roof' in a riddling sense), that is, the timbers which 'spread apart' the standing walls. The biblical narrative states (1 Kings 6:9) that the ceilings of Solomon's Temple were finished with boards of cedar. The poet's shift from exterior to interior perspective would appear to be the kind of trick used more than once in the Old English riddles, for example, in the *fæst* 'sealed off' island of *Wulf and Eadwacer* 5. See the discussion of that poem in Part One above.

also make a workable riddle on the color of cedarwood and would shift the mind's eye from the outside roof of the literal ruin to the inside [h]rof 'ceiling' (line 31) of the Temple. Thus, whereas an eighth-century Anglo-Saxon poet could not possibly have seen wooden structures at Bath, he could easily have imagined the roof timbers that once sheltered the wonders both of Bath and of the Temple itself. A visionary ruin at the heart of the poem not only allows such otherwise impossible details as wooden beams but also accounts for the poet's impersonal and unelegiac tone.[23]

In imitation of Scripture the allegorical ruin appears to focus the mind on the interior of the house of God. Thus the compound hrostbeag (line 31) literally 'roost ring,' besides perhaps alluding to the roof vaulting at Bath, might also describe an even more central place in the allegorical ruin. The great round sea in Solomon's Temple rests on the backs of twelve cast figures of oxen (1 Kings 7:25). In riddlic logic this elaborate stand would make a properly disguised 'roost' for the beag 'ring' of the bath itself. Thus the word hrostbeag of line 31 might easily designate the same scriptural object as the hringmere of line 45. Both words together, along with the most probable emendation and reading of hri[n]geat as 'ring gate,' i.e., 'gate of a ring' (line 4), appear to disclose a riddlic circular 'bath' which 'roosts' on a stand above the ground. Such an object would resemble more closely the great bath of the Temple than the round pool at Bath, which in any case belonged to the frigidarium rather than the thermal system of the Roman baths.[24] With its implied biblical affinities the

[23] The objection to the ruin as a wooden structure is offered by Wentersdorf, "Observations on The Ruin," p. 176. There is no need to argue, as Hume does ("The 'Ruin Motif'," p. 353) that the poet shows no personal grief because he is thinking of a city, "hence a relatively large and impersonal" thing. Leslie, Three Old English Elegies, pp. 26–28, 34–36, suggests an early-eighth-century date for the poem on (confessedly slender) linguistic evidence and on the probable state of the ruins at Bath during the eighth century. An eighth-century date would also fit the probable influence of Bede's allegorical treatise De Templo on this poem.

[24] Barry Cunliffe, The Roman Baths: A Guide to the Baths and Roman Museum,

*hringmere* in *The Ruin*, perhaps also the same as the *hrostbeag*, seems to play on the idea of a baptismal font, the likely end and source of the waters that have flowed especially through the middle poems of *The Easter Riddle*. As a whole, the disguised allegorical ruin appears to be an edifice in the poet's mind, built from the long scriptural history of the house of God but including also the Church of Anglo-Saxon times. The literal ruin, almost surely a portrayal of Bath influenced by the tradition of the *encomium urbis*, seems to serve as a riddlic diversion from the deeper truth.[25]

In comparison to the hard lines about the crumbled roof, the remaining enigmas of *The Ruin* have somewhat plainer echoes from Scripture. The lost glory of the city and the departed splendor of its ancient inhabitants (lines 32b–37) recall both the abundant gold surrounding the Ark of the Covenant and the riches of the several temples: the magnificence of Solomon's Temple and bejeweled throne (1 Kings 6:7), the gold and silver returned to the Temple by Sheshbazzar at the restoration (Ezra 5:14–15), and the collections of precious stones (*eorcanstan*, line 36) in the Temple of Jesus' time (Luke 21:5–6). The one *stream* of line 38 and the plural *streamas* of line 43 correspond to the stream of Ezekiel's vision (Ezek. 47), a river which issues from beneath the foundations of the Temple, divides into three branches, and gradually rises beyond wading depth until the prophet cannot cross. Earlier, toward the end of *The Descent into Hell*, the Easter riddler has already made Ezekiel's river into the Jordan, which not all land dwellers could swim through.

Bound to the previous manuscript poems in a single allegorical purpose, *The Ruin* can take several other such backward glances through *The Easter Riddle*, and through scriptural his-

---

pp. 18–20 (schematic maps of the baths), 21. There is, of course, no guarantee that the thermal system could be distinguished from the *frigidarium* in the perplexing eighth-century rubble at the site.

[25] The general scholarly doubt of ever knowing the authorial intention of *The Ruin* is perhaps most directly stated by Lee, "*The Ruin*: Bath or Babylon?" p. 435. I think of *The Ruin* as a kind of *encomium urbis* on the New Jerusalem.

tory, particularly at those places where God has been seen to dwell in men. The long-dead *beorn* 'man' of *The Ruin*, imagined in shining *wighyrstum* 'war gear' (lines 32b–34), is the fallen hero of past ages who also recalls the warrior girded in the armor of faith—just such a warrior as John the Baptist awaiting the ascent from hell. The heroes of *The Ruin* were once *wlonc* 'proud' (line 34a), the word used of the men and women sharing the kiss of peace in *Riddle 30b*. Just as the ancient city dwellers were *wingal* 'elated from wine' (line 34a), their riddlic counterparts the Apostles seemed drunk when at Pentecost they were visited with "the spirit poured out on mankind" (Acts 2:13–17). The allegorical 'wine' once found in *meodoheall monig* 'many a mead hall' of the ruined city thus becomes the drink poured *ofer meodu[-bence]* in *The Husband's Message*. Similarly, the baths of the ruin once gave *hat on hreþre* 'heat in the heart' (line 41a), as the spreading Light of *Homiletic Fragment II* first shone *beorht on br[eostum]* of Mary and then penetrated the hearts of all the faithful as the Easter Fire of *Riddle 30b*.

But in the dramatic present time of *The Ruin* the hot streams are empty, just as the fires of *Judgment Day* are imagined to be cooled. *The Ruin*, then, is more than just an allegory of Doomsday, for it closes *The Easter Riddle* with a genuine celestial promise.[26] As a recent reading of line 31b also suggests, the poet imagines himself in a present moment when *hryre wong gecrong* 'the place,' or even 'the world,' has toppled along with its 'corruption,' perhaps a fleeting allusion to the fall of Babylon in Rev. 17–18.[27] But in line 41b the poet again looks backward

[26] Kjell Meling, "Cruciform Runes in the Manuscripts of Some Old English Poems" (Ph.D. diss., SUNY/Binghamton, 1972), pp. 218–34, argues elaborately that *The Ruin* is a Doomsday poem. M. J. Swanton, "*The Wife's Lament* and *The Husband's Message*: A Reconsideration," *Anglia* 82 (1964): 284, also speculates that *The Ruin* might be a poem about the Last Days.

[27] Wentersdorf, "Observation on *The Ruin*," pp. 177–78, rightly observes that if line 31b begins a new clause *wong* must be the masc. sing. subject of *gecrong*. Reading *hryre* as instrumental, he translates the line 'the place fell (or: was ruined) by decay' to emphasize ruin by a gradual process, probably weather instead of violence. But the references to *woldagas* (line 25), a probable allusion to

in imaginary time to memorialize the baths, presumably the earthly waters made warm with the power of baptism, as *hyðelic* 'fitting, convenient.' For after 'mighty Providence' has taken all bold men and their works (lines 24–27), the faithful promise of the Husband will still remain.

As the marginal *invisibilium* by the graphic solver of *The Husband's Message* tells, the mixed wonder and sadness of *The Ruin* is borrowed from the mixed terror of Doomsday and joy of salvation, the paradox considered at great length in *Judgment Day I*. From the celestial vision of this mystery in the book of Revelation *The Ruin* borrows image upon image, thought after thought.

The 'broad domain' of earth (line 37b), the Babylon of Revelation in the widest sense, has fallen in the *woldagas* 'days of plague' poured upon the world in Rev. 18:4–8. In *The Ruin* 22, *heresweg micel* 'a great noise of armies,' probably the imagined clamor of the Apocalypse (Rev. 18:11ff.), has died away. Treasures of dead men and their wasted homeland, many of the same riches that shall perish with Babylon (Rev. 18), have vanished in *The Ruin* 35–36. In line 42a the unwritten but grammatically necessary 'they' cannot be surely identified because of the damaged lines. After the still-legible words *Leton geotan* some missing words probably referred to the joyful and 'convenient' pouring of life-giving waters in heaven (Rev. 21:6, 22:1, 17), for the remaining scraps of the last lines seem to return to the spirit of the word *wrætlic* which opens the poem—not the horror of

---

the blood and boil plagues of God's wrath in Rev. 16, and to *heresweg micel* 'great noise of armies' (line 22) suggest that *hryre* might be a dat. of accompaniment, the ruinous decadence that attends the Apocalypse. Grein, *Sprachschatz*, reads *wong* as the acc. object of *gecrong*, whose subject would then be [*h*]*rof* in line 31a: 'the roof of the roost ring, broken to mounds, crumbled the place by means of ruin' (Grein). The unlikely tautology of *hryre* as instr. aside, Grein's reading is possible only if *teaforgeapa*, line 30a, is taken as the subject of *sceadeð* in line 30b. But parallels in *geap* (*The Ruin* 11) and *horngeap* (*Beowulf* 82 and *Andreas* 668) suggest that *teaforgeapa* is an adj. (see discussion and n. 21 above). I agree with Keenan ("The Ruin as Babylon") that the world as Babylon receives a passing glance or two in the poem, but not that Babylon or Babylon Magna is the central ruin of the text.

final destruction so much as the wonder that follows it, the sight of heaven itself.

The history of the earthly Temple in *The Ruin*, like the poet's model in Revelation, would thus have culminated in a vision of heavenly Jerusalem. This vision would have been available to any eighth-century poet who knew Bede's allegorical treatise *De Templo*, wherein the literal and historical Temple of Solomon attains fourfold significance as the (allegorical) church, the (tropological) body of Christ, the (anagogical) joys (of the glorified body) in heaven. Like the buildings of the ancient Temple, the heavenly city is measured with a rod, and the celestial riches are described in familiar earthly terms (Rev. 21 : 15–21). The streets of heaven are of gold, the walls of many kinds of precious stones, the *wrætlic wealstan* and *eorcanstan* of *The Ruin*. The *heresweg* of Revelation does not stop with the din of battle but continues in the loud praise of God by his victorious hosts. Ezekiel's threatening river and the apocalyptic pouring of blood shall pass, and in place of them life-giving crystal waters are seen to issue from beneath God's throne. The images of *The Ruin* also signify these heavenly things. Once, when the text was whole, the streams at the end of the poem might have had the consummate warmth of the blood of redemption. Without much doubt the words *burg* 'city' and *cynelic þing* 'kingly thing,' lucky survivals amid the ruined final lines, played on the first and last royal builders of the Temple, Solomon and God.

At the center of the New Jerusalem, however, is to be imagined only God himself: there is no temple except the Lord himself and the Lamb (Rev. 21 : 22–23). God becomes, as the Husband's messenger has partly said, the place *ofer eald gebeot*, the Temple of infinite sacrifice. In *The Ruin* the *wrætlic wealstan* and *eorcanstan* are finally none other than Christ, who is also called *weallstan*, *goldhord*, and *eorcanstan* in the Exeter Book poem that bears his name.[28] He is the Ruin of all ruins, the once-rejected

---

[28] Leslie, *Three Old English Elegies*, p. 75 n. on line 36, remarks on the "oddity" of the singular word *eorcanstan* as pointed out by J. E. Cross, "Notes on Old English Texts," *Neophil* 39 (1955): 204–205. "Oddity" is the right word, for *eor-*

cornerstone (Luke 20:17; 1 Pet. 2:6–7) and riddlic Temple of flesh that was destroyed and rebuilt in three days.[29] They are the three days in the symbolical and liturgical journey of *The Easter Riddle*.

To faithful "hearers" such as the Husband's messenger, the open tomb, an occasion for exclamation in *The Descent into Hell*, is the gateway to the *wrætlic wealstan* which evokes similar wonder in *The Ruin*. The ruin of all mortal things will mean the end of death as well, when once and for all the restored Bridegroom will summon Ecclesia his Bride (Rev. 18:7–9, 21:2–3, 22:17). The last two runic texts of *The Easter Riddle* invite contemplation of that wedding day, when all obedient flesh becomes *M. dreama full* 'M[an] full of joys.' Then, as perhaps the odd punctuation of both the *m* rune and its manuscript line was intended to show, *wyrd seo swiþe* 'Fate the strong' (line 24b) will be complete for men. The long exile of the Wife's *eald eorðsele*, her weary temple of mortal flesh, will be no more, for the treasures promised in *The Husband's Message* and the ruin of the mortal body will be one and the same happiness.[30] The self-contained answer of the

---

*canstan* and *wealstan*, both singular, are riddle words for the precious "building stone" of the New Jerusalem. In riddling terms this material is the glorified flesh of Christ and his faithful followers. For the poetic use of *weallstan* in apparent reference to Roman ruins, see Leslie, p. 67 n. on line 1. On *weallstan*, *eorcanstan*, and *goldhord* as metaphors for Christ in *Christ* 2, 787, and 1195, see E. G. Stanley, "Old English Poetic Diction and the Interpretation of *The Wanderer*, *The Seafarer*, and *The Penitent's Prayer*," *Anglia* 73 (1956): 424, 431. Here, as elsewhere in the riddles, certain prominent images can be found again in earlier texts of the Exeter Book. For a similar matching of words, images, and themes in *Riddles 42/43* and in the Guthlac poems, see my article "Two Spliced Riddles of the Exeter Book," pp. 66–69.

[29] This scriptural riddle of Christ as Temple is found in Matt. 26:61, 27:40; Mark 14:58, 15:29; John 2:19–21; and (without reference to the three-day rebuilding period) Acts 6:14.

[30] Thus the "shock" of proceeding abruptly from the promised wealth and splendor of *The Husband's Message* to the destruction of *The Ruin* becomes, as Renoir has surmised ("Constrastive Structure," pp. 155–56), a deliberately arranged effect. But in my view that effect belongs first to *The Easter Riddle* specifically and only incidentally to the Exeter Book as a whole.

eighth-century *Ruin*, as well as the central figure of the great tenth-century *Easter Riddle* of the Exeter Book, is *M*, 'Man,' a creature now ruined by death, but heir through Christ the God-Man to a fullness of joys. This is the hidden divinity toward which the solver is urged to strive. And to find that wisdom, readers of the Easter Riddler's day would have had to do much the same thing as we: playfully abandon some of their firmest notions about the forms, genres, and subjects of their traditional poetry.

THE EASTER RIDDLE

# The Texts

*The Wife's Lament*
*Judgment Day I*
*Resignation*
*The Descent into Hell*
*Almsgiving*
*Pharaoh*
*The Lord's Prayer I*
*Homiletic Fragment II*
*Riddle 30b*
*The Husband's Message*
*The Ruin*

# [THE WIFE'S LAMENT]

   Ic þis giedd wrece    bi me ful geomorre,
   minre sylfre sið.   Ic þæt secgan mæg
   hwæt ic yrmþa gebad    siþþan ic up weox,
   niwes oþþe ealdes,   no ma þonne nu.
5  A ic wite wonn    minra wræcsiþa.
   Ærest min hlaford gewat    heonan of leodum
   ofer yþa gelac;   hæfde ic uhtceare
   hwær min leodfruma    londes wære.
     Ða ic me feran gewat    folgað secan,
10  wineleas wræcca,    for minre weaþearfe.
     Ongunnon þæt þæs monnes    magas hycgan
   þurh dyrne geþoht,   þæt hy todældon unc,
   þæt wit gewidost   in woruldrice
   lifdon laðlicost,   ond mec longade.
15  Het mec hlaford min   her heard niman.
   Ahte ic leofra lyt    on þissum londstede,
   holdra freonda.   Forþon is min hyge geomor.

Note: As in *Riddle 1*, the established scholarly titles and separate line numbering of the poems in the Easter Riddle have been retained.

3: *weox*. Followed by ASPR 3. W. S. Mackie, ed., *The Exeter Book, Part II, Poems IX–XXXII* (hereafter cited as Mackie), and Roy F. Leslie, ed., *Three Old English Elegies: The Wife's Lament, The Husband's Message, The Ruin* (hereafter cited as Leslie), emend to [*a*]*weox*.

6: ASPR 3 and Leslie show a paragraph division here. Mackie, following the MS, shows none.

9: A raised point followed by the small capital of *Ða* gives the first paragraph division in the MS. Thus the wife appears to begin her story with what she conceives to be the alpha and omega of her endless miseries. The first clue to the falsity of her thinking therefore seems to be the scribe's work.

10: *wrecca*. Followed by Mackie. Leslie and ASPR 3 give *wræcca*.

11: In the MS a raised point after *weaþearfe* and the small capital of *Ongunnon* isolate lines 9–10 as the second paragraph. The wife's legal maneuver, described as *folgað secan*, thus becomes a distinct step in her narrative.

15: *her heard*. MS *her*/*heard*, separated by the end of a MS line. Thus older editors, not wishing to place alliterative stress on *her*, variously emended to *hearg*,

# [THE WIFE'S LAMENT]

I'll recite this song of myself most sad,
a tale of my own. Then I can tell
what sorrows I've suffered since I grew up,
new ones and old ones, no more than right now.
5  I know always the woe of my wanderings in exile.
First my lord fled hence from the land,
over the welling of waves; I had worry in darkness
where my liege lord on land would be.
   So I left to go plead for my rightful place
10  as patronless outcast, in my piteous need.
   Then the former man's kinsmen began to conspire
with secret scheming so that they might divide us,
so that farthest apart in the world we lived
in utmost agony, and I ached with longing.
15  My overlord told me to take up a home here.
I had few loved ones in this plot of land,
loyal defenders. This is why my mind is downcast.

---

*hearh*, etc., and read the two words as a compound *heargeard, herheard.* Mackie
reads *her heard* and translates *her heard niman* 'be taken here.' ASPR 3 reads
*herheard.* Leslie emends to *her eard* and in his note argues cogently for stress on
*her*, as well as for *heard* either in scribal error for *eard* or as unetymological inser-
tion of *h* before words beginning in a vowel. This phenomenon in fact produces
the spelling *heard* for *eard* once in Anglo-Saxon law (see Felix Liebermann, *Die
Gesetze der Angelsachsen* , 2 : 1, 59, under *eard*). Leslie thus thinks, as I do, of *eard
niman* 'to take up one's abode,' which he finds in Ps. 131 of the Paris Psalter, and
also in *Christ* 61–63. Heinrich Leo, *Angelsächsisches Glossar*, p. 74, 4, gives two ci-
tations from *Genesis*; and C. W. M. Grein, *Sprachschatz der angelsächsischen Dichter*,
gives an instance of *eard niman* in Ps. 64 : 8. There is little doubt that the off verse
means *her eard niman* 'to take up a home here.' Because the spelling *heard* for *eard*
is recorded elsewhere, I have retained the MS reading, which might be not a mis-
take but a kind of riddle on *heard* and *eard.* Leslie objects to the unusual b verse
alliteration of *her heard*, but perhaps the reader was supposed to discover that the
*h* on *heard* was not to be pronounced.

   17–18: Some editions, notably ASPR 3, coordinate *forþon* . . . *ða* 'thus is
my mind sad, because,' etc. But the raised point after *geomor* in the MS and the

Ða ic me ful gemæcne    monnan funde
heardsæligne,    hygegeomorne,
20  mod miþendne,    morþor hycgend[n]e,
bliþe gebæro.    Ful oft wit beotedan
þæt unc ne gedælde    nemne deað ana,
owiht elles.    Eft is þæt onhworfen,
is nu        swa hit no wære
25  freondscipe uncer.    S[c]eal ic feor ge neah
mines felaleofan    fæhðu dreogan.
Heht mec mon wunian    on wuda bearwe,
under actreo    in þam eorðscræfe.
*115b*    Eald is þes eorðsele;    eal ic eom oflongad. /
30  Sindon dena dimme,    duna uphea,
bitre burgtunas    brerum beweaxne,
wic wynna leas.    Ful oft mec her wraþe begeat
fromsiþ frean.    Frynd sind on eorþan,
leofe lifgende,    leger weardiað,
35  þonne ic on uhtan    ana gonge,
under actreo,    geond þas eorðscrafu.

---

small capital of *ða* argues against Mackie's enjambed sense 'And so my heart is sad, since I found," etc. With Leslie, I read the words *forþon is min hyge geomor* as closed syntax. These words are the emotional summation of the misfortunes given in the paragraph from line 11 to line 17—the kinsmen's secret plotting and the wife's subsequent separation from her lord. Leslie shows a paragraph division at line 15, but the MS does not.

20: *hycgende*. Generally emended to *hycgend[n]e*, in parallel with the other acc. complements of *monnan* in lines 19–20a.

21: *bliþe gebæro*. The grammar and syntax are ambiguous, I think perhaps deliberately so. Mackie and ASPR 3 represent the scholarly view which begins a new clause with *bliþe gebæro* as an (instrumental?) description of the spirit in which the marriage vows in the following lines were first made. With Leslie I view *bliþe gebæro* as acc. grammar, unambiguously reduplicated in line 44. It ends the husband's disturbing states of mind in the lines before with an ostensible paradox. But in the hidden allegory of *The Easter Riddle* the paradox is resolved, for 'with a calm manner' describes Christ's heroic composure during his trial and *morþor* 'murder' (line 20). The wife as Church, i.e., in one sense the apostles,

Then I had found the man fully matched to me
grim in his spirit, gloomy in mind,
20   concealing his mind, dwelling on murder
[but] peaceful in manner. Many's the time that we two
    promised
no cause would divide us except death alone,
no other thing. That's since turned around:
  our love is now
25   as if it never had been. I have far and near
my dearly beloved's blood feud to bear.
I have been told to go live in a grove of the wood,
under an oak tree, in this earthen cave.
    Old in this earth hall; I'm all worn out with longing.
30   Dim are the dales, the hills rising high,
cruel citadels crept over with briars,
a cheerless abode. Often indeed my husband's departure
has seized me here harshly. On earth there are
    helpmates,
loving ones living, keeping their couches,
35   while I pace alone in the midnight darkness,
under an oak tree, around and around these pits in the
    earth.

---

thinks backward from line 20b on Christ's often-repeated promises in the
Gospels.

    24: The on verse is defective, though there is no gap or erasure in the MS.
Leslie fills the verse as *is nu [fornumen]*, a reasonable guess. Mackie simply follows
the MS. Following ASPR 3, I indicate a missing word or words without filling
them in, since the gist of the sentence is clear.

    25: *s[c]eal*. MS *seal*, clearly an error, which suggests that the omission in the
previous line was also a careless mistake.

    28: A raised point after *eorðscræfe* closes another paragraph in the MS.
Lines 18–28 thus form the riddlic heart of the wife's complaint, the abandon-
ment by her husband which (as she feels) has put her beneath the oak tree of
death.

    29: The small capital of *Eald* begins the long last division of this text. In
lines 29–53 the wife bitterly compares the (allegorical) scene of her exile with the
imagined woes of her husband but insinuates (lines 52b–53) that hers is the
worse suffering. The raised point after *oflongad* (line 29b) ends fol. 115a.

Þær ic sitta[n] mot     sumorlangne dæg;
þær ic wepan mæg     mine wræcsiþas,
earfoþa fela.    Forþon ic æfre ne mæg

40    þære modceare     minre gerestan,
ne ealles þæs longaþes    þe mec on þissum life begeat.
A scyle geong mon     wesan geomormod,
heard heortan geþoht.    Swylce habban sceal
bliþe gebæro,    eac þon breostceare,

45    sinsorgna gedreag,    sy æt him sylfum gelong
eal his worulde wyn,    sy ful wide fah
feorres folclondes.    Þæt min freond siteð
under stanhliþe,    storme behrimed,
wine werigmod,    wætre beflowen

50    on dreorsele!    Dreogeð se min wine
micle modceare:    he gemon to oft
wynlicran wic.    Wa bið þam þe sceal
of langoþe    leofes abidan.

---

37: *sitta*[*n*]. Emended from MS *sittam*, an error. The acc. ending -*ne* of MS *sumor langne* has been entered over an erasure. The letters *ne*, expansively written and perhaps by another hand, do not fill the erased space, which originally had *lang-* plus an ending or another word filling about three letter spaces more

There I must sit out a long day of summer;
there I may beweep my wanderings in exile,
my many misfortunes. For I never can rest
40    from my misery of mind,
nor from all the longing that's seized me in this life.
A young man should always be stern in his mind,
hardened the thought of his heart. In this way he shall
      have
cheerful bearing and breast care besides,
45    a throng of ceaseless sorrows, be all his joy in the world
from himself alone, be he banned a long way
in a far-off kingdom. [Ah,] that my friend sits
beneath a stone cliff, iced over by storm,
a friend weary in spirit, flooded round by water
50    in a dreary hall! This friend of mine suffers
great anguish of mind: too much he remembers
a happier house. Woe be unto him
who, compelled by longing, must wait for a loved one.

---

than *langne*. Possibly the erased reading was *langostan*, a reference to the sum-
mer solstice which was corrected because it did not fit the allegory of *The Easter
Riddle*.

# [JUDGMENT DAY I]

Ðæt gelimpan sceal    þætte lagu floweð,
flod ofer foldan.    Feores bið æt ende
anra gehwylcum.    Oft mæg se þe wile
in his sylfes sefan    soð geþencan.
5 Hafað him geþinged hider    þeoden user
on þam mæstan dæge;    mægencyninga / hyhst
wile þonne forbærnan,    brego moncynnes,
lond mid lige.    Nis þæt lytulu spræc
to geheganne.    Hat bið onæled
10 siþþan fyr nimeð    foldan sceatas,
byrnende lig    beorhte gesceafte;
bið eal þes ginna grund    gleda gefylled,
reþra bronda,    swa nu rixiað
gromhydge guman,    gylpe strynað,
15 hyra hlaforde    gehlæges tilgað,
oþþæt hy beswicað    synna weardas,
þæt hi mid þy heape    helle secað,
fleogað mid þam feondum.    Him bið fyr ongean,
droflic wite.    Þær næfre dæg scineð
20 leohte of lyfte,    ac a bilocen stondeð
siþþan þæs gæstes gryre    agiefen weorþeð.
Ufan hit is enge    ond hit is innan hat;
nis þæt betlic bold,    ac þær is brogna hyhst,
ne noht hyhtlic ham,    ac þær is helle grund,
25 sarlic siðfæt    þam þe sibbe ful oft
tomældeð mid his muþe.    Ne con he þa mircan
gesceaft,
hu hi butan ende    ece stondeð
þam þe þær for his synnum    onsægd weorþeð,
ond þonne a to ealdre    orleg dreogeð.

116a (margin, line 6)

---

1: The initial Ð of this poem, of about the same size and ornateness as the initial *I* of *The Wife's Lament*, is one of the more successful large capitals of the MS.

# [JUDGMENT DAY I]

It shall come to pass that a wave shall pour,
a flood over the earth. The life of each and every thing
will be at an end. In his own mind whoever desires
can often reflect upon that fact.
5  Our Prince has pledged himself to come hither
on the Last Day; the highest among mighty kings,
the Counselor of humankind, will then burn up
the lands with flame. That is no light judgment
to carry out. The heat will be increased
10  after fire consumes the corners of earth,
once the burning flame grips bright Creation.
All this wide earth will be filled with embers,
with fierce fires. No matter that cruel-minded men
hold sway now, get all the glory,
15  stir up scorn for their Lord,
so much that the wardens of sins deceive them,
that among that mob they go to hell,
flying with fiends. Fire will greet them,
surging pain. There day never shines
20  in light from the air, but stops, endlessly barred,
once the soul's sentence of terror is given.
It is blocked from above and hot from within;
it is not a grand dwelling, but the direst of dreads there,
no joyful home, but depths of hell there instead—
25  a sad journey's end for whoever from habit
separates friends with his mouth. He does not know that
    murky creation,
how it lasts forever, without an end
for him who is sacrificed there for his sins
and then bears that fate forever and ever.

---

9: *onæled*. Generally emended from MS *onhæled*.
23: *bold*. Generally emended from MS *blod*.

30    Hwa is þonne þæs ferðgleaw    oþþe þæs fela cunne,
       þæt æfre mæge heofona    heahþu gereccan,
       swa georne þone godes dæl,    swa he gearo stondeð
       clænum heortum,    þam þe þisne cwide willað
       ondrædan þus deopne?    Sceal se dæg weorþan

35    þæt we forð berað    firena gehwylce,
       þeawas ond geþohtas;    þæt bið þearlic gemot,

*116b*    heardlic / heremægen.    Hat biþ acolod.
       Ne biþ þonne on þisse worulde    nymþe wætres sweg
                                  fisces eþel;

40    ne biþ her ban ne blod,    ac sceal bearna gehwylc
       mid lice ond mid sawle    leanes fricgan
       ealles þæs þe we on eorþan    ær geworhtan
       godes oþþe yfles.    Ne mæg nænig gryre mare
       geweorþan æfter worulde,    ond se bið wide cuð.

45    Ne tytaþ her tungul,    ac biþ tyr scæcen,
       eorþan blædas.    Forþon ic a wille
       leode læran    þæt hi lof Godes
       hergan on heahþu    hyhtum to wuldre,
       lifgen in geleafan,    ond a lufan dryhtnes

50    wyrcan in þisse worulde,    ær þon se wlonca dæg
       bodige þurh byman    brynehatne leg,
       egsan oferþrym.    Ne bið nænges eorles tir
       leng on þissum life,    siþþan leohtes weard
       ofer ealne foldan fæþm    fyr onsendeð.

---

30: *ferðgleaw*. Emended, as in ASPR 3, from MS *forð gleaw*. W. S. Mackie, ed., *The Exeter Book, Part II, Poems IX–XXXII* (hereafter cited as Mackie), reads *forðgleaw* 'very wise,' a compound not found elsewhere. *Ferhðgleaw* 'wise of mind' occurs in *Judith* 41 and *Elene* 327 and would make of line 30 the kind of hidden challenge to the reader which is occasionally found elsewhere among the riddles, especially in words such as *snottor* and *gleaw*. For an example of such a challenge made with the noun *rynemenn* in *Riddle 42* see my "Two Spliced Riddles of the Exeter Book," *In Geardagum* 5 (June, 1983): 57–75.

39: The on verse of this line of *f* alliteration is missing, though the MS has no gap or erasure at this point.

30 Who, after all, is so clever, or could know so much
    that he might ever reckon the height of the heavens,
    or know as fully that region of good as it stands ready
    for clean hearts, those who will dread this deep
    decree that follows? The day shall come
35 when we carry forth each of our crimes,
    our habits and thoughts. It will be a merciless meeting,
    a cruel clash of armies. The heat will be cooled.
    Then there will be naught in this world but noise of
        water,
                                    the dominion of fish.
40 Here there will be neither bone nor blood; but instead
      each man
    with body and soul shall discern his wages
    for all of the good or evil on earth
    which we have done. No mightier dread
    can come over the world, and it will be known far and
      wide.
45 Here no star will gleam, but the glory will be gone,
    the splendors of earth. Thus I want always
    to teach the people to lift the praise
    of God to the heights in hope of glory,
    to live in faith, and always to win the Lord's love
50 in this world, before that dread day
    herald by trumpet the burning-hot flame,
    the unchecked force of fear. In this life no man's fame
    will last any longer once the Keeper of Light
    sends fire over all the reaches of earth.

---

    42: *geworhtan*. Emended from MS *ge weorhtan* as in ASPR 3. Mackie re-
tains the MS reading but understands 'wrought.' As in *The Wife's Lament* 24–25,
the omission of words in line 39 is almost immediately followed by another error.
This time the scribe was perhaps looking ahead to *geweorþan* in line 44.
    52: *oferþrym*. Abbreviated *oferþrȳ* in the MS.

55     Lixeð lyftes mægen,     leg onetteð,
       blæc byrnende;     blodgyte weorþeð
       mongum gemeldad,     mægencyninges þrea.
       Beofað eal beorhte gesceaft,     brondas lacað
       on þam deopan dæge,     dyneð upheofon.
60     Þonne weras ond wif     woruld alætað,
       eorþan yrmþu,     seoð þonne on ece gewyrht.
       Þonne bið gecyþed     hwa in clænnisse
       lif alifde;     him bið lean gearo.
       Hyht wæs a in heofonum     siþþan user hælend wæs,
65     middangeardes meotud,     þurh þa mæstan gesceaft
       on ful blacne beam     bunden fæste
       cearian clomme.     Crist ealle wat
       gode dæde;     no þæs gilpan þearf
       synfull sawel     þæt hyre sie swegl ongean,
70     þonne he gehyrweð / ful oft     halge lare,
117a    brigdeð on bysmer.     Ne con he þæs brogan dæl,
       yfles ondgiet,     ær hit hine on fealleð.
       He þæt þonne onfindeð,     þonne se fær cymeþ,
       geond middangeard     monegum gecyþeð
75     þæt he bið on þæt wynstre weorud     wyrs gescaden
       þonne he on þa swiþran hond     swican mote,
       leahtra alysed.     Lyt þæt geþenceð,
       se þe him wines glæd     wilna bruceð,
       siteð him symbelgal,     siþ ne bemurneð,
80     hu him æfter þisse worulde     weorðan mote.
         Wile þonne forgieldan     gæsta dryhten
       willum æfter þære wyrde,     wuldres ealdor,
       þam þe his synna nu     sare geþenceþ,
       modbysgunge     micle dreogeð.

---

     63: *him.* MS *hī*, at the end of a line. Between lines 52 and 63 MS *þoñ* appears three times. These lines give no visible clue for the rather unusual frequency of these common abbreviations.

     64: *hælend.* Generally corrected from MS *hæ lendes*, an error caused by inattention as the scribe syllabificated at the end of a line.

     70: *ful.* Generally corrected from MS *fol*, the first word on fol. 117a.

     72: *ondgiet.* MS *7giet.* Shorthand 7 occurs frequently for *ond* in the Exeter Book.

55   The aery force will ignite, the flame will quicken,
      burning brightly; bloodshed will be reported
      to many, the assault of the King of strength.
      All fair Creation will tremble, and fire will leap
      on that awful day; high heaven will resound.
60   Then men and women will give up the world,
      the woes of earth, then to see their eternal task.
      Then will be disclosed who in cleanness
      has lived out his life; his reward will stand ready.
      There has been joy in heaven since the moment our
         Healer,
65   Lord of this earth, by the loftiest plan
      on a tree of great brightness was immovably bound
      in a grievous grasp. Christ knows all
      good deeds. The sinful soul
      will be granted no boast that heaven is near him,
70   for again and again he flouts holy teaching
      and turns it to shame. His share of the terrors,
      of the end of evil, he does not know before it befalls him.
      He first finds it out when the peril approaches,
      reveals to many in this middle earth
75   that in the left-hand assembly he is worse assigned
      than if he might withdraw to the right-hand half,
      released from his sins. Little he thinks
      who wastes his pleasures in joy of wine,
      sits flushed with feasting, feels no care for his fate,
80   what could become of him after this world.
         Then the Lord of souls, Governor of glory,
      will freely repay in accord with his plan
      the one who now sorrowfully ponders his sins,
      who struggles with great distress of mind;

---

74: *monegum.* Generally corrected from MS *mongegum.*

75: *gescaden.* Corrected from MS *geaceaden* as in ASPR 3. Mackie retains the MS reading, which may be a deliberate phonetic spelling. The *e* of *ea* in *gesceaden* appears to have been crowded in later between *c* and *a*.

80: *æfter.* MS *efter*, with the shadow of *a* in the ligature still visible.

81: From the very large and relatively ornate initial *W* here, of similar decoration to the initial *W* of *Deor* 1 (fol. 100a) but somewhat smaller, *Judgment Day I*

85   Him þæt þonne geleanað   lifes waldend,
      heofona hyrde,   æfter heonansiþe
      godum dædum,   þæs þe he swa geomor wearð,
      sarig fore his synnum.   Ne sceal se to sæne beon,
      ne þissa larna to læt,   se þe him wile lifgan mid Gode,
90   brucan þæs boldes   þe us beorht fæder
      gearwað togeanes,   gæsta ealdor.
      Þæt is sigedryhten   þe þone sele frætweð,
      timbreð torhtlice.   To sculon clæne,
      womma lease,   swa se waldend cwæð,
95   ealra cyninga cyning.   Forþon cwicra gehwylc,
      deophydigra,   dryhtne hyreð,
      þara þe wille heofona   heahþu gestigan.
      Hwæþre þæt gegongeð,   þeah þe hit sy greote
                                bepeaht,
*117b*   lic mid / lame,   þæt hit sceal life onfon,
100   feores æfter foldan.   Folc biþ gebonnen,
      Adames bearn   ealle to spræce.
      Beoð þonne gegædrad   gæst ond bansele,
      gesomnad to þam siþe.   Soþ þæt wile cyþan
      þonne we us gemittað   on þam mæstan dæge;
105   rincas æt þære rode   secgað þonne ryhta fela,
      eal swylce under heofonum gewearð   hates ond
                                      cealdes,
      godes oþþe yfles.   Georne gehyreð
      heofoncyninga hyhst   hæleþa dæde.
      Næfre mon þæs hlude   horn aþyteð
110   ne byman ablaweþ   þæt ne sy seo beorhte stefn
      ofer ealne middangeard   monnum hludre,

---

turns from a poem of warning to a poem of hope. This is the only paragraphing and a major turning point of the poem, and it might be the place where the Easter riddler spliced together two originally separate texts on the Judgment Day theme. It signals the change of heart, from bitterness to obedience, which the speaker must also undergo in *Resignation*. The bottom end of the initial is

85    for that the Lord of life, the heavens' Keeper,
will requite him with kindnesses after his passing,
because he has thus become mournful,
sorry for his sins. He must not be too careless,
too remiss in these teachings, he who wants to reside with
    God,
90    delight in that lodging which the radiant Father,
the Prince of souls, will prepare to receive us.
It is the Lord of triumphs who trims that hall,
frames it in brightness; the faultless shall go there,
those free of stains, as the Sovereign declared,
95    the King of all kings. Therefore each living man,
each man of deep mind, will hear the Lord,
who wants to rise to the heights of heaven.
It will come to pass still, though the corpse be covered
with clods and clay, that it shall assume life,
100   essence above earth. All folk will be called,
the offspring of Adam, to the judgment.
Then the soul and its bone house will be assembled,
gathered together to make their journey. The truth will
    be shown
when we meet again on that greatest of days;
105   then men under the Rood will say many right things,
all such as under the heavens occurred, both hot and
    cold,
whether good or evil. The highest of the kings of heaven
will hear in earnest the acts of men.
Never shall horn be blared nor trumpet blown
110   to bray so loudly that that bright voice,
the Master's word, be not louder to men

---

missing because of a small hole in the page, the first hint of the increasing textual
damage in the last fourteen leaves of the MS.

    95: *gehwylc*. Generally corrected from MS *gewylc*.

    103: *cyþan*. Generally corrected from MS *cyþam*.

    108: *hæleþa*. Generally corrected from MS *hæle/la*, at the end of a line.

waldendes word.    Wongas beofiað
for þam ærende    þæt he to us eallum wat.
Oncweþ nu þisne cwide:    "Cuþ sceal geweorþan
115    þæt ic gewægan ne mæg    wyrd under heofonum.
Ac hit þus gelimpan sceal    leoda gehwylcum
ofer eall beorht gesetu,    byrnende lig.
Siþþan æfter þam lige    lif bið gestaþelad.
Welan ah in wuldre    se nu wel þenceð."

throughout all middle earth. The world will waver
at the message that he will mean for us all.
Echo now this decree: "It shall be proclaimed
115   that I cannot hinder fate under the heavens.
But it shall thus come to pass for every people
throughout all bright abodes, a burning fire.
Then, after that flame, life will be fixed firm.
He who thinks well now will own rich goods in glory."

# [RESIGNATION]

Age mec se ælmihta God,
helpe min se halga dryhten!    Þu gesceope heofon ond
                       eorþan
ond wundor eall,    min wundorcyning,
[þe] þær on sindon,    ece dryhten,
5   micel ond manigfeald.    Ic þe, mære God,
mine sawle bebeode    ond mines sylfes lic,
ond min word ond min weorc,    witig dryhten,
*118a*  ond eal / min leoþo,    leohtes hyrde,
ond þa manigfealdan    mine geþohtas.
10  Getacna me,    tungla hyrde,
þær selast sy    sawle minre
to gemearcenne    meotudes willan,
þæt ic þe geþeo    þinga gehwylce,
ond on me sylfum,    soðfæst cyning,
15  ræd arære.    Regnþeof ne læt
on sceade sceþþan.    Þeah þe ic scyppendum,
wuldorcyninge,    waccor hyrde,
ricum dryhtne,    þonne min ræd wære,
forgif me to lisse,    lifgende God,
20  bitre bealodæde.    Ic þa bote gemon,
cyninga wuldor,    cume to, gif ic mot.
    Forgif þu me, min frea,    fierst ond ondgiet
ond geþyld ond gemynd    þinga gehwylces
þara þu me, soþfæst cyning,    sendan wylle
25  to cunnunge.    Nu þu const on mec

---

1: At the left of the large, bold, but unadorned initial *A* of this poem is a hastily penciled cross, no doubt by the same hand that entered the cross at *The Soul's Address* 1, fol. 98a. The first short MS line of *Resignation*, *Age mec se ælmihta God*, lies near the top of the initial and was overlooked by Thorpe (Benjamin Thorpe, ed. and trans., *Codex exoniensis: A Collection of Anglo-Saxon Poetry, etc.*,) and by Grein (C. W. M. Grein, *Bibliothek der angelsächsischen Poesie*) but corrected by later editors. See the discussion of the poem in the Introduction to Part Two.

# [RESIGNATION]

May the almighty God own me,
the holy Lord help me! You shaped both heaven and
    earth
and all the wonders, my wondrous King,
that lie thereon, my Lord eternal,
5   great things, and manifold. To you, great God,
I consign my soul and my very own body,
and my words and my works, wise Lord,
and all my limbs, Keeper of light,
and the manifold thoughts of my mind.
10  Show me a sign, Shepherd of stars,
where for my soul it were wisest
to mark the way of the Maker's will,
that for you I may flourish in all my affairs,
and increase, righteous King,
15  your ends in myself. Let not the arch-thief
strike from the shadow. Though I've served the Creator,
the King of glory, Lord for all kingdoms,
more feebly than was my first aim,
in your mercy forgive, God ever-living,
20  my bitter bad deeds. With my mind on atonement,
O Glory of kings, I come near, if I may.
    Lend me, my Lord, some repose and insight
and patience and purpose to meet all things
that you will send me, sound King of truth,
25  to know me in trials. Now you know of me

---

4: *þe*. Not in MS and not entered or noted by Mackie (W. S. Mackie, ed., *The Exeter Book*; *Part II*: *Poems IX–XXXII*; hereafter cited as Mackie). I follow ASPR 3, which supplies the word.

22: The raised point after *mot* and the small capital *F* of *Forgif* mark the speaker's turn from acknowledgment of the Creator's power and her own sinful weakness to a petition for forgiveness. The paragraphing at lines 41, 59, and 105 seems to mark further spiritual milestones on the way to reconciliation with God.

firendæda fela;    feorma mec hwæþre,
meotod, for þinre miltse,    þeah þe ic ma fremede
grimra gylta    þonne me God lyfde.
Hæbbe ic þonne þearfe    þæt ic þine seþeah,
30    halges heofoncyninges,    hyldo getilge
leorendum dagum,    lif æfter oþrum
geseo ond gesece,    þæt me siþþan þær
unne arfæst God    ecan dreames,
lif alyfe,    þeah þe lætlicor
35    bette bealodæde    þonne bibodu wæron
halgan heofonmægnes.    Hwæt, þu me her fela
           forgeafe.    Gesette minne hyht on þec,
forhte foreþoncas,    þæt hio fæstlice
stonde gestaðelad.    Onstep minne hige,
40    gæsta god cyning,    in gearone / ræd.
*118b*    Nu ic fundige to þe,    fæder moncynnes,
of þisse worulde,    nu ic wat þæt ic sceal
ful unfyr faca;    feorma me þonne,
wyrda waldend,    in þinne wuldordream,
45    ond mec geleoran læt,    leofra dryhten,
geoca mines gæstes.    Þonne is gromra to fela
æfestum eaden,    hæbbe ic þonne
æt frean frofre,    þeah þe ic ær on fyrste lyt
earnode arna.    Forlæt mec englas seþeah
50    geniman on þinne neawest,    nergende cyning,
meotud, for þinre miltse,    þeah ðe ic mana fela
æfter dogrum dyde.    Ne læt þu mec næfre deofol
               seþeah
þin lim lædan    on laðne sið,
þy læs hi on þone foreþonc    gefeon motan

---

27: *þe ic ma*. The words appear to be written over thorough erasure of a considerably longer word or phrase.

37: The *s*-alliteration word has apparently been omitted from the on verse. If, as I guess, the context here suggests that *forgeafe* means 'had given,' then the omitted word might be *sæla*, or some other *s* word meaning 'riches, blessings,' etc. If, as seems less probable, *forgeafe* meant 'had forgiven,' the missing *s* word might have been *synna*.

many monstrous deeds; yet admit me,
O Judge, in your mercy, though I have done more
grievous wrongs than God forgave me.
Therefore I have need to obtain nonetheless
30    some kindness of you, good heavenly King,
in my dwindling days, to see and desire
life hereafter, so that then gracious God
may give me there gladness eternal,
allow me to live, though I've purged my offenses
35    more slowly than meets the commands
of the holy Power of heaven. Hear me, for you had given
    me here
many               . I put my hope in you,
my fearful precautions, that fixed and firm
it may stand established. Lift up my spirit,
40    good King of souls, to the profit already prepared.
    Now I hasten to you, Father of humankind,
away from this world, now that I know I'll
depart in a very short while. Welcome me, then,
Guide of all fates, into your glorious joy,
45    and let me pass, Lord of beloved ones,
preserve my soul. When too many foes
are given to hatreds, then I have help
from the Lord, though in my time I earned little
honor. But let angels yet take me
50    into your presence, preserving King,
O Measurer, for your mercy's sake, though I've done
    many
evils day after day. But never let devils
lead me, your limb, on the loathsome journey,
lest they might be pleased with their ancient plotting

---

41: The point after *ræd*, raised in the MS, and the small capital *N* of *Nu* mark the speaker's turn from prayers begging forgiveness to expressions of confidence in God's mercy and salvation.

55 þy þe hy him sylfum     sellan þuhten,
   englas oferhydige,     þonne ece Crist.
   Gelugon hy him æt þam geleafan;     forþon hy longe
                                        scul[.],
   werge wihta,     wræce þrowian.
      Forstond þu mec ond gestyr him,     þonne storm cyme
60 minum gæste ongegn;     geoca þonne,
   migtig dryhten,     minre sawle,
   gefreoþa hyre ond gefeorma hy,     fæder moncynnes,
   hædre gehogode;     hæl, ece God,
   meotod meahtum swiþ.     Min is nu þa
65 sefa synnum fah,     ond ic ymb sawle eom
   feam siþum forht,     þeah þu me fela sealde
   arna on þisse eorþan.     Þe sie ealles þonc
   meorda ond miltsa,     þara þu me sealdest.
119a No ðæs earninga     ænige wæron [mid . . .] /
70 hwæþre ic me ealles þæs     ellen wylle
   habban ond hlyhhan     ond me hyhtan to,
   frætwian mec on ferðweg     ond fundian
   sylf to þam siþe     þe ic asettan sceal,
   gæst gearwian,     ond me þæt eal for gode þolian
75 bliþe mode,     nu ic gebunden eom
   fæste in minum ferþe.     Huru me frea witeð
   sume þara synna     þe ic me sylf ne conn
   ongietan gleawlice.     Gode ic hæbbe
   abolgen, brego moncynnes;     forþon ic þus bittre wearð
80 gewitnad fore þisse worulde,     swa min gewyrhto wæron

---

57: *scul*[.]. Either *sculō* or *sculon*, with one or two letters missing because of a small hole at the right-hand margin. This is the first damaged word of *The Easter Riddle*.

59: The raised point and small capital *F* in the MS turn the argument from the weakness and fall of the rebellious angels to the speaker's need for God's protection against them. This interrupted paragraph might once have led to the speaker's confession of specific sins.

69–70: The ellipsis and brackets after the word *mid*, the last word on fol. 118b, represent an entire leaf missing from the MS. See the discussion of *Resignation* (Introduction to Part Two).

55 by which they, the arrogant angels,
  to themselves seemed better than Christ eternal.
  In that belief they deluded themselves; thus they must
   long
  endure exile, cursed creatures.
   Stand by me and repel them whenever a storm may
    come
60 against my spirit; then spare
  my soul, mighty Sovereign,
  defend it, sustain it, Father of men,
  (it is) busied with cares. Cure it, God of ages,
  O Judge with strong might. My heart is stained
65 even now with sins, and for my soul I am
  sometimes afraid, though for me you have furnished
  many honors on this earth. To you be all thanks
  for the goodness and kindness which you have given me.
  No merits for this were in me [among . . .]
70 yet from it all I will find strength
  and be happy, and hope for myself,
  adorn myself for the journey hence, and myself make
   haste
  toward the pilgrimage I must depart on,
  make my soul ready, and for my own good suffer it all
75 with a glad bearing, now that I'm girded
  fast in my heart. The Lord surely levies against me
  certain sins which I cannot myself
  clearly discover. I have provoked
  God, champion of men, for which I was chastized
80 thus bitterly before the world, so that my works

---

80: *fore*. MS *fo*[.], with part of the *r* visible at the edge of the hole in the right margin. Mackie reads *fore* and understands 'in the sight of.' ASPR 3 reads *for* but notes that the word might have been either *for* or *fore*. Mackie takes *swa* to mean 'just as' and the whole clause of lines 79b–82a as a contrite admission of just deserts for previous evil works.

 *min gewyrhto*. For MS *mingie wyrhto*, an error. Because of the missing folio leaf between the present fols. 118 and 119, fol. 119 shows considerably more

micle fore monnum,     þæt ic martirdom
deopne adreoge.     Ne eom ic dema gleaw,
wis fore weorude;     forþon ic þas word spræce
fus on ferþe,     swa me on frymðe gelomp
85  yrmþu ofer eorþan,     þæt ic a þolade
geara gehwylce     —Gode ealles þonc!—
modearfoþa     ma þonne on oþrum,
fyrhto in folce;     forþon ic afysed eom
earm of minum eþle.     Ne mæg þæs anhoga,
90  leodwynna leas,     leng drohtian,
wineleas wræcca:     is him wrað meotud.
Gnornað on his geoguþe,
ond him ælce mæle     men fullestað,
ycað his yrmþu,     ond he þæt eal þolað,
95  sarcwide secga,     ond him bið a sefa geomor,
mod morgenseoc.     Ic bi me tylgust
secge þis sarspel     ond ymb siþ spræce,
longunge fus,     ond on lagu þence,
nat min
100  hwy ic gebycge     bat on sæwe, /
119b  fleot on faroðe;     nah ic fela goldes
ne huru þæs freondes,     þe me gefylste
to þam siðfate,     nu ic me sylf ne mæg
fore minum wonæhtum     willan adreogan.
105  Wudu mot him weaxan,     wyrde bidan,
tanum lædan;     ic for tæle ne mæg
ænigne moncynnes     mode gelufian
eorl on eþle.     Eala dryhten min,
meahtig mundbora!     þæt ic eom mode [.]eoc,

---

damage than fol. 118. The *w* and most of the *y* in *wyrhto* are legible, and the
upper halves of *rht* extend beyond the upper edge of a hole at midpage. The *o* is
entirely visible, so that the whole word can be read.

81: *martirdom*. For MS *martir dom*, with the upper part of *t* and only the
upper tips of *i* and *r* visible above the hole. A letter space followed, after which
the *d* of *dom* is almost unscathed.

92: A half-line has been omitted in copying. The missing words may have
been either the on verse or the off verse, and they cannot be exactly located.

were great before men, that I might undergo
a harsh martyrdom. I am not a just judge,
wise before multitudes; thus I speak these words
with a sorrowing heart, since there once came
85  hardships to me upon the earth. I bore it always,
year after year—thank God for it all!—
miseries of mind more than anything else,
fear among the folk; thus I am driven
poor from my homeland. Against this the lone pilgrim,
90  without joy of his people, can no longer last,
a patronless outcast: the Lord is angry with him.
Men of his following mourn,
and so each time assist him,
add to his agonies, and he suffers it all,
95  the wounding words of men, and his heart is ever sad,
his mind downcast at dawn. Of myself most especially
I tell this sad tale, and speak of a journey,
saddened by longing, and think of the sea.
My                                  does not know
100  with what I might buy a boat on the sea,
a ship on the main. I have not much gold,
nor, indeed, the friend who might foster me
for the voyage. Devoid now of means,
I cannot myself fulfill my desire.
105      The wood may flourish of itself, expect its fate,
shoot forth its branches; because of calumny I cannot
love in my heart anyone who is human,
no man in my homeland. Alas, my Lord,
my mighty Spokesman! how sick I am in my spirit,

---

99: Most of this line, which would have fallen in the last MS line of fol.
119a, has been omitted, perhaps because the scribe was already thinking ahead,
completing the syntax as far as *sæwe* (line 100b) on the recto of the leaf.

104–105: A raised point after *adreogan* and the small capital *w* of *Wudu* in
the MS begin the final paragraph of the poem. The references to the wood and
to branches, to the speaker's isolation through *tæle* 'calumny' (line 106)—her own
sin against her lord as well as her enemies' sin against her—and her final gnomic
wisdom identify her with the speaker of *The Wife's Lament*.

110    bittre abolgen!    Is seo bot æt þe
       gelong æfter [. .]fe.    Ic on leohte ne mæg
       butan earfoþum    ænge þinga
       feascæft hæle    foldan [. . .]unian;
       þonne ic me to fremþum    freode hæfde,
115    cyðþu gecwe[. . . .]    me wæs a cearu symle
       lufena to leane,    swa ic alifde.
       Nu giet biþ þæt [selast]    þonne mon him sylf ne mæg
       wyrd onwendan,    þæt he þonne wel þolige.

109: *[.]eoc.* The *s* has been obliterated by a hole at the left margin.

111: *[. .]fe.* The *li* of *life,* the second arsis of the on verse, has disappeared in the hole at the left margin.

113: *foldan.* All of the word is legible but part of the *n,* which has disappeared into the hole at midpage. As Mackie notes, a trace of a *w* as in *[w]unian* is to be seen. But the space between *foldan* and *[w]unian,* now taken up by the hole in the page, is too wide for Mackie's reading *foldan wunian* and too narrow for the four letter spaces given in ASPR 3. Furthermore, *wunian* would normally require a preposition, e.g., *on foldan wunian,* where none appears. Probably the damaged word was *gewunian,* which fits the available space and does not require a preposition. The use of *gewunian* here would also riddle thematically on *gewunadest* in lines 100 and 104 of *The Descent into Hell.*

115: *gecwe [. . . .] me.* The final *-e* is legible only as a shadow and there are

110    how bitterly hurt! The cure comes from you
       after this life. I cannot live
       free of afflictions in this earth's light
       by any means, miserable being;
       when for myself I had shelter from strangers,
115    fitting kinsfolk, for me woe was always
       the reward of loves such as I've lived.
       As yet it's still best, when one cannot himself
       foil his fate, that he then suffer well.

---

four or five damaged letter spaces before *me.* Two of the spaces are actually on surviving parchment and appear to be blank. ASPR 3 therefore notes that "the spacing before *me* seems . . . to have been wider than usual" (p. 355), but the damage is severe enough to make such a judgment uncertain. ASPR 3 accepts Mackie's suggestion *gecwe*[*me*], whose sense appears to be right.

117: *biþ þæt* [*selast*]. The *bi* and a good part of *þ* are clear, and *þæt* can barely be discerned as a shadow in a badly discolored spot on the page. The on verse needs an alliteration word, which is missing from the MS. Both Mackie and ASPR 3 supply *selast*, which would make a riddlic answer to the prayer using the same word at lines 10–12.

118: *þonne.* Expanded from MS *þon,* almost certainly *þoñ* before this place was badly discolored. Here *þolige* is used intransitively, in the meaning 'suffer,' a clever thematic look backward at the final sentence of *The Wife's Lament.*

# [THE DESCENT INTO HELL]

ONgunnon him on uhtan     æþelcunde mægð
gierwan to geonge;     wiston gumena gemot
æþelinges lic     eorðærne biþeaht.
Woldan werigu wif     wope bimænan
5     æþelinges deað     ane hwile,
reon[g]e bereotan.     Ræst wæs acolad,
heard wæs hinsið.     Hæleð wæron modge
þe hy æt þam beorge     blið[e] f[u]ndon.
Cwom seo murnende     Maria on dægred;
10     heht hy oþre mid     eorles dohtor.
Sohton sarigu tu     sigebearn Godes
ænne in þæt eorðærn     þær hi ær wiston
þæt hine gehyddan     hæleð Iudea.
Wendan þæt he on þam beorge     bidan sceolde,
15     ana in þære Easter / niht.     Huru þæs oþer þing
120a     wiston þa wifmenn     þa he on weg cyrdon.
Ac þær cwom on uhtan     an engla þreat;
behæfde heapa wyn     hælendes burg.
Open wæs þæt eorðærn.     Æþelinges lic
20     onfeng feores gæst;     folde beofode,
hlogan helwaran.     Hagosteald onwoc
modig from moldan;     mægenþrym aras
sigefæst ond snottor.     Sægde Iohannis,
hæleð helwarum,     hlyhhende spræc
25     modig to þære mengo     ymb his mæges [. . .]:
"Hæfde me gehaten     hæland user,
þa he me on þisne sið     sendan wolde,

---

1: *ONgunnon.* The word begins with a bold and modestly decorated initial *O*, smaller than the initials of previous poems, and a bold block capital *N*.

6: *reon[g]e.* Generally emended from MS *reone.*

8: *blið[e] f[u]ndon.* Corrected from MS *bliðne*, an error, and probably *fondon*. Over the stem vowel *o* the tips of a *u* protrude, as though *u* was super-

# [THE DESCENT INTO HELL]

At midnight the highborn women began
to prepare themselves to depart. The people assembled
knew that the Lord's corpse was enclosed in an earth
    vault.
The saddened women wished to bewail
5   with tears the Lord's death for a time,
grieve in their sadness. The grave had grown cold,
his passing was hard; [yet] the heroes were keen
whom they found exultant beside the tomb.
The Mary who mourned came at dawn;
10  she ordered another earl's daughter to follow.
The two sad ones sought God's victorious Son
alone in the earth vault, where they'd already learned
that townsmen among the Jews had entombed him.
They thought he would have to stay in the sepulchre,
15  alone on that Easter night. Yet the women knew
otherwise when they went back by the same way.
For at midnight a crowd of angels had come there;
the best of hosts hedged round the Savior's retreat.
Open was the earth vault! The Lord's body
20  had received the spirit of life. The earth shook,
and hell dwellers rejoiced. The young warrior awoke
bold from the ground; his great glory arose
certain of victory and sure in wisdom. John said,
bold hero of dwellers in hell, spoke smiling
25  to the crowd of his kinsman's [journey]:
"Our Preserver had promised me
as he prepared to despatch me on this trek

---

imposed without erasure. But most of the letter has been either erased or
washed away by dampness or a liquid spill on the letter, which has a puzzling
appearance.

    25: A hole at the right-hand margin has swallowed a small word needed to
fill out the syntax. The word *sið* is commonly supplied.

þæt he me gesoht[. . . . . .]iex monað,
ealles folces fruma.     Nu [. . . . . . . . .] sceacen.
30   Wene ic ful swiþe     ond witod [. . . . .
     . . . . . .] to dæge     dryhten wille
     [. . . . .] gesecan, sigebearn Godes."
       Fysde hine þa to fore     frea moncynnes;
     wolde heofona helm     helle weallas
35   forbrecan ond forbygan,     þære burge þrym
     onginnan reafian,     reþust ealra cyninga.
     Ne rohte he to þære hilde     helmberendra,
     ne he byrnwigend     to þam burggeatum
     lædan ne wolde,     ac þa locu feollan,
40   clustor of þam ceastrum.     Cyning in oþrad;
     ealles folces fruma     forð onette,
     weorud[a] wuldorgiefa.     Wræccan þrungon,
     hwylc hyra þæt sygebearn     geseon moste,
     Adam ond Abraham,     Isac ond Iacob,
45   monig modig eorl,     Moyses ond Dauid,
     Esaias     ond Sacharias,
*120b*   heahfædra fela,     swylce eac / hæleþa gemot,

---

28: *me gesoht [. . . . . .]iex monað*. For *me* ASPR 3 reads *mec* with *c* erased, a reading which explains the wide space and faint shadows of ink between *me* and *gesoht*. At the left edge of the hole the cross stroke of the *t* can still be seen, and at the right edge a legible portion of the *i*. The five or perhaps six letter spaces between are commonly filled so that the restored space reads *gesoht[e ymb s]iex monað*.

29: *Nu*. Virtually all of the *n* and a readable portion of the *u* are clear, and the word *sceacen* is unscathed. The nine or ten letter spaces of the hole are best filled so that the verse reads *nu [is se fyrst] sceacen*. Mackie (W. S. Mackie, ed., *The Exeter Book, Part II: Poems IX–XXXII*; hereafter cited as Mackie) adopts this reading from older editors.

30–31: The hole has swallowed thirteen or fourteen letter-spaces of lines 30b and 31a. Various suggestions for filling the space are *witod [talige, þætte us] to dæge*; *witod [telle, þæt usic] to dæge* (Mackie); *witod[lice, þæt usic] to dæge*. The word *usic* would match the tail of a long descending stroke about three letter spaces before *to*. But although enough parchment survives to show part of the *ic* of *usic*, the spaces before *to* are blank. Probably, therefore, as ASPR 3 notes (p. 357), the *ic* of *usic* was erased to read *us*. Similar erasures, including the alteration of *mec* to *me* already noted in line 28, are visible at several other places in this text.

that he'd seek me out [after] six months,
the Prince of all peoples. [The time has] now passed.
30  I hope with all strength, and [? hold to be] true,
[that for us] today the Redeemer will
[himself] be seeking, God's conquering Son."
    Then the Lord of the human race hastened his
        journey;
the defender of heaven wished to break and unbuild
35  the ramparts of hell, begin to rob
the strength of that fortress, the sternest of kings.
For the battle he wanted no helmet wearers,
nor wished to guide byrnied men to the gates
of the fortress; but the locks fell off,
40  the bars from the keeps. The King rode up inside,
the Prince of all peoples charged ahead,
glory giver of hosts. The exiles pressed near
to try who could see the triumphant Son:
Adam and Abraham, Isaac and Jacob,
45  many an earl of great daring, Moses and David,
Isaiah and Zacharias,
patriarchs many, heroes marshaled as well,

---

32: The fourth letter space from the left margin shows the tail of a long
descender. Then the bottom loop of a *yogh* and vestiges of an *e* can be seen.
There is a letter space of parchment before *secan*. So [*sylfa*]*ge secan*, the com-
monly suggested reading, fits perfectly.

33: With a raised point after *Godes*, John's first speech ends. The new para-
graph, marked by the small capital *F* of *Fysde*, shifts to Christ as he quickens his
march toward hell.

42: *weorud*[*a*]. The usual correction of MS *weorud*.

43: *hwylc*. Originally *wylc*, but with *h* later crowded in after the *n* of *þrun-
gon* (line 42b). The MS spelling *gewylc* of *Judgment Day I* 95, already noted, to-
gether with the scribal correction here, would perhaps suggest an unaspirated
pronunciation of the word.

46: Mackie suggests that the off verse of this line has been omitted by the
scribe, but it is also possible that the line was left short. The poet has completed
the traditional list of patriarchs' names as it is found in the Benedictine office
and the rite of baptism (see the discussion in the Introduction to Part Two). Or
perhaps a word has been omitted in the on verse: [*snottor*] *Esias ond Sacharias*, or
the like.

witgena weorod,      wifmonna þreat,
fela fæmnena,     folces unrim.
50   Geseah þa Iohannis     sigebearn Godes
mid þy cyneþrymme     cuman to helle,
ongeat þa geomormod     Godes sylfes sið.
Geseah he helle duru     hædre scinan,
þa þe longe ær     bilocen wæron,
55   beþeahte mid þystre.     Se þegn wæs on wynne.
   Abead þa bealdlice     burgwarena [o]rd
modig fore þære mengo     ond to his mæge spræc,
ond þa wilcuman     wordum grette:
"Þe þæs þonc sie,     þeoden user,
60   þæt þu us [. . . . . . .] ige     secan woldest,
nu we on þissum bendum     bidan [. . . . . . . . . .]
þonne monige bindeð     broþorleasne

     55–56: A raised point after *wynne* and a small script capital *A* of *Abead*
mark another paragraph division. The description of Christ's approach to hell
ends, and John steps forward to greet him. The top part of an *o* can be seen in
the damaged word at the left margin. The reading *word* has been offered in
scholarship, but the correct word is almost certainly *ord*, who here encounters
Christ, the *ordfruma* of *Homiletic Fragment II* 20. In the later poem the *ordfruma*
brings light to the world just as he has cast light on the doors of hell in lines
53–55a of this text. For the riddling which shows the *burgwarena ord* here to be
John himself, see the discussion in the Introduction to Part Two.

     58: *þa* has an intact *a*, and the long descender of the *þ* is visible below the
hole at the left margin. The letters *wor* of *wordum* are damaged but legible above
the top of the hole.

     60: Seven letter spaces of the on verse are missing; after the hole the let-
ters *ige* of an adjective can be read. Between *us* and the front edge of the hole is
enough blank parchment to suggest an original reading *usic* with the *ic* erased, as
several times elsewhere in this poem. The various suggestions for filling the hole
depend on whether one reads *us* or *usic* before it. It has not been remarked,
however, that the one letter space between *us* and the hole rules out the sugges-
tion *us ic*. Ferdinand Holthausen's reading *usic sarige* ("Zur altenglischen Liter-
atur. v. 21. 'Christi Höllenfahrt,'" *Anglia Bleiblatt* 19 [1908]: 49–53; hereafter
cited as Holthausen) would probably be too short for the available space unless,
perhaps, the scribe had written *us ic*, an unlikely word division unless done by
mistake. Moritz Trautmann's reading (at first accepted by Holthausen) *us sorg-
cearige* ("Zur Botschaft des Gemahls," *Anglia* 16 [1894]: 207–25) should show the

a host of prophets, a press of women,
many a maiden, numberless folk.
50  Then John saw God's victorious Son
amid his royal might coming toward hell;
then, girded in mind, he spied God's own progress.
He saw the gates of hell gleam brightly,
the ones which had long been locked before,
55  enwrapped with darkness. The thane was in rapture.
The foremost of fortress-dwellers then called out
boldly,
full of courage before the crowd, and spoke to his
kinsman,
greeting with words the welcome one:
"Thanks be to you, our Prince of thanes,
60  for wanting to seek us unlucky ones;
now that we many [? have had] to endure [. . . . . .] in
these bonds,
since [. . . . . .] binds the brotherless

---

descending stroke of an *s* below the hole, and Mackie's *us þus sarige* should likewise show the downstroke of the *þ*. But no downstroke appears below the leading edge of the hole. Moreover, there has already been talk of rejoicing and exultant laughter among the hell dwellers in earlier lines. Thus I would suggest either *usi[c unsæl]ige*, with *usic* altered to *us* before the MS was damaged, or else *us [unsæl]ige*, with emphasis on the hell dwellers' unlucky imprisonment rather than on any idea of their present sadness.

61: All of *bidan* is clear; then follow nine or ten letter spaces of missing text. The abbreviated word *þoñ* (for *þonne*) of line 62 is partly damaged but readable above the upper edge of the hole. The hole sweeps directly through the MS line at this point, so that the off verse after *bidan* is irrestorably lost. For the various conjectures of early scholarship see ASPR 3:357n.

62: The on verse is unmetrical, but also impossible to correct, since too much of line 61b has been lost. MS *monige* is followed by ASPR 3, but Mackie adopts an older emendation to *monig[n]e*. There is no compelling need to emend without knowing the object of *bidan* in line 61 or the syntactical function of the missing language after *wræccan* in line 63. The available syntax of lines 62–63a gives a subordinate clause with singular verb and singular object and a lost singular subject, perhaps a word for the devil. Presumably the pronoun *he* of lines 63b ff. refers to the *broþorleasne wræccan* 'brotherless exile' of lines 62–63. Probably *monige* agrees with *we* of line 61a. Lines 61–63 would then read 'now that we

wræccan [. . . . . . . . . . .]    (He við wide fah.)
Ne við he no þæs nearwe    under niðloc[.n],
65  [. . .] þæs bitre gebunden    under bealuclommum,
þæt he þy yð ne mæge    ellen habban
þonne he his hlafordes    hyldo gelyfeð,
þæt hine of þam bendum    bicgan wille.
Swa we ealle to þe    an gelyfað,
70  dryhten min se dyra.    Ic adreag fela
siþþan þu end to me    insiþadest
þa þu me gesealdest    sweord ond byrnan,
helm ond heoroscearp    (a ic þæt heold nu giet),
ond þu me gecyðdest,    cyneþrymma wyn,
75  þæt þu mundbora    minum wære.
    Eala Gabrihel,    hu þu eart gleaw ond scearp,
milde ond gemyndig    ond monþwære,
*121a*  wis on þinum gewitte /    ond on þinum worde snottor!
Þæt þu gecyðdest    þa þu þone cnyht to us
80  brohtest in Bethlem.    Bidan we þæs longe,
set[t]an on sorgum,    sibbe oflyste,
wynnum ond wenum,    hwonne we word Godes
þurh his sylfes muð    secgan hyrde.
    Eala Maria,    hu þu us modigne
85  cyning acendest    þa þu þæt cild to us
brohtest in Bethlem!    We þæs beofiende
under helle doru[m]    hearde sceoldon

---

many endure [? hell pains], [? when ? since] [someone or something] binds the brotherless exile . . . . . . . (He is banned far and wide.)' But even this reading, which accommodates the grammar of the available words, is uncertain.

    63: The word *wræccan* is intact. Of about twelve missing letter spaces following *wræccan*, the first and fourth had long descending strokes, and the second may have had a shorter descender. Thus the on-verse alliterated on *w*, perhaps *wr*. Nothing else can be restored. At the right-hand edge of the hole the *h* of *he* is damaged but readable, so that the words *he við wide*, ending at the right margin, are certain.

    64: The *e* of *under* is beheaded but readable. The *c* of *niðloc* is largely present, and the feet of the final *n* are visible. The word is *niðlocan* without much doubt. There are then three letter spaces before the right-hand margin.

    65: [. . .]. The second of the three spaces at the end of the MS line shows a

[exile. . . . . . .] (He is banned far and wide.)
Yet none is so closely or bitterly bound
65    under cursed locks or evil clutches
that he could not the more freely have courage
when he believes in his Lord's faithfulness,
that he will buy him out of those bonds.
So we all believe in you alone,
70    my Lord, my beloved. I've endured much
since the other time you came inside me,
the time you bestowed on me sword and byrnie,
helmet and war gear (I've always held it, even till now),
and you made known to me, noblest of rulers,
75    that you would be my flock's defender.
    O Gabriel, how shrewd and sharp you are,
how generous and thoughtful and gentle,
wise in your mind and prudent with words!
You made it known when you brought the boy
80    to us in Bethlehem. Long we awaited it,
sitting in sorrows, longing for peace,
full of joy and hope when we heard God's word
spoken through a mouth sent from himself.
    O Mary, how courageous a king
85    you bore for us when you brought the babe
to us in Bethlehem! Trembling in bonds
beneath hell's doors, we had to await it

---

trace of what was probably the leading serifed foot of an *n*. Although ASPR
3 : 357–58n. records guesses of *to* and *oððe*, the first word of line 65 would more
logically have been *no*, giving parallel *no þæs* constructions to lines 64–65.

76, 84, 99, 103: A raised point after *wære* and a small capital *E* open the
apostrophe to Gabriel with a new paragraph. Identical paragraphing occurs for
the apostrophes to Mary, Jerusalem, and the Jordan. All have a thematic connection
with John and are therefore parallel or "equal" in a riddlic sense (see the
discussion in the Introduction to Part Two). The scribe therefore treats the four
apostrophes with graphic "equality" as well.

87: *doru*[*m*]. MS *doru*, with an unusually wide space after *helle*, suggesting
that the word was entered over an erasure. Probably the MS reading is an error
for *dorū*.

    bidan in bendum.    Bona weorces gefeah;
    wæron ure ealdfind    ealle on wynnum
90   þonne hy gehyrdon    hu we hreowen [. .
    . . . . .]on murnende    mægburg usse,
    oþþæt [. . . . . . . . .]    sigedryhten God,
    bimengdes[. . . . . . . . . . .    . . . . .] gust ealra cyninga.
    [. . . . . . . . . . . . . . . .]    nu us mon modge þe
95   ageaf from usse geogoðe.    We þurh gifre mod
    beswican us sylfe;    we þa synne forþon
    berað in urum breostum    to bonan honda,
    sculon eac to ussum feondum    freoþo wilnian.
        Eala Hierusalem    in Iudeum,
100 hu þu in þære stowe    stille gewunadest!
    Ne mostan þe geondferan    foldbuende
    ealle lifgende,    þa þe lof singað.
        Eala Iordane    in Iudeum,
    hu þu in þære stowe    stille gewunadest!
105 Nales [mostan] þ[e] geondflowan    foldbuende;
    mostan hy þynes wætres    wynnum brucan.

88: *bona*. A readable word, with the latter half of the *a* swallowed in the hole at the right-hand margin.

89: *wynnum*, like *bona*, missing the latter half of the *m*.

90–91: The *n* of *hreowen* is partly cut away by the leading edge of the hole. Then follow seven letter spaces of lost text and the word ending -*on*. C. W. M. Grein (*Bibliothek der angelsächsischen Poesie*, vol. 1; hereafter cited as Grein) suggested *hreowen* [*de mænd*]*on*, and both Mackie and ASPR 3 adopt this very probable guess.

92: *oþþæt* is readable even though the leading edge of the hole slices upward on a slant through all the letters except *o*. The first letter of the next word had a long ascending stroke: ASPR 3 guesses at *þu*. Then follow nine or ten completely obliterated letter spaces, after which the long descending tail of the *s* and most of the *i* of *sige* are visible.

93: *bimengdes*, with only the very top of the *s* still visible above the hole, almost certainly once read *bimengdest*. Then follow some sixteen letter spaces. If, as ASPR assumes, the word ending in legible -*gust* was part of the *m* line with *bimengdest*, then the broken word was probably [*modi*]*gust*, which would make the off verse a lexical variant for *reþust ealra cyninga*, line 36b. Mackie puts [. . . . .]*gust ealra cyninga* on a separate poetic line, an inferior solution. From this point on, Mackie's line numbering differs from the present text (which follows ASPR 3) by one.

in woeful trial. In his work the slayer rejoiced;
our ancient foes were all in raptures
90 when they found out how [? in our affliction]
we [? clamored our grief], mourning our kindred,
until [? you . . . . . . . . . .], Lord God triumphant,
deigned to consort [. . . . . . . . . .] of all kings most
[?dauntless].
[. . . . . . . . . . . . . . . .] brave, since someone has
brought
95 you to us from our youth. By the greed in our hearts
we betray ourselves; and thus the sins
in our breasts we bear into the slayer's hands,
and we must implore reprieve from our foes.
O Jerusalem amid the Jews,
100 how you have stood undisturbed in that place!
Those who dwell in the world could not walk through
you,
not all those living who laud you in song.
O Jordan amid the Jews,
how you have stood undisturbed in that place!
105 Earth's citizens [could] not at all stream through [you];
all had leave to use your water with joy.

---

94: A raised point and generous space after *cyninga*, at the right-hand
margin, suggests that there may have been another small capital and a new para-
graph, perhaps also beginning with *Eala*, at the left margin. In lines 94–98 the
theme seems rather different from the apostrophe to Mary and God in the previ-
ous lines. But beginning at the left margin, the hole now completely eliminates
seventeen or eighteen letter spaces. Following the hole, the words *nu us mon
modge þe* are visible, but Mackie judges them to be "corrupt." The word *us* origi-
nally read *usic*, but the *ic* has been badly erased and is still readable.

95: *from*. The word, at the left-hand margin, shows only the descending
tail of the *f* and the bottom portion of the *r*. The word is fairly legible.

96: *us*. Originally *us/ic*, divided at the end of the MS line. The letters *ic*, at
the left margin, have been only halfheartedly erased.

101: *þe*. Originally *þec*, with the shadow of the erased *c* still visible.

105: *Nales* [*mostan*] [*þe*] *geondflowan foldbuende*. MS *Nales þu geondflowan fold-
buende*, an ungrammatical line, has been variously emended: *nales þu geondflowan
mostes foldbuende*; *naldes þu geondflowan foldbuende*; and *mostes þu geondflowan fold-
buende*, finally suggested by Grein, who, like many other scholars, was troubled
by the negative particles in lines 101a and 105a. Mackie follows this latter sugges-

   Nu ic þe halsie,   hæland user,
*121b*  deope in gedyrstum   (þu eart drihten Crist), /
   þæt þu us gemiltsie,   monna scyppend.
110 Þu fore monna lufan   þinre modor bosm
   sylfa gesohtes,   sigedryhten God,
   nales fore þinre þearfe,   þeoda waldend,
   ac for þam miltsum   þe þu moncynne
   oft ætywdest,   þonne him wæs are þearf.
115 Þu meaht ymbfon   eal folca gesetu,
   swylce þu meaht geriman,   rice dryhten,
   sæs sondgrotu,   selast ealra cyninga."
    "Swylce ic þe halsige,   hælend user,
   fore [.] inum cildhade,   cyninga selast,
120 ond fore þære wunde,   weoruda dry[. . . .
   . . . . r] þinum æriste,   æþelinga wyn,
   ond fore þinre me[d . . . . . . . . . . . ar]ian nama,
   þa ealle hellwara   hergað ond lof[. . .

---

tion; and ASPR 3:358–59 describes it as the most plausible emendation yet
offered, except for the apparently awkward repetition of *mostan* in line 106. But
the negative particles of this passage belong to an allegorical riddle about Jerusa-
lem and the Jordan, culminating in a second speaker's desire to imitate the bap-
tism of John and Christ as the poem ends. Thus line 101 can be read to make
good sense as it stands in the MS, and line 105 can be emended to make the same
point about the Jordan in exactly parallel grammar: *Nales* [*mostan*] *þ*[*e*] *geond-
flowan foldbuende*. For more details of the argument, see the discussion in the In-
troduction to Part Two.

  107: With a raised point after *brucan* and a bold small block capital *N* of
*Nu*, John turns from the four apostrophes to address Christ directly once again
and to make a brief final plea for deliverance from hell.

  114: A raised point after *þearf* is generously spaced, and perhaps the scribe
intended an additional paragraph here. But his *þ* opening line 115 is not cer-
tainly a capital.

  118: With a raised point after *cyninga* and the unambiguous small capital *S*
of *Swylce* a concealed second speaker, someone other than John but of themati-
cally discoverable identity, begins to address Christ *swylce* 'likewise,' i.e., in an ar-
gument of riddlic similarity to John's. See the discussion in the Introduction to
Part Two.

Now, our Savior, I beseech you
fervently in affliction (you are Christ the Lord)
that you show us mercy, O Shaper of men.
110   For love of men in your mother's bosom
you alighted yourself, Lord God of triumphs,
not at all for your own needs, Ruler of nations,
but because of the mercies which to mankind
you often have given when it needed grace.
115   You could surround all peoples' settlements,
just as you, mighty Ruler, could also reckon
the sand grains of the sea, O best of all kings."
    [*A second speaker pleads for Christ's presence in this world*]
    "Likewise I, too, beseech you, our Savior,
by your childhood, choicest of kings,
120   and by the wounding, Warder of hosts,
and by your arising, best of rulers,
and by your mo[ther . . . . . . . . Mar]y is the name,
whom all hell's inhabitants laud and pr[aise

---

119: The first letter of the second word has totally disappeared into the hole at the left margin. The missing letter is *þ*, as the intact *þinum* in line 121 shows.

120–21: The *y* of *dry* is broken but recognizable, and the *þ* of *þinum* is almost whole. The top of the letter preceding *þ* looks like *r*. The parallel phrases in *ond fore* in lines 120 and 122 leave no doubt of the seven or eight letter spaces: the text once read *dry[hten 7 for]*.

122: At midline an *me-* and the forward trace of a looped letter are visible. Then follow about twelve obliterated letter spaces. At the right-hand edge of the hole *-ian* is preceded by the upper traces of two letters reasonably taken to be *a* and *r*. The two words on either side of the hole are therefore probably *me[der]* and [*Mar*]*ian*. As noted in ASPR 3:359, the missing words would have led to the nom. sing. grammar of *nama* at the end of the line. Perhaps, then, the line once read *ond fore þinre me[der, þære is Mar]ian nama*, with a dative of interest denoting possession: 'and by your mother, of whom Mary is the name' (i.e., 'whose name is Mary').

123: In the off verse the word *lof-* also shows the bottom part of an *i* and barely the lower front edge of an *a*. The whole word, in series with *hergað*, is *lof[iað]*.

. . . . . . . . . . . . . . .]lum    þe þe ymb stondað,
125    þa þu þe lete sittan    [. . . . . . . . . . . . . . .] hond,
       þa þu us on þisne wræcsið,    weoroda dryhten,
       þurh þines sylfes geweald    secan woldest,
       ond [fore] Hierusalem    in Iudeum
       (sceal seo burg nu þa    bidan efne swa þea[h],
130    þeoden leofa,    þines eftcymes),
       ond for Iordane    in Iudeum:
       Wit unc in þære burnan    baþodan ætgædre.
       Oferwurpe þu mid þy wætre,    weoruda dryhten,
       bliþe mode    ealle burgwaran,
135    swylce git Iohannis    in Iordane
       mid þy fullwihte    fægre onbryrdon
       ealne þisne middangeard.    Sie þæs symle meotude
                                          þonc."

124: After the projected end of *lof*[*iað*], some fifteen or sixteen letter spaces lead to a broken word ending in -*lum*. The third letter space before -*lum* has the tip of a high-looped *e* of the type consistently written before *n*. With *ymb* as the alliterating word of the off verse, and with the reference to creatures who 'stand around' Christ in heaven, the line may be restored [*ond fore þam eng*]*lum þe þe ymb stondað*, as the notes in ASPR 3:359 also argue. Mackie has [*ond fore þinum eng*]*lum*, which seems a bit too long for the available space.

125: After *sittan*, the rest of the MS line, some sixteen letter spaces, is missing all the way to the right margin. The traces of descending strokes after *sittan* fit the usual suggestion *on þa swiþran*, which does not, however, fill the MS line. I suspect an intensive comparative, [*on þa swiþorran*] *hond* 'on your very strong right hand,' which would still produce the shortest MS line on the entire page.

and by the ang]els who stand around you,
125 whom you caused to sit [on your very strong right] hand
since you, Lord of hosts, willed to seek us out
of your own accord in this journey of exile,
and by Jerusalem among the Jews
(even though that city must still await
130 your reappearance, beloved Prince),
and by Jordan among the Jews:
we two bathed in that spring together.
May you splash with that water, Warden of hosts,
with a blithe spirit all burghers everywhere,
135 just as you and John in the Jordan
by that baptism inspired with beauty
all this middle earth. For that be always thanks to God."

---

126: *us.* MS *us* was once again originally *usic* but was altered by erasure. This is the last of the mysteriously erased accusative pronouns of the poem, which alone among the poems of *The Easter Riddle* has such changes. Possibly the scribe (or corrector) preferred the leveled forms *me*, *þe*, and *us* to the older accusative forms, or perhaps he did not want the lettes *ic* to be mistaken for the first-person pronoun.

128: In fitting the word *Hierusalem* neatly to the right-hand margin, the scribe seems to have inadvertently left out the syntactically necessary *fore*, which virtually all editors supply.

129: *þeah.* MS *þean*, again fitted to the right-hand margin, is corrected by Mackie to *þeana*, but is more probably, as ASPR 3 suggests, a simple error for *þeah*.

# [ALMSGIVING]

Wel bið þam eorle    þe him on innan hafað,
*122a*   reþehyg / dig wer,    rume heortan.
Þæt him biþ for worulde    weorðmynda mæst,
ond for ussum dryhtne    doma selast.
5   Efne swa he mid wætre    þone weallendan
leg adwæsce,    þæt he leng ne mæg,
blac byrnende,    burgum sceððan,
swa he mid ælmessan    ealle toscufeð
synna wunde,    sawla lacnað.

In the text of this poem (fols. 121b–122a) there are no irregularities or difficulties.

# [ALMSGIVING]

It is well for the earl, an upright man,
who has inside him an ample heart.
It is his best stamp of worth in the eyes of the world,
and in the sight of our Lord the soundest of judgments.
5   As he might wash out with water
the welling flame brightly burning,
so that it can no longer scathe the cities,
so through almsgiving he dispels all
wounds from sins and thus heals souls.

# [PHARAOH]

"Saga me hwæt þær weorudes    wære ealles
on Farones fyrde,    þa hy folc Godes
þurh feondscipe    fylgan ongunn[.]."
"Nat ic hit be wihte,    butan ic wene þus,
5  þæt þær screod[a] wære    gescyred rime
siex hu[n . . . . . . . .]a    searohæbbendra;
þæt eal fornam [yþ . . . . . . . . . . .
w]raþe wyrde    in woruldrice."

3: The hole at the right margin has consumed only one letterspace. Thus the word *ongunnon* was probably written *ongunn[ō]*, like MS *fornā* for *fornam* in line 7.

5: Again at the right-hand margin only the front half of the final *-a* in *screoda* is visible.

6: The letters *hu* are intact, and the first part of an *n* shows at the leading edge of the hole. Mackie restores the number as *siex hun[d þusend]a*, a suggestion which does not fit the scriptural source for this poem, Exod. 14:6–7. As ASPR 3 notes (p. 360), the missing number must be either *siex hu[nd]*, followed by a six- or seven-letter adjective ending in the nearly intact *-a* after the hole, or *siex hu[ndred]* followed by four missing letters before the *-a*. Since the biblical source states that "six hundred chariots of the first class" were lost in the Red Sea, Ferdinand Holthausen's old proposal *siex hu[ndred godr]a* ("Zur altenglischen Litera-

# [PHARAOH]

"Tell me in full what troop strength there was
in Pharaoh's army, when for enmity's sake
they began to pursue the people of God."
    "I don't know it right on the nose, but I believe this,
5   that of cars there were by measured count
six hu[ndred . . . .] of men harnessed in armor;
the wave [. . . . . . . . . .] swept it all away
by the cruel fortune of this worldly kingdom."

---

tur. v. 21. 'Christi Höllenfahrt,'" *Anglia Beiblatt* 19 [1908]: 49–53) seems to hit on
the right theme even if it cannot certainly restore the second lost word.

    7: The letters *y* and the upward stroke of *þ* are reasonably certain through
a badly discolored spot at the forward edge of the hole, since *fornam* suggests
waves as the destructive agents in the Red Sea. After the upstroke of *þ* are eleven
letter spaces, variously conjectured as *yþ[a geblond]*, *yþ[a flodas]*, and *y[þa
streamas]*, of which the last proposal, in ASPR 3:360, would best fill the damaged
space. Less satisfactory for the paleographer, but more likely as a formula than
*yþa streamas* (which does not occur elsewhere), would be *yþ[a gewealc]*, an impor-
tant verse formula in the Exeter Book, since it occurs twice in *The Seafarer* (lines
6, 46). L. Whitbread, "The Old English Poem 'Pharaoh,'" *N&Q* 190 (1946):53b,
suggests *yþ[a færgripe w]raþe*, also a reasonably good paleographical fit.

    8: At the end of the hole the broken but readable *w* of *wraþe* appears.

# [THE LORD'S PRAYER I]

[. . . . . . . . . . g fæ]der,    þu þe on heofonum eardast,
ge[we]or[ð]ad wuldres dreame.    Sy þinum weorcum
   halgad
noma niþþa bearnum;    þu eart nergend wera.
Cyme þin rice wide,    ond þin rædfæst willa
5    aræred under rodores hrofe,    eac þon on rumre
   foldan.
Syle us to dæge    domfæstne blæd,
hlaf userne,    helpend wera,
þone singalan,    soðfæst meotod.
Ne læt usic costunga    cnyssan to swiþe
10    ac þu freodo[m] gief,    folca waldend,
from yfla gehwam,    a to widan feore.

1: All but the top of a serifed vertical stroke of a large bold initial has dis-
appeared in the large hole that spreads to the left margin. After the initial came
eleven or twelve letter spaces. Then appears a broken but readable *g* of an adjec-
tive ending in -*ig*, the discolored lower traces of the letters *fæ*, and the somewhat
more complete and readable *de* of the word *fæder*, whose final *r* is undamaged.
ASPR 3:360 correctly notes that the missing word ending in -*ig* should be *halig*
to alliterate with *heofonum* in the off verse but that *halig* alone will not fill the
damaged space. *Ure halig fæder* is also improbable, because the remnant of the
large initial looks like neither *U* nor *V* but instead like the top of either *H* or *L*.
We would then appear to be dealing not with the pronoun *Ure* at all but instead
with some expletive of direct address. But the context of the Lord's Prayer dis-
qualifies the common expletives in *h*: *huru* is used for logical argument rather
than direct address, and *hwæt* is too indecorous for calling on God. We are left, I
think, with *La*, a properly respectful word of rather frequent use in poetry,
though not otherwise recorded in the Exeter Book. Of all other initials in this
codex the larger bold *L* of *Wulf and Eadwacer* (fol. 100b) most nearly resembles

# [THE LORD'S PRAYER I]

[. . . . . . . . . . Fa]ther, who make your home in the
    heavens,
adored in the gladness of glory. Because of your works
be your name hallowed by the sons of men; you are men's
    savior.
Your kingdom come far and wide, and your wise will
5  be exalted below heaven's roof, as also on this ample
    earth.
Lend us today a lawful blessing,
our loaf of bread, Benefactor of men,
the eternal one, Lord true-sworn.
Let not temptations assault us too strongly,
10  but give us deliverance, Leader of nations,
from every evil until endless ages.

---

what little remains of the initial for this poem. Assuming on these circumstantial
grounds that the opening word of *The Lord's Prayer I* could have been *La*, I would
suggest for the remaining space the word *eallhalig*, which would fit quite well.
This word occurs only once in poetry, in the metrical version of Ps. 131. But, as a
lexical comparison of *The Easter Riddle* with the Benedictine office will show, yet
another borrowed word from the vocabulary of poetic psalmody associated with
the singing of the hours would be no surprise here. I think, therefore, that the
opening verse of *The Lord's Prayer I* might originally have been [*La, eallhali*]*g
fæder*.

    2: *ge*[*we*]*or*[*ð*]*ad*. Ms *ge*/[*we*]*or*[*ð*]*ad*, divided at the end of a MS line. The
damaged letters are at the left-hand margin, where the tail of a *w* and the bottom
portion of an *e* are visible. The following *o* is quite readable, the *r* nearly intact,
and the *ð* apparently visible except for its upper part and cross stroke. Conceiv-
ably the scribe mistakenly wrote *geweordad*, but the meaning *geweorðad* is obvious
from the context.

    10: *freodo*[*m*]. For MS *freo don*, an error.

# [HOMILETIC FRAGMENT II]

|  | Gefeoh nu on ferðe ond to frofre geþeoh, |
|---|---|
|  | dryhtne þinum, ond þinne dom arær. |
| *122b* | Heald hordlocan: hyge fæste bind / |
|  | mid modsefan. Monig biþ uncuþ |
| 5 | treowgeþofta; teora∂ hwilum, |
|  | waciaþ wordbeot. Swa þeos woruld fareð: |
|  | scurum scyndeð ond gesceop dreogeð. |
|  | An is geleafa. An lifgende, |
|  | an is fulwihte. an fæder ece, |
| 10 | an is folces fruma se þas foldan gesceop, |
|  | duguðe ond dreamas. Dom siþþan weox, |
|  | þeah þeos læne gesceaft longe stode |
|  | heolstre gehyded, helme [.]edygled, |
|  | biþeaht wel treowum, þystre oferfæðmed. |
| 15 | Siþ[.]an geong awe[ox] |
|  | mægeð modhwatu mid moncynne. |
|  | ðær gelicade þa[m . . . . . . .]op |
|  | in þam hordfæte halgan gæste. |

8–9: Small script capital *A* for the first word of both verses of line 8 and raised points after each verse in these two lines perhaps mark the splicing in of these well-known phrases from Eph. 4:5–6 and also provide a clue to the credal nature of the poem. See the discussion in the Introduction to Part Two.

9: *Fulwihte*. Corrected to *fulwiht* in ASPR 3. Both occur as nom.

11: *dreamas. Dom*. The MS words *dreamas dom* have been written over an erasure.

13: [.]*edygled*. The hole at the left margin has swallowed all of the prefixal *g* and about the front half of the following *e*, which is nevertheless readable.

15: *Siþ*[.]*an . . . awe*[*ox*]. MS *siþ*/[.]*an*, with the destroyed *þ* at the left edge of the MS line. At the top of the hole in midpage the readable upper part of an *x* confirms the damaged word as *awe*[*ox*], even though the *o* is practically all lost.

17: Since the *ð* of *ðær* is not certainly a small capital, a paragraph division might or might not have been intended with the raised point following *moncynne*

# [HOMILETIC FRAGMENT II]

Rejoice now in spirit and thrive in your solace,
which is your Lord, and lift up your honor.
Defend the treasure vault: fast in your heart
bind up your thoughts. Many a man is unsteady
5   among one's sworn friends; they sometimes fail,
words of promise will weaken. So this world goes:
it slips past amid turmoil and suffers its doom.
    [But] one is the faith, one living God,
there is one baptism, one Father eternal,
10  there is one Prince of peoples, who fashioned men's
    fields,
their wonders and joys. The glory then grew
(though this unrealized world long had lain
hidden in darkness, cloaked under covering,
well shrouded by trees, wrapped in shadow).
15  Then a young maid grew up,
deep-minded among men.
There, in that treasure cup, it contented
the Holy Spirit, [who inspired all life].

---

(line 16). At midpage, after the front portion of what is probably *m*, seven or eight letter spaces are completely lost except for perhaps the upper tip of a *c*. ASPR 3:361 notes Ferdinand Holthausen's old restoration þa[*m þis leoht gesce*]*op* ("Zur altenglischen Literatur. V. 21. 'Christi Höllenfahrt,'" *Anglia Beiblatt* 19 [1908]: 49–53; hereafter cited as Holthausen), which is somewhat too long for the available space and would require the awkward repetition of the word *leohtes* in line 20. Mackie's proposal þa[*m þe lif gesc*]*op* (W. S. Mackie, ed., *The Exeter Book, Part II: Poems IX–XXXII*; hereafter cited as Mackie), "accounts very well for the number of letters lost in the MS" (ASPR 3) only in the unlikely event that the scribe wrote the lost words with practically no spacing. Despite the desirable regularity of the verse as Mackie restores it, there is hardly room in the hole for more than þa[*mþe lif sc*]*op*, with the *li* of *lif* closely written and rather small spaces between words.

Beorht on br[eos . . . . . . . . . . . . .]e scan.
20   Se wæs ordfruma     ealles leohtes.

19: At the bottom of the hole at midpage traces of the letters *eos* confirm
the damaged on verse as either *beorht on br[eostum]* (Holthausen, followed by
ASPR 3) or *beorht on br[eoste]* (Mackie). Holthausen restored the off verse as
[*bearn leoht]e scan*, which is one or two letter spaces too long for the hole and
which again demands the awkward repetition of *leoht*. Mackie suggests [*bearn
hadr]e scan*, an attractive possibility on both paleographical and lexical grounds.
Adopting Holthausen's suggestion for the on verse, Mackie's for the off verse, I
would guess that line 19 once read *beorht on br[eostum bearn hadr]e scan*. But, as
ASPR 3 cautions, the off verse is very uncertain, and it is possible that the allit-
erating word there was also a riddle word such as *bryne* (for the fire of the Holy
Spirit) or *byrne* (hearkening back to the riddlic "armor" of John the Baptist in *The
Descent into Hell*).

Bright in her breast [. . . . . . . . . . . . .] shone:
20  this was the primordial point of all light.

# [RIDDLE 30b]

Ic eom lig bysig,    lace mid winde,
w[uldre bewunden,    we]dre gesomnad,
fus forðweges,    fyre gemylted,
bear[u] blowende,    byrnende gled.
5    Ful oft mec gesiþas    sendað æfter hondum;
þær mec weras ond wif    wlonce gecyssað.
Þonne ic mec onhæbbe,    hi onhnigað to me,
modge miltsum,    swa ic mongum sceal
ycan upcyme    eadignesse.

2: After a fairly readable *w* at the beginning of the line lower traces of the letters *u* and *l* can be seen. In the second letter space after *l* is the tail of a long downstroke. Then about thirteen more letter spaces are virtually obliterated all the way to the righthand margin. Luckily the closely comparable verse in *Riddle 30a* (fol. 108a) reads *bewunden mid wuldre*. With the help of these words the traces of the damaged letters in *Riddle 30b*, and the letters *dre* at the left margin right

# [RIDDLE 30b]

I am a busy flame; I float with the wind,
[surrounded with splendor,] joined with [the air],
for departure impatient, melted by fire,
blowing wood, burning embers.
5  High companions often pass me around in their hands;
there men and women in majesty kiss me.
When I left myself up, they bend low to me,
sincere in their meekness. Thus for many I'll bring
elevation in bliss.

---

after the damaged part, we can safely restore line 2 as *w[uldre bewunden   we]dre gesomnad*, an exact paleographical fit.

3: *gemylted*. Below the hole the word is intact except for the upward stroke of the *d*.

4: *bear[u]*. The lower traces of *bear* are visible before the right-hand margin, but *u* has completely vanished into the hole. The word is certain as *bear[u]* by comparison with *Riddle 30a*, fol. 108a.

# [THE HUSBAND'S MESSAGE]

    Ic wæs be sonde,    sæwealle neah,
    æt merefaroþe,    minum gewunade
    frumstaþole fæst.    Fea ænig wæs
    monna cynnes    þæt minne þær
5    on anæde    eard beheolde;
    ac mec uhtna gehwam    yð sio brune
    lagufæðme beleolc.    Lyt ic wende
*123a*    þæt ic ær oþþe sið /    æfre sceolde
    ofer meodu[bence]    muðleas sprecan,
10    wordum wrixlan.    Þæt is wundres dæl,
    on sefan searolic    þam þe swylc ne conn,
    hu mec seaxe[s] ord    ond seo swiþre hond,
    eorles ingeþonc    ond ord somod,
    þingum geþydan,    þæt ic wiþ þe sceolde
15    for unc anum twa[m]    ærendspræce
    abeodan bealdlice,    swa hit beorna ma
    uncre wordcwidas    widdor ne mænden.
    Nu ic onsundran þe    secgan wille

1–17: These lines are known as "Riddle 60" in Mackie (W. S. Mackie, ed., *The Exeter Book, Part II: Poems IX–XXXII*; hereafter cited as Mackie), ASPR 3, and nearly all other older editions. Craig Williamson, ed., *The Old English Riddles of the Exeter Book* (1977) still edits them separately as "Riddle 58." But in line with important statements by F. A. Blackburn ("The 'Husband's Message' and the Accompanying Riddles of the Exeter Book," *JEGP* 3 [1901]: 1–13,) hereafter cited as Blackburn), Robert E. Kaske ("A Poem of the Cross in the Exeter Book: 'Riddle 60' and 'The Husband's Message,' *Traditio* 23 [1967]: 41–71), Margaret Goldsmith ("The Enigma of The Husband's Message," in Lewis E. Nicholson and Dolores Warwick Frese, eds., *Anglo-Saxon Poetry: Essays in Appreciation for John C. McGalliard*, pp. 242–63), and John C. Pope ("Palaeography and Poetry: Some Solved and Unsolved Problems in the Exeter Book, in M. B. Parkes and Andrew G. Watson, eds., *Medieval Scribes, Manuscripts and Libraries: Essays Presented to N. R. Ker*, pp. 25–65, hereafter cited as Pope), I have incorporated these lines into *The Husband's Message*, though for reasons quite different from those my predecessors have offered. See the discussion in the Introduction to Part Two.

9: *meodu[bence]*. A hypothetical correction from MS *meodu*, without a gap or erasure. Of various suggestions made to fill out the defective meter of the verse,

# [THE HUSBAND'S MESSAGE]

I was by the sand, near the seashore,
near the waves from the deep, dwelt
firm in my first home. Few there were
of humankind who would ever behold
5  my spot there in that solitude;
but each dawn the bright breaker
lapped me instead with its wet embrace. Little I thought
that early or late I ever should speak
without mouth over mead [bench]
10  traffic in words. A great wonder it is,
strange skill to his mind who knows not such things,
how the dagger's point and the dextral hand,
an earl's inner thought and the point together,
thus connected me closely with you, so that I'd
15  boldly announce for us both as one
a message in speech, so more children of men
should not tell it more widely, our dealing in words.
    I want now to say aside to you

---

C. W. M. Grein's reading *meodu*[*bence*] (*Bibliothek der Angelsachsischen Poesie*, vol. 1),
adopted by Mackie, ASPR 3, and recently also by Pope, makes the best versifica-
tion and thematic sense. See ASPR 3:362n. and the discussion in the Introduc-
tion to Part Two.

    12: *seaxe*[*s*]. MS *seaxeð*, an error. ASPR 3:362 recalls the plausible sugges-
tion of Georg Herzfeld (*Die Räthsel des Exeterbuches und ihr Verfasser*, p. 64) that
the following word, *ord*, rather awkwardly repeated in the next line, was also a
mistake, perhaps for *ecg*. The scribe's eye might have inadvertently slipped down
a line too far in the MS he was copying, in which case he would mistakenly have
written the word *ord* twice. A similar error, with more confusing results, may
have happened in *The Ruin* 3–4.

    15: *twa*[*m*]. MS *twan*, an error.

    17–18: In the MS the word *mænden*, followed by a colophon, takes up a
short MS line by itself. Then, without extra space between MS lines, the block
capital initial of *Nu* begins line 18. This block *N*, the smallest and plainest of the
four initials in the poem, marks a riddlic change in the speaker's audience, not
yet in the speaker. See the discussion in the Introduction to Part Two.

[. . . . . . . . .] treocyn[ne]    ic tudre aweox.
20 I[w] mec [?æ]ld[. . . . . . . . . . . .] sceal    ellor londes
sett[an . . . . . . . . . . . . . . . . . . e]c    sealte streamas
[. . . . . . . . . . . . . . . . . . . . . . . . . .]sse.
Ful oft ic on bates [. . . . . . . . . . . . . . . . . . . .] gesohte,
þær mec mondryhten    min [. . . . . . . .]
25 ofer heah hofu.    Eom nu her cumen
on ceolþele,    ond nu cunnan scealt
hu þu ymb modlufan    mines frean
on hyge hycge.    Ic gehatan dear
þæt þu þær tirfæste    treowe findest.
30 Hwæt, þec þonne biddan het    se þisne beam agrof
þæt þu sinchroden    sylf gemunde

19–24, 50–56: These two passages in the poem, badly damaged by the large hole through fol. 123, have been ingeniously patched with letters and words borrowed from other parts of the Exeter Book and photographed in their new places. The discussion and photographs can be seen in Pope, pp. 25–65. As he would be the first to warn, the photographs of his work, despite perfect paleographical matches of every detail around the edges of the hole in the page, cannot establish certain readings everywhere. But since Pope's judicious handling of both paleography and themes confirms my own views of the damaged passages, I have borrowed his readings for those parts almost wholesale. The following notes indicate the extent of my borrowing and summarize as objectively as possible the evidence for Pope's astute guesswork. Without exception, his readings make excellent fits, letter stroke for letter stroke around the edges of the hole, letter space for letter space inside the hole.

19: Into the nine letter spaces after *wille*, Pope fits the words *of hwylcum*, following an old suggestion of Imelmann's (*Forschungen zur altenglischen Poesie*, p. 148), which Imelmann himself rejected on wrong thematic grounds. MS *treo cyn*, damaged by a hole at the right-hand margin, may have been spelled *treo cyne*, since only one letter appears to be missing. But Pope emends to the more usual spelling *treocynne*.

20: Pope reads the first broken word in this line as *iw* 'yew,' specifying the *treocyn* referred to in line 19. Then follow the readable word *mec* and a damaged word, which Pope restores as *ælde* 'men.' The whole line, in Pope's restoration, reads *i[w] mec [æ]ld[e hatað, ac ic] sceal ellor londes*.

21: Pope has *setta[n siþas mine þonne me]c sealte streamas*, with *siþas* as a guess at theme and *þonne* as a guess at syntax.

22: Except for a final word ending in *-sse*, this line is totally destroyed. Taking a cue from *Maldon* 41, *on flot feran*, Pope restores the on verse as *on flot*

[. . . . . . . .] kind of tree, [? from what] kinship I grew.
20  [Yew] me [? men . . . . . . . . . . . . .] shall in another land
[? set . . . . . . . . . . . . . . . . . .] salt streams
[. . . . . . . . . . . . . . . . . . . . . . . .]
I very often on a boat's [. . . . . . . . . . . . . . . . . . . . .]
    sought,
where my liege lord me [. . . . . . . .]
25  over high seas. Now I've come hither
on a big ship's planks, and now you shall know
how you should think in your thoughts
of my lord's deep love. I dare to pledge
that there you shall find an honor-bound promise.
30      Hear! He who engraved this wood then ordered to ask
            you,
    O ring-covered one, yourself to recall

---

*fergað.* The off verse he supplies as *frean to lisse,* an attractive suggestion because the identity of the *frea* 'lord' is a major riddlic challenge of the poem.

23: Between *bates* and *gesohte,* mostly readable, are twenty-one letter spaces of destroyed text. Pope restores the entire lines as *Ful oft ic on bates* [*stefne burgstede þær*] *gesohte,* a possible if rather unusual hypermetric line.

24: After *min,* beginning again at the left margin, there are nine letter spaces of obliterated text, followed by the lower part of an *o* in the readable word *ofer* (line 25a). Pope supplies the missing word as *gelædde,* a reasonable thematic guess.

25: *hofu.* Leslie (Roy F. Leslie, ed., *Three Old English Elegies: The Wife's Lament, The Husband's Message, The Ruin;* hereafter cited as Leslie) and Pope emend to *h[a]fu,* which is surely the right meaning. But the spelling *hofu* may be simply phonetic, indicating a pronunciation [hɔvu]. Compare, for example, the word *gopes* in *Riddle 48* 3 and its relation to ON *gapa,* and the preferred Exeter Book spellings *hond, long, ond* (exclusively), etc.

29: *treowe findest.* MS *treo* / [runover mark] *we findest,* with a short line preceded by a runover mark at the right margin. The runover mark, one of thirteen in the entire codex, resembles a reversed open block *S* with periods inside both ends. It was placed to make the short right-hand line visible, since it competes with a significant initial *H* at the left margin.

30: A rather large, graceful, and modestly decorated initial *H,* more significant than the smaller and plainer block *N* at line 18, is the graphic clue of the change to a human speaker, who also signals his own presence by calling the previous speaker *þisne beam.* See the discussion in the Introduction to Part Two.

on gewitlocan     wordbeotunga
þe git on ærdagum     oft gespræcon,
þenden git moston     on meoduburgum
35  eard weardigan,     an lond bugan,
freondscipe fremman.     Hine fæhþo adraf
of sigeþeode;     heht hu sylfa þe
123b  lustum     læran þæt þu lagu drefde /

siþþan þu gehyrde     on hliþes oran
40  galan geomorne     geac on bearwe.
Ne læt þu þec siþþan     siþes getwæfan,
lade gelettan     lifgendne monn.
    Ongin mere secan,     mæwes eþel,
onsite sænacan,     þæt þu suð heonan
45  ofer merelade     monnan findest.
Þær se þeoden is     þin on wenum.
Ne mæg him [on] worulde     willa [gelimpan]
mara on gemyndum,     þæs þe he me sægde,
þonne inc geunne     alwaldend God
50  [þæt git a]etsomne     siþþan motan
secgum ond gesiþum s[inc . . . . . . . . .],

    38: *drefde* is the last word on fol. 123a. The inverted drypoint drawing of horse and rider, shown here as a line drawing, is approximately centered in the bottom margin between the last MS line and the edge of the page. The drawing here is from a pencil rubbing of the impression in the photofacsimile edition of the Exeter Book. On the authority of my notes about the drypoint impression in the MS, the rubbing was corrected in one or two slight details. The MS drawing is about 7 cm long and 5.5 cm high.
    43: A large, bold, decorated initial *O* followed by a smaller block capital *N*

in your mind those commitments in words
that you two often uttered in earlier days,
while yet in the mead towns you both had the might
35 to watch your domain, live in one land,
further your friendship. A feud drove him away
from this glorious nation. Gladly now he himself has
   commanded
that you make ready to drive through the deeps
as soon as you've heard on the high cliff's head
40 the woeful cuckoo's cry in the wood.
Do not suffer yourself to be kept from the voyage;
let no man living delay your going.
   Go seek out the ocean, the seagull's home:
mount the seagoing ship, so that off to the south,
45 over the course of the main, you find your man.
There the prince is expecting you.
No wish in the world can [? be]
more on his mind, since he told me himself
when almighty God should willingly grant
50 [? that you two] together may thenceforth [? mete out]
to true men and retainers [? your costly treasures],

---

marks the final paragraph of the poem, a turn to the human messenger's long
declaration of the husband's abiding love for the wife, his success and prepara-
tion to receive her in his new land, his runic oath and promise of their mystical
reunion, and the final clue to his divine identity. See the discussion in the Intro-
duction to Part Two.

47: A short word, supplied by most editors as *on*, appears to have been
erased by accidental smudging rather than by intention. Although there is no
gap in the MS, the off verse is incomplete. Most editors have supplied *gelimpan*,
to which there is no good objection.

49: *alwaldend God*. MS *al/waldend*, divided by the end of a line, with the bow
of *w* visible at the edge of a small hole at the left margin. Before the leading edge
of the hole in midpage, the letters *go* and the characteristic upper tip of *d* are
visible.

50: [*þæt git a*]*etsomne*. According to the practically inescapable conclu-
sions of earlier editors, Pope fills the gap in the on verse with [*þ git a*]*etsomne*,
and I have merely expanded the abbreviation *þ* to *þæt*, as I have done silently
elsewhere.

51: After *gesiþum*, at the front edge of the hole, there is the long down-

næglede beagas.　　He genoh hafað
fedan go[ldes . . . . . . . . . . . . . . . .
　. . . . . . .]d elþeode　　eþel healde,
55　fægre fold[an . . . . . . . . . . . . . . . . . . . . .
　. . . .] ra hæleþa,　　þeah þe her [herra] min
　win[. . . . . . . . . . . . . . . . . . . . . .]
　nyde gebæded,　　nacan ut aþrong,
　ond on yþa ge[? belg　　? ana] sceolde,
60　faran on flotweg,　　forðsiþes georn,
　mengan merestreamas.　　Nu se mon hafað
　wean oferwunnen;　　nis him wilna gad,
　ne meara ne maðma　　ne meododreama,
　ænges ofer eorþan　　eorlgestreona,
65　þeodnes dohtor,　　gif he þin beneah.
　Ofer eald gebeot　　incer twega

─────────

stroke of an *s*. Pope follows the suggestion of earlier editors, *s[inc bryttian]*, an excellent paleographical fit.

52: *næglede beagas*. The words are badly broken and faded but readable, at the upper edge of the hole.

53: *fedan go[ldes*. The words *fedan go[l]* are readable before the front edge of the hole. Pope fills out the line as *fedan go[ldes, feohgestreona]*, an acceptable paleographical fit and an attractive thematic suggestion, parallel with *eorlges-treona* in the undamaged line 64.

54: If the spacing of *feohgestreona* is accepted for the previous verse, there are eight more letter spaces to the right-hand edge of the gap. With somewhat generous but not objectionable spacing, Pope fills in the damaged on verse with [þ he mi]d elþeode.

55: From the words *fægre fold[an]*, readable all but the larger part of *a* and the final *n*, Pope proceeds all the way to the margin with [nalæs he þær fea teleð], and translates 'There he counts not a few,' a shrewd thematic guess. The *l* of Pope's word *teleð* is matched up with the first of three vertical upstrokes toward the right-hand margin.

56: The vertical ascenders whose tips show above the last two letter spaces match perfectly with [hold], an established editorial suggestion, which also squares well with the margin. The on verse is therefore [hold]/ra hæleþa without much doubt. In the off verse, where other editors have þeah þe her min win[e], Pope keenly assumes an unemphatic *her* and an erroneously omitted alliteration word. Thus his off verse becomes þeah þe her [herra] min—speculation, to be

riveted rings. He has enough
of hammered go [ld . . . . . . . . . . . . . . . .
. . . . . . .] a foreign folk have his home,
55   fair field[s . . . . . . . . . . . . . . . . . . . . . .
? of loyal] heroes, though here my [lord]
friend [. . . . . . . . . . . . . . . . . . . . . .]
driven by need, shoved his ship out,
and had to [? go alone] onto the [? lashing] of waves,
60   travel the floodpath, take flight in haste,
stir the sea streams. Now the man has
won out over woes; he lacks no delights,
neither horses nor jewels nor joys of mead,
nothing on earth of an earl's treasures,
65   if he may have, noble's daughter, enough of you.
Above the old vow of your common devotion

---

sure, but based on a very possible scribal slip with two adjacent words *her* and
*herra*, and potentially a vast improvement of the text.

57: Pope's ingenious suggestion for line 56 left him free to begin line 57,
left totally blank in all other editions, with the readable letters *win* upon which to
build a line of *w* alliteration. His solution is *wi[neleas gewat of wicstede]*, a fascinat-
ing reemergence (whether consciously proposed or not) of the word *wineleas* and
the important riddle word *wic* in *The Wife's Lament*. Pope's line here is only a
guess, but I have high stakes in wishing him to be right.

59: The word after *yþa* begins with a virtually undamaged *g* and ends with
the lower loop of another *g*. After the first *g* the letter *e* with a low horizontal
stroke is visible. Of the next letter only the bottom of the loop can be seen, and
the next two marks look like the serifed feet of an *n*. Though most editors read
*geong*, Pope argues that the looped letter is too narrow for the scribe's typical *o*
and is more probably a *b*. Also, as Pope notes, the readable *e* has a low loop, not
the characteristic high-looped *e* that makes a partial ligature in *eo*. Pope there-
fore suggests that the word is not *geong* but *gebelg* and translates *yþa gebelg* as
'swelling' or 'surge of waves.' The remaining letter spaces to the right margin are
then filled in with the old proposal *ana* 'alone.' This solution improves the verse
of these lines: line 59 can now be ended with a comma, as I have done but Pope
did not, so that *sceolde / faran* (lines 59–60) need not be read as awkward enjamb-
ment. The phrases *faran on flotweg* (line 60a) and *mengan merestreamas* (line 61a)
can then be read in the complete apposition which a skillful Anglo-Saxon poet
would almost certainly have preferred.

ge[h]yre ic ætsomne   ·S·R· geador,
·EA·W· ond ·D·,   aþe benemnan
þæt he þa wære   ond þa winetreowe
70   be Him lifgendum   læstan wolde,
þe git on ærdagum   oft gespræconn.

67: *ge[h]yre.* MS *ge[.]yre,* a problematical reading. Blackburn, Ernst A. Kock ("Interpretations and Emendations of Early English Texts, *VIII*," *Anglia* 45 [1921]: 105–31), and ASPR 3:364, read *ge[c]yre.* But despite the confidence expressed in ASPR 3, the faint and discolored traces of the missing letter do not look like *c,* and Pope justly dismisses *gecyre* as "totally erroneous." Kaske reads *genyre,* with the ingenious but obscure meaning 'constrain together.' The letter could be *h* just as well as *n,* so that the combined paleographical, grammatical, and thematic evidence most strongly favors *ge[h]yre* 'I hear.' See the discussion in the Introduction to Part Two, which explains *ge[h]yre* as a likely riddle word on a major theme of the poem. Moritz Trautmann ("Zur Botschaft des Gemahls," *Anglia* 16 [1894]: 207–25, hereafter cited as Trautmann), Ferdinand Holthausen ("Zur altenglischen Literatur. V. 21. 'Christi Höllenfahrt,'" *Anglia Beiblatt* 19 [1908]: 49–53), Ernest Sieper (*Die Altenglische Elegie*), Henry Bradley (review of Henry Morley, *English Writers, II, Academy* 33 [1888]: 197–98), Leslie, and Pope all read *ge[h]yre* as well.

I [?hear] in a sum *S, R* together,
*EA, W*, and *D* declare with an oath
that by him who is living he would fulfill
70   the pledge of faith and the partners' promise
that you two often uttered in former days.

---

67–68: In the MS the boldly written runes are individually surrounded by raised points, and have therefore been variously interpreted as separate rune names concealing a symbolic message (R. M. W. Elliott, *Runes: An Introduction*, and Pope), as personal names (Nora Kershaw, *Anglo-Saxon and Norse Poems*, p. 42), or as personal and rune names in combination (Trautmann). But, as Leslie reminds us, the similarly punctuated runes of *Riddle 24* are simply an anagram for the word *higora* 'magpie' or 'jay.' Of course, there have been various unsuccessful anagrammatic solutions for the runes in *The Husband's Message*, including my own *sweard* (ModE *sward*) 'parchment.' But the archaeological evidence reviewed in the discussion in the Introduction to Part Two suggests that the most probable anagram, in keeping with the legal theme of the poem, is *sweard* (*swearð*) 'swearing,' with perhaps a pun on Sedgefield's old idea *sweard* (*sweord*) 'sword' (W. J. Sedgefield, *An Anglo-Saxon Verse Book*). The last word of line 68, *benemnan*, is somewhat smudged by the same accident, perhaps a drop of perspiration or other small liquid spill, that erased the crucial stem consonant of *ge*[.]*yre* in line 67.

# [THE RUIN]

Wrætlic is þes wealstan,    wyrde gebræcon.
*124a*   Burgstede / burston,    brosnað enta geweorc.
Hrofas sind gehrorene,    hreorge torras,
hri[n]geat berofen,    hrim on lime,
5   scearde scurbeorge    scorene, gedrorene,
ældo undereotene.    Eorðgrap hafað
waldend wyrhtan,    forweorone, geleorene,
heard gripe hrusan,    oþ hund cnea
werþeoda gewitan.    Oft þæs wag gebad
10   ræghar ond readfah    rice æfter oþrum,
ofstonden under stormum.    Stea[þ], geap, gedreas.
Wonað giet se[o . . . . . . . . . . . .]rum gehea[w]en,
felon [u . . . . . . . . . . . . . . . . . . . . . . . . e]

4: [*hrungeat*] *berofen,*   *hrim on lime.* MS *hrim geat torras berofen hrim on lime.* The scribe's attention to his work seems to have lapsed here. The word *torras* makes the on verse unmetrical, and is probably a mistaken repetition of the same word, correctly placed, in line 3b. In line 4 the word *torras* is deleted by most editors, though Grein included an emended form of the word in the reading *hrimge edoras*, then read *hrungeat-torras* somewhat later (C. W. M. Grein, *Bibliothek der angelsächsischen Poesie*, vol. 1 [1857]). This later reading was kept by Wülcker in his revised 2d ed. of Grein's work (vol. 1, 1881, p. 296), and *hrungeat berofen* appears in both W. S. Mackie, ed., *The Exeter Book, Part II: Poems IX–XXXII* (hereafter cited as Mackie), and ASPR 3. Since MS *hrim geat* seems to be a mistake caused by glancing ahead at the word *hrim* in line 4b, some kind of emendation is probably needed. However, the easiest paleographical solution, *hrungeat*, would be a unique compound of doubtful reference: ? 'rung gate,' ? 'barred gate.' Almost as good paleographically, and lexically much more probable, is Friedrich Kluge's suggeston *hringeat* 'ring-gate' (*Angelsächsisches Lesebuch*; hereafter cited as Kluge), adopted by Levin L. Schücking, *Kleines angelsächsisches Dichterbuch*. Together with the words *hringas* (line 19) and *hringmere* (line 45), the word *hringeat* (for *hring-geat* 'gate of the ring') was probably intended as part of a riddlic theme on circularity. The circle, especially the *hringmere* 'circular sea,' is a prominent detail of the Roman ruins at Bath, the Temple of Solomon, and the Christian baptistery. See the discussion in the Introduction to Part Two.

8: *cnea.* The word has *ea* written in a partial ligature with a high-looped *e*, as always in the Exeter Book, but with a script *a* rather than the usual insular *a*.

# [THE RUIN]

Wondrous is this wall stone, broken by Fate.
Strongholds have split; giants' works rot away.
Roofs are caved in, towers in ruin,
the [ring gate] broken in, rime on mortar,
5   gaping roofs weakened and shorn away,
gnawed through by age.    The earth has in its grasp
both kings and their builders, dead and decayed,
the hard grip of the ground; up to a hundred clans
of people have passed. Often this wall,
10   splotched mold gray and red, outlived rule after rule,
stood strong under storming. High and wide, it has
    fallen;
still more the [. . . . . .] weakens, hewn by [hard
    weather?],

---

11: *Stea[þ]*. Only the top left corner of the *þ* escaped the hole at the right-hand margin.

12: MS *wonað* is quite readable at the top edge of the hole in the photofacsimile, but ASPR 3 notes the word as very badly damaged in the MS. The lower part of the loop on the *g* of *giet* is lost. Only the *se* of the next word is seen at the front edge of the hole, but Leslie very probably restores the *o* because the *e* has the high-looped letter of the *eo* partial ligature. However, the letter after *se* might also have been *a, m, n,* or *r*. After the letters *se* follow about thirteen destroyed spaces, then a word which ended either in *-num* (Mackie and ASPR 3) or *-rum* (Roy F. Leslie, ed., *Three Old English Elegies: The Wife's Lament, The Husband's Message, The Ruin*; hereafter cited as Leslie). If Leslie is right, as the remnant of the broken letter suggests, then Kluge's and Mackie's reading [*wealstan wæþ*]*num* is impossible for both words. The restoration [*wæþ*]*num* has influenced the emendation of MS *geheapen* to *gehea[w]en*, which also satisfies the strong verb grammar. I have followed Leslie in the reading [*wede*]*rum gehea[w]en* 'hewn by hard weather,' which, however, cannot be thematically favored over [*wæþ*]*num gehea[w]en*. Karl P. Wentersdorf, "Observations on *The Ruin*," *MÆ* 66 (1977): 178–79, also suggests [*winte*]*rum* or [*wæte*]*rum gehea[w]en*, neither of which seems to fit the riddlic theme especially well.

13: Most of this line is destroyed. The word *felon* is readable in the on verse. Mackie translates 'by files' as a consequence of the emended reading *gehea[w]en* grimme gegrunde[n . . . . . . . . . . . . .

15    . . . . . . . . . . . . . .] scan heo [. . . . . . . . . . .

     . . . . . . . . . . . . . . . .]g orþonc,   ærsceaft [. . . . . .

     . . . . . . . . . . . . . . . .]g[.]   lam rindum beag.

     Mod mo[. . . . . . . . m]yne swiftne gebrægd,

     hwætred in hringas   hygerof gebond

20    weallwalan wirum   wundrum togædre.

     Beorht wæron burgræced,   burnsele monige,

     heah horngestreon,   heresweg micel,

     meodoheall monig .   . M . dreama full,

     oþþæt þæt onwende   wyrd seo swiþe.

25    Crungon walo wide,   cwoman woldagas,

     swylt eall fornom   secgrof[ra] wera;

     wurdon hyra wigsteal   westenstaþolas.

     Brosnade burgsteall,   betend crungon

---

in the previous line. But Leslie suggests 3d pret. pl. of *feolan* 'to penetrate.' At the very edge of the hole rests, as Leslie observes, what resembles the foremost stroke of a *u*. Some twenty-six destroyed letter-spaces later the other edge of the hole shows the mere wisp of a letter. Leslie notes that this letter can be read from the MS, though not from the photofacsimile, as *e*.

14: Virtually all of the on verse can be read, though only the characteristic top of the final *n* in *gegrunden* can be seen. The rest of the line is obliterated.

15: Before the unscathed word *scan* appear the bottom parts of two letters, probably either *rð* (Leslie) or *rd*. As Leslie indicates, the following letters *heo* might be either the feminine pronoun or the remnant of a word such as *heo*[*lde*] or *heo*[*fon*]. By reason of syntax, *scan* probably ended the on verse in this line. The letters *heo* end a MS line about two letter spaces short of the right-hand margin, a spacing which suggests the pronoun *heo* rather than some longer word. The rest of the line, which began at the left margin, is lost except for mere tips of letters in about the first four spaces of the new MS line. The second or third letter appears to have had a high ascender, and the letter following might have been a thorn with crossed ascender, the frequent abbreviated form of *þæt*.

16: At the end of the hole the loop of a *g* is visible. It may be followed by the slightest trace of another letter. Then, virtually undamaged to the end of the MS line, appear the words *orþonc*   *ærsceaft*, probably the second arsis word in the on verse and the alliterating arsis word in the off verse.

17: The loop of a *g* shows at the end of the hole, and the trace of another letter follows, possibly the very bottom of a *d* or *ð*. The top of the *l* in *lam* is gone, but the word is quite legible, and the rest of the MS line is undamaged.

[pierced?] [. . . . . . . . . . . . . . . . . . . . . . . .]
ground up grimly [. . . . . . . . . . . . .
15  . . . . . . . . . . . . .] shone. [. . . . . . . . . . . . . .
 . . . . . . . . . . . . . . . .] skillful thought, ancient work
   [. . . . . .
 . . . . . . . . . . . . . . . . . .] clay sagged in its crusts.
[A subtle?] mind wove a swift design—
resolved and resourceful, bound wall stems together
20 with wires, wondrously shaped them into rings.
Bright were the borough halls, many the bathhouses,
high gable ornament, great noise of armies,
many a mead hall, M[an] full of joys,
until Fate the strong disturbed it all.
25 The fated fell everywhere, times of pestilence came,
death swept away all manly men,
their temples fell to foundations of rubble.
The fortress decayed; its restorers fell,

------

18: *mod mo*/[. . . . . . . . *m*]*yne swiftne gebrægd*. The damaged word is syllabifi-
cated at the end of a MS line. About eight letter spaces are missing. Leslie thinks
that the broken space calls for a verb and suggests *mo*[*nade*]. But this guess does
not fill the required space, and an adjective for *mod* would also satisfy the rules of
syntax. A reasonable fit both of the space and of the scribe's practice of word
division would be *mo*[*nigfeald*], and the line would then mean 'a manifold [i.e.,
subtle] mind wove a swift design,' an appropriate riddlic play on the mind of
man, the mind of the poet himself, and the mind of God, Creator of the
"temple" of Man. In poetry the word *monigfeald* is several times linked with
thought and the mind, as in *þa manigfealdan mine geþohtas, Resignation* 9. At the
end of the hole the three feet of an *m* and the characteristic tail of a *y* make the
word [*m*]*yne* practically certain.

19: *hygerof*. The *h*, largely destroyed, is nevertheless readable.

23: In the MS a bold runic *M*, surrounded by raised points, is at the left
margin. I have translated its verse as *mon dreama full* 'Man full of joys,' as a refer-
ence to the restored "temple" of Man. But *mondreama full* 'full of human joys' is
also possible: cf. *Beowulf* 1702a, *eald eðelwear*[*d*], where the *eðel* rune forms part
of the compound word. For the possibility that *The Ruin* has been spliced here,
with punctuation like *Riddles 42/43* and *47/48* and finished by a tenth-century
poet reflecting on the coronation of Edgar at Bath in 973, see the Introduction to
Part Two and nn. 21–23.

26: *secgrof*[*ra*]. MS *secgrof*, generally emended to *secgrof*[*ra*] to modify *wera*,
partitive gen. complement of *eall*.

hergas to hrusan.    Forþon þas hofu dreorgiað
30   ond þæs teaforgeapa    tigelum sceadeð
*124b*   hrostbeages [h]rof.    Hryre / wong gecrong,
gebrocen to beorgum.    Þær iu beorn monig,
glædmod ond goldbeorht,    gleoma gefrætwe[d],
wlonc ond wingal    wighyrstum scan,
35   seah on sinc, on sylfor,    on searogimmas,
on ead, on æht,    on eorcanstan,
on þas beorhtan burg    bradan rices.
   Stanhofu stodon,    stream hate wearp
widan wylme,    weal eall befeng
40   beorhtan bosme    þær þa baþu wæron,
hat on hreþre.    Þæt wæs hyðelic [þing].
Leton þonne geotan    [þ . . . . . . . . . . . . . .]
ofer ha[rn]e stan    hate streamas
un[. . . . . . . . . . . . . . . . . . . . . . . . . . .
45   o]þþæt hringmere    hate [. . . . . . .

31: *hrostbeages [h]rof*. So emended from MS *hrost beages rof* by ASPR 3 and
Leslie. Mackie reads *hrostbeages rof*. For *hrostbeages* as a thematic reading, see the
discussion in the Introduction to Part Two. The emendation [h]*rof* is mainly to
prevent misreading as *rof* 'bold, strong, brave,' etc.

33: *gefrætwe[d]*. Commonly corrected from MS *gefrætweð*, a simple error.

38: There is a bold raised point after *rices*, but the first letter of *Stanhofu* is
very little bigger than the *s* of *stodon* or *stream* in the same line. I follow Leslie's
paragraph division here, for at least the poet has returned to viewing the ruin
through his own eyes rather than those of the imagined ancient inhabitants of
previous lines. If *The Ruin* is a spliced eighth- and tenth-century production (see
Introduction to Part Two and note to line 23 above), perhaps this is where the
splice occurs.

41: In the MS the off verse reads *þæt wæs hyðelic*, but Leslie recalls an old
suggestion by Ferdinand Holthausen ("Zur altenglischen Literatur: V. 21. 'Christi
Höllenfahrt,'" *Anglia Beiblatt* 19 [1908]: 49–53) to correct the defective meter by
adding [*þing*], as in line 48b. Although Leslie does not enter the corrected line in
his text, I have done so here because of the additional possibility of a scribal
omission. If the scribe was looking ahead to the small capital of the word after
*hyðelic* and also thinking of justifying the right-hand margin, which he has done
with *þonn̄* for *þonne*, he might easily have overlooked a small word in the line.

42: The raised point after *hyðelic* and the unambiguous small capital *L* of
*Leton* make a separate paragraph of the final eight lines. Badly damaged as they

whole armies to earth. Thus these courtyards loom
    dreary,
30  and from its tiles the tiver-spanned roof
of the roost-ring parts. The place has toppled with its
    corruption,
ground into gravel heaps. There many a man,
glad-hearted and gold-burnished, dressed in splendors,
proud and elated from wine, once shone in his war gear,
35  gazed at treasure, at silver, at well-set gems,
at wealth, at rich goods, at wonderful stone,
at these bright cities of the broad domain.
    There stone courts stood; a stream gushed up heat
in a wide surging. A wall enclosed everything
40  with its bright bosom, where the baths were,
the heat in the heart. It was fitting, [this thing].
    Then they let pour [. . . . . . . . . . . . . .]
the hot streams over gray stone
    [. . . . . . . . . . . . . . . . . . . . . . . . . . .]
45  until the round pool hot [. . . . . . .]

---

are, these lines appear to have riddled on the Crucifixion (lines 42–43), baptism
(lines 45–46), and the heavenly Jerusalem (lines 48–49), the major themes for
each of the three days of the Easter triduum. Thus these last eight lines appear
to have been a secret thematic summation of the Easter Riddle. After *geotan* the
upstroke of a letter is preserved above the edge of the hole. I agree with Leslie
that the letter was probably *þ*. About fifteen destroyed letter spaces follow, but
the off verse is not restorable.

    43: The word *ofer* is nearly intact, the word *h[ar]ne* much obscured by dis-
coloration at the top of the hole. Nevertheless, the entire line is readable.

    44: Except for the letters *un*, probably the first letters in this line, nothing
else can be read. Leslie's text has [*d*] after *un*, but this reading, which cannot be
confirmed by the very small fragment of the letter in the photofacsimile, goes
unexplained in Leslie's notes.

    45: A shadowy arc of the *o* in *oþþæt* is visible at the edge of the hole. After
*hate*, at the front edge of the hole, the tail of a descender is visible. ASPR 3 notes
that the remnant suggests the kind of *s* which forms part of the consonant cluster
*st*. Leslie concurs and even enters [*st*] in his text. Following ASPR 3, Leslie thinks
of *streamas*, which would mean that line 45b repeated line 43b just as line 40b is
repeated in line 46b. But *hate* might also be an adverb, and the following de-
scender of line 45b might have been part of a *þ* as well as of an *s*. The line seems

. . . . . . . . . . . . . . . . . . . . . .] þær þa baþu wæron.
Þonne i[s . . . . . . . . . . . . . . . . . . . .
. . . . . . . . . . .]re.    Þæt is cynelic þing,
hu se [b . . . . . . . . . . . . . . . . . . .] burg[. . . . . .]

to call for a verb after *hate* rather than a noun: if the following letters were *st*, perhaps *stiemde*.

46: Only the off verse, once probably a riddlic repetition of line 40b, can now be seen.

47: The *s* of *is* has slight damage at its top. In the second letter space after *is* appears a mark which Leslie explains, on the authority of the MS itself, as the shadow of a *g* from the other side of the page. Leslie explains the mark in the following letter space the same way, but in the photofacsimile it looks like the tail of a descender in this line.

48: The ending *-re* of a lost syllabificated word is at the left margin. The entire off verse, with a barred thorn as shorthand for *þæt*, is preserved.

49: MS *huse*, lacking the upper half of the *e*, can be read at the front edge of the hole. ASPR 3 read *huse*, but Mackie and Leslie read *hu se*, in explanatory apposition to line 48b, the probable syntax. After *se* the bottom portions of two letters are visible. The first of these has the curve of a *b*. Together with the damaged but readable word *burg* of the off verse, this letter fragment suggests that the final line of *The Ruin* had *b* alliteration. I have therefore accepted Leslie's reading of *b* after *se* as virtually certain. The rest of the on verse, and perhaps a

. . . . . . . . . . . . . . . . . . . . . .] where the baths were.
Then i[s . . . . . . . . . . . . . . . . . . . .
. . . . . . . . . . . . .] It is a kingly thing,
how the [. . . . . . . . . . . . . . . . . . . .] city [. . . . . .]

_____

short word or two of the off verse (which may well have been a prepositional phrase), have been lost in the hole, which extends to the right-hand edge of the page. Assuming that the minute trace of a letter after the *g* in *burg* is a shadow from the broken *m* of [*m*]*yne* in line 18 on the other side of the page, the descenders in the second and fourth letter spaces after *burg* would suggest a compound word written as separate elements. Leslie suggests that the descenders fit the consonant cluster *str-*, and there is a compound *burgstræt*, otherwise unknown in poetry. On the other hand, the descenders would also fit the compound *burgwara*, frequently used in poetry, and prominently located in *The Easter Riddle* in *The Descent into Hell* 56, where John the Baptist has been called *burgwarena ord* (see the discussion of *The Descent into Hell* in the Introduction to Part Two). At the end of *The Ruin*, which closes *The Easter Riddle* with allegorical suggestions of the heavenly Jerusalem, the poet might logically have compared the hope of all believers with the joyful release of the faithful *burgwarena* from hell. I therefore suspect that the final verse of *The Ruin* was on the order of *mid þam burgwarum*, or perhaps *ealle burgwaran*, both familiar half lines in other Anglo-Saxon poetry. Such words would have closed *The Easter Riddle* with the triumphant arrival of all resurrected flesh in the fortress of salvation.

# WORKS CITED

Adams, John F. "'Wulf and Eadwacer': An Interpretation." *MLN* 73 (1958): 1–5.

Alexander, Michael, trans. *Old English Riddles from the Exeter Book*. London: Anvil Press, 1980.

Amira, Karl von. *Grundriss des germanischen Rechts*. 3d ed. Strassburg: Karl J. Trübner, 1913.

Anderson, Earl R. "*The Husband's Message*: Persuasion and the Problem of *Genyre*." *ES* 56 (1975): 289–94.

———. "Voices in *The Husband's Message*." *NM* 74 (1973): 238–46.

Anderson, George K. *The Literature of the Anglo-Saxons*. Princeton, N.J.: Princeton University Press, 1949.

Anderson, James E. "*Deor, Wulf and Eadwacer*, and *The Soul's Address*: How and Where the Exeter Book Riddles Begin." In Martin Green, ed. *The Old English Elegies: New Essays in Criticism and Research*. Rutherford, Madison, and Teaneck, N.J.: Fairleigh-Dickinson University Press; London and Toronto: Associated University Presses, 1983, pp. 204–31.

———. ON *víkingr* and the OE *Wife's Lament*." *MScan* 12 (forthcoming).

———. "Strange, Sad Voices: The Portraits of Germanic Women in the Old English Exeter Book." Ph.D. dissertation, University of Kansas, 1978.

———. "Two Spliced Riddles of the Exeter Book." *In Geardagum* 5 (June, 1983): 57–75.

Arnold, Thomas, ed. *Memorials of St. Edmund's Abbey*. 3 vols. Rolls Series 96. London: Eyre and Spottiswoode for Her Majesty's Stationery Office, 1890–96.

Arntz, Helmut. *Handbuch der Runenkunde*. 2d ed. Halle: Max Niemeyer, 1944.

ASPR 3. See Krapp and Dobbie, eds.

Attenborough, F. L. *The Laws of the Earliest English Kings*. Cambridge: Cambridge University Press, 1922.

Bachtold-Stäubli, Hanns. *Handwörterbuch des deutschen Aberglaubens*. 4 vols. Berlin and Leipzig: de Gruyter, 1930–31.

Baker, Peter S. "The Ambiguity of *Wulf and Eadwacer*." *SP* 78 (1981): 39–51.

Bambas, Rudolph C. "Another View of the Old English *Wife's Lament*." *JEGP* 62 (1963): 303–309.

Bammesberger, Alfred. *Beiträge zu einem etymologischen Wörterbuch des Altenglischen. Berichtigungen und Nachträge zum Altenglischen etymologischen Wörterbuch von Ferdinand Holthausen.* Anglistische Forschungen 139. Heidelberg: Carl Winters Universitätsverlag, 1979.

Berkhout, Carl T. "Some Notes on the Old English 'Almsgiving.'" *ELN* 10 (1972): 81–85.

———. "The Speaker in *Resignation*: A Biblical Note." *N&Q* 219 (1974): 122–23.

Bestul, Thomas H. "The Old English *Resignation* and the Benedictine Reform." *NM* 78 (1977): 18–23.

Blackburn, F. A. "The 'Husband's Message' and the Accompanying Riddles of the Exeter Book." *JEGP* 3 (1901): 1–13.

Blank, S. H. "Riddle." *The Interpreter's Dictionary of the Bible.* New York and Nashville, Tenn.: Abingdon Press, 1962, pp. 78b–79b.

Bliss, A. J. *An Introduction to Old English Metre.* Oxford: Basil Blackwell, 1962.

———, and Allen J. Frantzen. "The Integrity of *Resignation*." *RES*, n.s., 27 (1976): 385–402.

Bloomfield, Morton. "The Form of *Deor*." *PMLA* 79 (1964): 534–41.

Bolton, W. F. "'The Wife's Lament' and 'The Husband's Message': A Reconsideration Revisited." *Archiv* 205 (1969): 337–51.

Bosworth, Joseph. *An Anglo-Saxon Dictionary.* Edited by T. Northcote Toller. Oxford: Clarendon Press, 1898.

Bouman, A. C. *Patterns in Old English and Old Icelandic Literature.* Leidse Germanistische en Anglistische Reeks, pt. 1. Leiden: Universitaire Pers, 1962.

Bradley, Henry. Review of Henry Morley, *English Writers, II. Academy* 33 (1888): 197–98.

Brandl, Alois. "Venantius Fortunatus und die ags. Elegien 'Wanderer' und 'Ruine.'" *Archiv* 139 (1919): 84.

Broch, Ada. *Die Stellung der Frau in der angelsächsischen Poesie.* Zürich: Zürcher und Furrer für die philosophischen Fakultät der Universität Zürich, 1902.

Bruder, Reinhold. *Die germanische Frau im Lichte der Runeninschriften und der antiken Historiographie.* Quellen und Forschungen zur Sprach- und Kulturgeschichte der germanischen Völker 57. Berlin: de Gruyter, 1974.

Budjuhn, Gustav. "Leodum is minum—ein ae. Dialog." *Anglia* 40 (1916): 256–59.

Cabrol, F. "Baiser. VII: L'osculatorium." *Dictionnaire d'archéologie chrétienne et de liturgie*, vol. 2, i, cols. 118–30.

Caie, Graham D. *The Judgment Day Theme in Old English Poetry*. Copenhagen: Nova, 1976.

Calder, Daniel G. "Perspective and Movement in *The Ruin*." *NM* 72 (1971): 442–45.

Campbell, Alistair. *Addenda and Corrigenda to An Anglo-Saxon Dictionary*. Oxford: Clarendon Press, 1972.

Chambers, R. W. *Widsith: A Study in Old English Heroic Legend*. Cambridge: Cambridge University Press, 1912.

————, Max Förster, and Robin Flower, eds. *The Exeter Book of Old English Poetry*. London: Dean and Chapter of Exeter Cathedral, 1933.

Cherniss, Michael D. *Ingeld and Christ: Heroic Concepts and Values in Old English Poetry*. Studies in English Literature 74. The Hague: Mouton, 1972.

Cockayne, Thomas Oswald, ed. *Leechdoms, Wortcunning and Starcraft of Early England*. 3 vols. London: Longman, Green, Longman, Roberts and Green, 1864–66. Reprint, London, 1961; reprint, Wiesbaden, 1965.

Condren, Edward I. "Deor's Artistic Triumph." *SP* 78, no. 5 (1981): 62–76.

Conner, Patrick W. "A Contextual Study of the Old English Exeter Book." Ph.D. dissertation, University of Maryland, 1975.

————. "The Liturgy and the Old English 'Descent into Hell.'" *JEGP* 79 (1980): 179–91.

Crenshaw, James L. "Riddle." *The Interpreter's Dictionary of the Bible, Supplementary Volume*. New York and Nashville, Tenn: Abingdon Press, 1976, pp. 749a–50a.

Cross, James E. "*Blickling Homily XIV* and the *Old English Martyrology* on John the Baptist." *Anglia* 93 (1975): 145–60.

————. "Notes on Old English Texts." *Neophil* 39 (1955): 203–206.

Crossley-Holland, Kevin, trans. *The Exeter Book Riddles*. Harmondsworth: Penguin Classics, 1979.

Crotty, Genevieve. "The Exeter *Harrowing of Hell*: A Reinterpretation." *PMLA* 54 (1939): 349–58.

Cunliffe, Barry. *The Roman Baths: A Guide to the Baths and Roman Museum*. Oxford: Institute of Archaeology for the Bath Archaeological Trust, 1978.

Dalbey, Marcia A. "Themes and Techniques in the Blickling Lenten Homilies." In Paul E. Szarmach and Bernard F. Huppé, eds. *The Old English Homily and Its Backgrounds*. Albany, N.Y.: SUNY Press, 1978, pp. 221–39.

Daly, Lloyd William, and Walther Suchier, eds. *Altercatio Hadriani Au-*

*gusti et Epicteti Philosophi*. Illinois Studies in Language and Literature 24, 1–2. Urbana: University of Illinois Press, 1939.

Davidson, Arnold E. "Interpreting *Wulf and Eadwacer*." *AnM* 16 (1975): 24–32.

Davidson, Clifford. "Erotic 'Women's Songs' in Anglo-Saxon England." *Neophil* 59 (1975): 451–62.

Davidson, Hilda Ellis. *Gods and Myths of Northern Europe*. Harmondsworth: Penguin Books, 1964.

Davis, Thomas M. "Another View of 'The Wife's Lament.'" *PELL* 1 (1965): 291–305.

Dix, Dom Gregory. *The Shape of the Liturgy*. 2d ed. Westminster: Dacre Press, 1945.

Dobbie, Elliott Van Kirk, ed. *The Anglo-Saxon Minor Poems*. The Anglo-Saxon Poetic Records 6. New York: Columbia University Press; London: Routledge and Kegan Paul, 1942.

Dunleavy, Gareth W. "A 'De Excidio' Tradition in the Old English *Ruin*?" *PQ* 38 (1959): 112–18.

———. "Possible Irish Analogues for *The Wife's Lament*." *PQ* 35 (1956): 208–13.

Düwel, Klaus. *Runenkunde*. Sammlung Metzler, Realienbücher für Germanisten, ser. C.: Sprachwissenschaft. Stuttgart: J. B. Metzlersche Verlagsbuchhandlung, 1968.

Eliason, Norman E. "On Wulf and Eadwacer." In Robert B. Burlin and Edward B. Irving, Jr., eds. *Old English Studies in Honour of John C. Pope*. Toronto: University of Toronto Press, 1974, pp. 225–34.

Elliott, R. M. W. *Runes: An Introduction*. Manchester: Manchester University Press, 1959.

———. "The Runes in the Husband's Message." *JEGP* 54 (1955): 1–8.

Ettmüller, Ludwig. *Engla and Seaxna Scopas and Boceras*. Quedlinburg and Leipzig: G. Bassi, 1850.

Fanagan, John M. "*Wulf and Eadwacer*: A Solution to the Critics' Riddle." *Neophil* 60 (1976): 130–37.

Förster, Max. "General Description of the Manuscript: 4. Ornamentation." In R. W. Chambers, Max Förster, and Robin Flower, eds. *The Exeter Book of Old English Poetry*. London: Dean and Chapter of Exeter Cathedral, 1933, p. 60.

———. *Keltisches Wortgut im Englischen*. Halle: Max Niemeyer, 1921.

Frankis, P. J. "*Deor* and *Wulf and Eadwacer*: Some Conjectures." *MÆ* 31 (1962): 161–75.

Frantzen, Allen J. *The Literature of Penance in Anglo-Saxon England*. New Brunswick, N.J.: Rutgers University Press, 1983.

Fritzner, Johan. *Ordbog over det gamle norske Sprog.* 2d ed. Kristiania (Oslo): Den norske Forlagsforening, 1883–96; reprint, Oslo: Tryggve Juul Møller Forlag, 1954.

Fry, Donald K. "Wulf and Eadwacer: A Wen Charm." *ChauR* 5 (1970): 247–63.

Gardner, John. *The Construction of Christian Poetry in Old English.* Carbondale: Southern Illinois University Press, 1975.

Goldsmith, Margaret. "The Enigma of *The Husband's Message.*" In Lewis E. Nicholson and Dolores Warwick Frese, eds. *Anglo-Saxon Poetry: Essays in Appreciation for John C. McGalliard.* Notre Dame, Ind.: University of Notre Dame Press, 1975, pp. 242–63.

Gordon, R. K., trans. *Anglo-Saxon Poetry.* Rev. ed. Everyman's Library 794. New York: Dutton, 1954.

Greenfield, Stanley B. *A Critical History of Old English Literature.* New York: New York University Press, 1965.

———. "*The Wife's Lament* Reconsidered." *PMLA* 68 (1953): 907–12.

Grein, C. W. M. *Bibliothek der angelsächsischen Poesie.* 2 vols. Göttingen: Georg H. Wigand, 1857–58; 2d ed., rev. and enl., by Richard Paul Wülcker. 2 vols. Kassel: Georg H. Wigand, 1881–88.

———. *Sprachschatz der angelsächsischen Dichter.* 2d ed. with collaboration of F. Holthausen, new ed. by J. J. Kohler. Heidelberg: Carl Winters Universitätsverlag, 1912; reprint, 1974.

———. "Zur Textkritik der angelsächsischen Dichter." *Germania* 10 (1865): 416–29.

Grimm, Jacob, Wilhelm Grimm, et al. *Deutsches Wörterbuch.* Leipzig: S. Hirzel, 1854–.

———, ———, et al. *Kinder- und Hausmärchen.* Leipzig: P. Reclam, 1843.

Grubl, Emily Doris. *Studien zu den angelsächsischen Elegien.* Marburg an der Lahn: Elwert-Gräfe u. Unzer, 1948.

Hain, Mathilde. *Rätsel.* Sammlung Metzler 1682. Stuttgart: J. B. Metzlersche Verlagsbuchhandlung, 1966.

Hall, J. R. Clark. *A Concise Anglo-Saxon Dictionary.* 4th ed., with Supplement by Herbert D. Meritt. Cambridge: Cambridge University Press, 1960.

Harris, Joseph. "A Note on *eorðscræf/eorðsele* and Current Interpretations of *The Wife's Lament.*" *ES* 58 (1977): 204–208.

Herzfeld, Georg. *Die Räthsel des Exeterbuches und ihr Verfasser.* Berlin: Mayer & Müller, 1890.

Hieatt, Constance B., trans. *Beowulf and Other Old English Poems.* 2d ed., rev. and enl. Toronto and New York: Bantam, 1983.

Hill, Joyce, ed. *Old English Minor Heroic Poems.* Durham and St. Andrews

Medieval Texts 4. Durham and Fife: Durham and St. Andrews Medieval Texts, 1983.

Hill, Thomas D. "Cosmic Stasis and the Birth of Christ: The Old English *Descent into Hell*, Lines 99–106." *JEGP* 71 (1972): 382–89.

Holoka, James P. "The Oral Formula and the Anglo-Saxon Elegy: Some Misgivings." *Neophil* 60 (1976): 570–76.

Holthausen, Ferdinand. "Zur altenglischen Literatur. V. 21. 'Christi Höllenfahrt.'" *Anglia Beiblatt* 19 (1908): 49–53.

Hoops, Johannes. *Reallexikon der germanischen Altertumskunde*. 4 vols. Strassburg: Karl J. Trübner, 1911–19.

Hotchner, Cecelia A. *Wessex and Old English Poetry, with Special Consideration of* The Ruin. Lancaster, Pa.: Lancaster Press, 1939.

Howlett, D. R. "Two Old English Encomia." *ES* 57 (1976): 289–93.

Hume, Kathryn. "The 'Ruin Motif' in Old English Poetry." *Anglia* 94 (1976): 339–60.

Hunt, R. W. Introduction. *St. Dunstan's Classbook from Glastonbury*. Umbrae Codicum Occidentalium 4. Amsterdam: North-Holland, 1961.

Imelmann, Rudolf. *Die altenglische Odoaker-Dichtung*. Berlin: J. Springer, 1907.

———. *Forschungen zur altenglischen Poesie*. Berlin: Weidmannschen Buchhandlung, 1920.

———. *"Wanderer" und "Seefahrer" im Rahmen der altenglischen Odoaker-Dichtung*. Berlin: J. Springer, 1908.

———. *Zeugnisse zur altenglischen Odoaker-Dichtung*. Berlin: J. Springer, 1907.

Irving, Edward B., Jr. "Image and Meaning in the Elegies." In Robert P. Creed, ed. *Old English Poetry: Fifteen Essays*. Providence, R.I.: Brown University Press, 1967, pp. 153–66.

Isaacs, Neil D. *Structural Principles in Old English Poetry*. Knoxville: University of Tennessee Press, 1968.

Jensen, Emily. "Narrative Voice in the Old English *Wulf*." *ChauR* 13 (1979): 373–83.

Jobes, Gertrude. *Dictionary of Mythology, Folklore, and Symbols*. 2 vols. New York: Scarecrow Press, 1962.

Johnson, William C., Jr. "*The Ruin* as Body-City Riddle." *PQ* 59 (1980): 397–411.

Jolles, André. *Einfache Formen*. Halle: Max Niemeyer, 1930; reprint, 1956.

———. "Rätsel und Mythos." In *Germanica: Festschrift für Eduard Sievers*. Halle: M. Niemeyer, 1925, pp. 632–45.

Jungmann, J. A. "Baptism (Liturgy of)." *New Catholic Encyclopedia* (1967 ed.). 2:58b–62a.

———. "Catechumenate." *New Catholic Encyclopedia* (1967 ed.). 3: 238a–240b.

———. *The Early Liturgy, to the Time of Gregory the Great*. Translated by Francis A. Brunner. London: Darton, Longman & Todd, 1960.

———. *The Mass of the Roman Rite: Its Origins and Development (Missarum Sollemnia)*. Translated by Francis A. Brunner. 2 vols. New York: Benziger Bros., 1955.

Kaske, Robert E. "The Conclusion of the Old English 'Descent into Hell.'" In Harry George Fletcher III and Mary Beatrice Schulte, eds. *Paradosis: Studies in Memory of Edwin A. Quain*. New York: Fordham University Press, 1976, pp. 47–59.

———. "A Poem of the Cross in the Exeter Book: 'Riddle 60' and 'The Husband's Message.'" *Traditio* 23 (1967): 41–71.

———. "The Reading *Genyre* in *The Husband's Message* Line 49." *MÆ* 33 (1964): 204–206 and facing p. 169.

Keenan, Hugh. "The Ruin as Babylon." *TSL* 11 (1966): 109–17.

Kellogg, Alfred L. "Susannah and the 'Merchant's Tale.'" *Speculum* 35 (1960): 275–79. Reprinted in Alfred L. Kellogg. *Chaucer, Langland, Arthur: Essays in Middle English Literature*. New Brunswick, N.J.: Rutgers University Press, 1972, pp. 330–38.

Kennedy, Charles W. *The Earliest English Poetry*. New York: Oxford University Press, 1943.

———. *Old English Elegies*. Princeton, N.J.: Princeton University Press, 1939.

Kershaw, Nora, ed. *Anglo-Saxon and Norse Poems*. Cambridge: Cambridge University Press, 1922; reprint, Ann Arbor: University Microfilms, 1978.

Kiernan, Kevin. "*Deor*: The Consolation of an Anglo-Saxon Boethius." *NM* 79 (1978): 333–40.

King, Archdale A. *Liturgies of the Past*. London: Longmans, 1959.

Kluge, Friedrich. *Angelsächsisches Lesebuch*. 2d ed. Halle: Max Niemeyer, 1897; 3d ed., 1902.

Kock, Ernst A. "Interpretations and Emendations of Early English Texts, VIII." *Anglia* 45 (1921): 105–31.

Krapp, George Philip, ed. *The Vercelli Book*. Anglo-Saxon Poetic Records 2. New York: Columbia University Press, 1932.

———, and Elliott Van Kirk Dobbie, eds. *The Exeter Book*. Anglo-Saxon Poetic Records 3. New York: Columbia University Press, 1936.

Kurath, Hans, Sherman M. Kuhn, and John Reidy. *Middle English Dictionary*. Ann Arbor: University of Michigan Press, 1952–.

Landrum, M. H. "A Fourfold Interpretation of 'The Wife's Lament.'" Ph.D. dissertation, Rutgers University, 1963.

Lawrence, W. W. "The Banished Wife's Lament." *MP* 5 (1908): 387–405.

Leach, Maria, and Jerome Fried, eds. *Funk and Wagnalls Standard Dictionary of Folklore, Mythology, and Legend.* New York: Funk and Wagnalls, 1972.

Lee, Anne Thompson. "*The Ruin*: Bath or Babylon?" *NM* 74 (1973): 443–55.

Lehmann, Ruth P. M. "The Metrics and Structure of 'Wulf and Eadwacer.'" *PQ* 48 (1969): 151–65.

Lehnert, Martin, ed. *Poetry and Prose of the Anglo-Saxons.* Vol. 1. Berlin: Deutscher Verlag der Wissenschaften, 1955.

Leo, Heinrich. *Angelsächsisches Glossar.* Halle: Verlag der Buchhandlung des Waisenhauses, 1877.

Leslie, Roy F., ed. *Three Old English Elegies: The Wife's Lament, The Husband's Message, The Ruin.* Manchester: Manchester University Press, 1961.

Liebermann, Felix. *Die Gesetze der Angelsachsen.* 3 vols. Berlin: Savigny-Stiftung, 1903–16; reprint, 1960.

Lucas, Angela M. "The Narrator of *The Wife's Lament* Reconsidered." *NM* 70 (1969): 282–97.

Luecke, Janemarie. "*Wulf and Eadwacer*: Hints for Reading from *Beowulf* and Anthropology." In Martin Green, ed. *The Old English Elegies: New Essays in Criticism and Research.* Rutherford, Madison, and Teaneck, N.J.: Fairleigh-Dickinson University Press; London and Toronto: Associated University Presses, 1983, pp. 190–203.

Mackie, W. S., ed. *The Exeter Book, Part II, Poems IX–XXXII.* EETS o.s. 194. London, 1934; reprint, 1958.

Magoun, Francis P., Jr. *The Anglo-Saxon Poems in Bright's Anglo-Saxon Reader.* Cambridge, Mass.: Harvard University Press, 1965.

Malone, Kemp. "An Anglo-Latin Version of the Hjaðningavíg." *Speculum* 39 (1964): 35–44.

———, ed. *Deor.* Methuen's Old English Library A2. London: Methuen, 1933.

———. "Mæðhild." *ELH* 3 (1936): 253–56.

———. "On *Deor* 14–17." In *Studies in Heroic Legend and Current Speech by Kemp Malone.* Edited by Stefan Einarsson and Norman E. Eliason. Copenhagen: Rosenkilde & Bagger, 1959, pp. 142–58.

———. "The Tale of Geat and Mæðhild." *ES* 19 (1937): 193–99.

———. *Ten Old English Poems Put into Modern English Alliterative Verse.* Baltimore, Md.: Johns Hopkins University Press, 1941.

———. "Two English *Frauenlieder*." In Stanley B. Greenfield, ed. *Studies in Old English Literature in Honor of Arthur G. Brodeur*. Eugene: University of Oregon Press, 1963, pp. 106–17.

Markland, Murray F. "*Deor: þæs ofereode, þisses swa mæg*." *AN&Q* 11, no. 3 (1972): 35–36.

Marquardt, Hertha. *Die altenglischen Kenningar*. Schriften der Königsberger Gelehrten-Gesellschaft 14, pt. 3. Halle: Max Niemeyer, 1938.

Martène, Edmond. *De antiquis ecclesiae ritibus libri ex variis insigniorum ecclesiarum . . . .* 4 vols. 2d ed. Antwerp: J. B. de la Bry, 1736–38; reprint, Hildesheim: Georg Ohms Verlagsbuchhandlung, 1967.

Mattox, Wesley S. "Encirclement and Sacrifice in *Wulf and Eadwacer*." *AnM* 16 (1975): 33–40.

Meling, Kjell. "Cruciform Runes in the Manuscripts of Some Old English Poems." Ph.D. dissertation, SUNY/Binghamton, 1972.

Meritt, Herbert D. *Fact and Lore About Old English Words*. Stanford University Publications in Language and Literature 13. Stanford, Calif.: Stanford University Press, 1954.

———. *Old English Glosses (A Collection)*. New York: Modern Language Society, 1945.

Merschberger, Gerda. *Die Rechtsstellung der germanischen Frau*. Mannus-Bücherei 57. Leipzig: Curt Rabitzsch, 1937.

Mullahy, B. I. "Kiss, Liturgical." *New Catholic Encyclopedia*. 1967 ed. 8:207a–b.

Murray, Sir James A. H., et al., eds. *Oxford English Dictionary*. 12 vols., supplements. Oxford: Oxford University Press, 1884–1928.

Musurillo, H. "Dialogue (Literary Genre)." *New Catholic Encyclopedia*. 1967 ed. 4:849a.

Nabers, Ned, and Susan Ford Wiltshire. "The Athena Temple at Paestum and Pythagorean Theory." *Greek, Roman, and Byzantine Studies* 21 (1980): 207–15.

Needham, G. I., ed. *Ælfric: Lives of Three English Saints*. Rev. ed. Exeter Medieval English Texts. Exeter: University of Exeter, 1976.

Nelson, Marie. "On *Resignation*." In Martin Green, ed. *The Old English Elegies: New Essays in Criticism and Research*. Rutherford, Madison, and Teaneck, N.J.: Fairleigh-Dickinson University Press; London and Toronto: Associated University Presses, 1983, pp. 133–47.

Norman, F. "Deor: A Criticism and an Interpretation." *MLR* 22 (1937): 374–81.

———. "Deor and Modern Scandinavian Ballads." *London Mediaeval Studies* 1, no. 2 (1937–39): 165–78.

Ogilvy, J. D. A. *Books Known to the English, 597–1066.* Cambridge, Mass.: Harvard University Press, 1967.

Orton, Peter. "The Speaker in 'The Husband's Message.'" *LeedsSE* 12 (1981): 43–56.

Osborn, Marijane. "The Text and Context of *Wulf and Eadwacer.*" In Martin Green, ed. *The Old English Elegies: New Essays in Criticism and Research.* Rutherford, Madison, and Teaneck, N.J.: Fairleigh-Dickinson University Press; London and Toronto: Associated University Presses, 1983, pp. 174–89.

O'Shea, W. J. "Easter Vigil." *New Catholic Encyclopedia.* 1967 ed. 5: 9a–13a.

*The Oxford English Dictionary.* Edited by James A. H. Murray et al. Oxford: Oxford University Press, 1888–1928.

Page, R. I. *An Introduction to English Runes.* London: Methuen, 1973.

Pope, John C. "Palaeography and Poetry: Some Solved and Unsolved Problems in the Exeter Book." In M. B. Parkes and Andrew G. Watson, eds. *Medieval Scribes, Manuscripts and Libraries: Essays Presented to N. R. Ker.* London: Scolar Press, 1978, pp. 25–65.

———. "An Unsuspected Lacuna in the Exeter Book: Divorce Proceedings for an Ill-matched Couple in the Old English Riddles." *Speculum* 49 (1974): 615–22.

Puntschart, Paul. *Schuldvertrag und Treugelöbnis des sächsischen Rechts im Mittelalter: Ein beitrag zur grundauffassung der altdeutschen obligation.* Leipzig: Veit, 1896.

Raffel, Burton, trans. *Poems from the Old English.* 2d ed. Lincoln: University of Nebraska Press, 1964.

Reichardt, Konstantin. *Runenkunde.* Jena: Eugen Diederichs Verlag, 1936.

Renoir, Alain. "The Old English *Ruin*: Contrastive Structure and Affective Impact." In Martin Green, ed. *The Old English Elegies: New Essays in Criticism and Research.* Rutherford, Madison, and Teaneck, N.J.: Fairleigh-Dickinson University Press; London and Toronto: Associated University Presses, 1983, pp. 148–73.

———. "A Reading of *The Wife's Lament.*" *ES* 58 (1977): 4–19.

———. "'Wulf and Eadwacer': A Non-Interpretation." In Jess B. Bessinger, Jr., and Robert P. Creed, eds. *Franciplegius: Medieval and Linguistic Studies in Honor of Francis Peabody Magoun.* New York: New York University Press, 1965, pp. 147–63.

Rissanen, Matti. "The Theme of 'Exile' in *The Wife's Lament.*" *NM* 70 (1969): 90–104.

Rowland, Beryl. *Birds with Human Souls: A Guide to Bird Symbolism.* Knoxville: University of Tennessee Press, 1978.

Rubin, Gary I. "MS Integrity, Lines 3a–4b of *The Ruin*." *Neophil* 63 (1979): 297–99.

Schofield, W. H. "Signy's Lament." *PMLA* 17 (1902): 262–95.

Schücking, Levin L. "Das angelsächsische Gedicht von der Klage der Frau." *ZfdA* 48 (1906): 436–49.

———. *Kleines angelsächsisches Dichterbuch*. Cöthen: Otto Schulze, 1919.

Sedgefield, W. J. *An Anglo-Saxon Verse Book*. Manchester: Manchester University Press, 1922.

Shippey, T. A. *Poems of Wisdom and Learning in Old English*. Cambridge: D. S. Brewer; Totowa, N.J.: Rowan and Littlefield, 1976.

Short, Douglas D. "The Old English Wife's Lament: An Interpretation." *NM* 71 (1970): 585–603.

Sieper, Ernst. *Die altenglische Elegie*. Strassburg: Karl J. Trübner, 1915.

Sisam, Kenneth. *Studies in the History of Old English Literature*. Oxford: Clarendon Press, 1953.

Smyser, H. M. "Ibn Fadlan's Account of the Rus with Some Commentary and Some Allusions to *Beowulf*." In Jess B. Bessinger and Robert P. Creed, eds. *Franciplegius: Medieval and Linguistic Studies in Honor of Francis Peabody Magoun*. New York: New York University Press, 1965, pp. 92–119.

Spamer, James B. "The Marriage Concept in *Wulf and Eadwacer*." *Neophil* 62 (1978): 143–44.

Stanley, E. G. "Old English Poetic Diction and the Interpretation of *The Wanderer*, *The Seafarer*, and *The Penitent's Prayer*." *Anglia* 73 (1956): 413–66.

Stenton, F. M. *Anglo-Saxon England*. 3d ed. Oxford: Clarendon Press, 1971.

Stephanovic, Svetislav. "Das angelsächsische Gedicht 'Die Klage der Frau.'" *Anglia* 32 (1909): 399–433.

Stevens, Martin. "The Narrator of 'The Wife's Lament.'" *NM* 69 (1968): 72–90.

Stubbs, William. "Memorials of St. Dunstan, Archbishop of Canterbury." *Historical Introduction to the Rolls Series*. London: Longmans, Green, 1902.

———. *Memorials of St. Dunstan, Archbishop of Canterbury*. Rolls Series 63. London: Longman & Co. and Trübner & Co., 1874.

Swanton, M. J. "*The Wife's Lament* and *The Husband's Message*: A Reconsideration." *Anglia* 82 (1964): 269–90.

Sweet, Henry. *A Student's Dictionary of Anglo-Saxon*. Oxford: Clarendon Press, 1896.

Taylor, Archer. *The Literary Riddle Before 1600*. Berkeley and Los Angeles: University of California Press, 1948.

Thompson, Stith. *Motif-Index of Folk Literature*. 5 vols. + index. Bloomington: Indiana University Press, 1955–58.

Thorpe, Benjamin, ed. and trans. *Codex exoniensis: A Collection of Anglo-Saxon Poetry, etc.* London: Society of Antiquaries of London, 1842.

Thrupp, John. *The Anglo-Saxon Home: A History of the Domestic Institutions and Customs of England, from the Fifth to the Eleventh Century*. London: Longman, Green, Longman, and Roberts, 1862.

Timmer, B. J. "The Elegiac Mood in Old English Poetry." *ES* 24 (1942): 33–44.

Toller, T. Northcote. *Supplement to An Anglo-Saxon Dictionary*. Oxford: Clarendon Press, 1921.

Trahern, Joseph B., Jr. "The *Ioca Monachorum* and the Old English *Pharaoh*." *ELN* 7 (1970):165–68.

Trask, Richard M. "*The Descent into Hell* of the Exeter Book." *NM* 72 (1971): 419–35.

Trautmann, Moritz. "Zur Botschaft des Gemahls." *Anglia* 16 (1894): 207–25.

Tuggle, Thomas. "The Structure of *Deor*." *SP* 74 (1977): 229–42.

Tupper, Frederick. *The Riddles of the Exeter Book*. Boston: Ginn and Co., 1910; reprint, Darmstadt: Wissenschaftliche Buchgesellschaft, 1968.

Ure, James M., ed. *The Benedictine Office: An Old English Text*. Edinburgh: Edinburgh University Press, 1957.

Webb, Suzanne S. "Imagery Patterns and Pagan Substructures: An Exploration of Structural Motifs in Five Old English Elegies." Ph.D. dissertation, Washington State University, 1973.

Wentersdorf, Karl P. "Observations on *The Ruin*." *MÆ* 66 (1977): 171–80.

———. "The Situation of the Narrator in the Old English *Wife's Lament*." *Speculum* 56 (1981): 492–516.

———. "The Situation of the Narrator's Lord in *The Wife's Lament*." *NM* 71 (1970): 604–10.

Whitaker, E. C. *The Baptismal Liturgy: An Introduction to Baptism in the Western Church*. London: Faith Press, 1965.

Whitbread, L. "Notes on Two Minor Old English Poems." *SN* 29 (1957): 123–29.

———. "The Old English Poem 'Pharaoh.'" *N&Q* 190 (1946): 52–54.

Williamson, Craig, ed. *The Old English Riddles of the Exeter Book*. Chapel Hill: University of North Carolina Press, 1977.

Wilson, R. M. *The Lost Literature of Medieval England*. London: Methuen, 1952.

Winzen, D. "Church, Symbols of." *New Catholic Encyclopedia*. 1967 ed. 3:724b–726b.

*Woordenboek der nederlandsche Taal*. The Hague: Martinus Nijhoff, 1916–.

Wrenn, C. L. *Beowulf with the Finnesburg Fragment*. Revised by W. F. Bolton. New York: St. Martin's Press, 1973.

———. *A Study of Old English Literature*. New York: Norton, 1967.

Wright, Joseph, ed. *The English Dialect Dictionary*. Oxford: Henry Frowde, 1905.

Wright, Thomas. *Old English Vocabularies*. Edited by Richard Wülcker. 2 vols. London: Trübner, 1883–84.

# INDEX